That's Ms. Bulldyke to you, Charlie!

By Jane Caminos

Madwoman Press 1992

This is a work of fiction. Any resemblance between characters in this book and actual persons, living or dead, is coincidental.

Printed in the United States on acid-free paper

Library of Congress Cataloging-in-Publication Data

Caminos, Jane, 1947–
    That's Ms. Bulldyke to you, Charlie! / Jane Caminos.
      p.   cm.
    ISBN 0–9630822–1–3 (soft cover–acid free paper) :
    1. Lesbians – – Caricatures and cartoons.   2. American wit and humor,
Pictorial.   I. Title.
NC1429.C25A4   1992
741.5'973—dc20

                                        92-60819
                                           CIP

That's MS. BULLDYKE to you, CHARLIE!

cartoons by
JANE CAMINOS

About the Author

Jane Caminos is a professional artist and illustrator who moved from Boston to live in a loft in New York City's Tribeca neighborhood with her delightful and understanding life partner, Christine, a joking black lab named Maude who is working on her issues around food, and a rapidly balding pussycat named Zoe, who is needy. Jane came out in the mid '70s, when it was not politically correct to have a sense of humor.

For dear Chrissie,
my muse, my prophet,
my dream come true,
Love of my life.

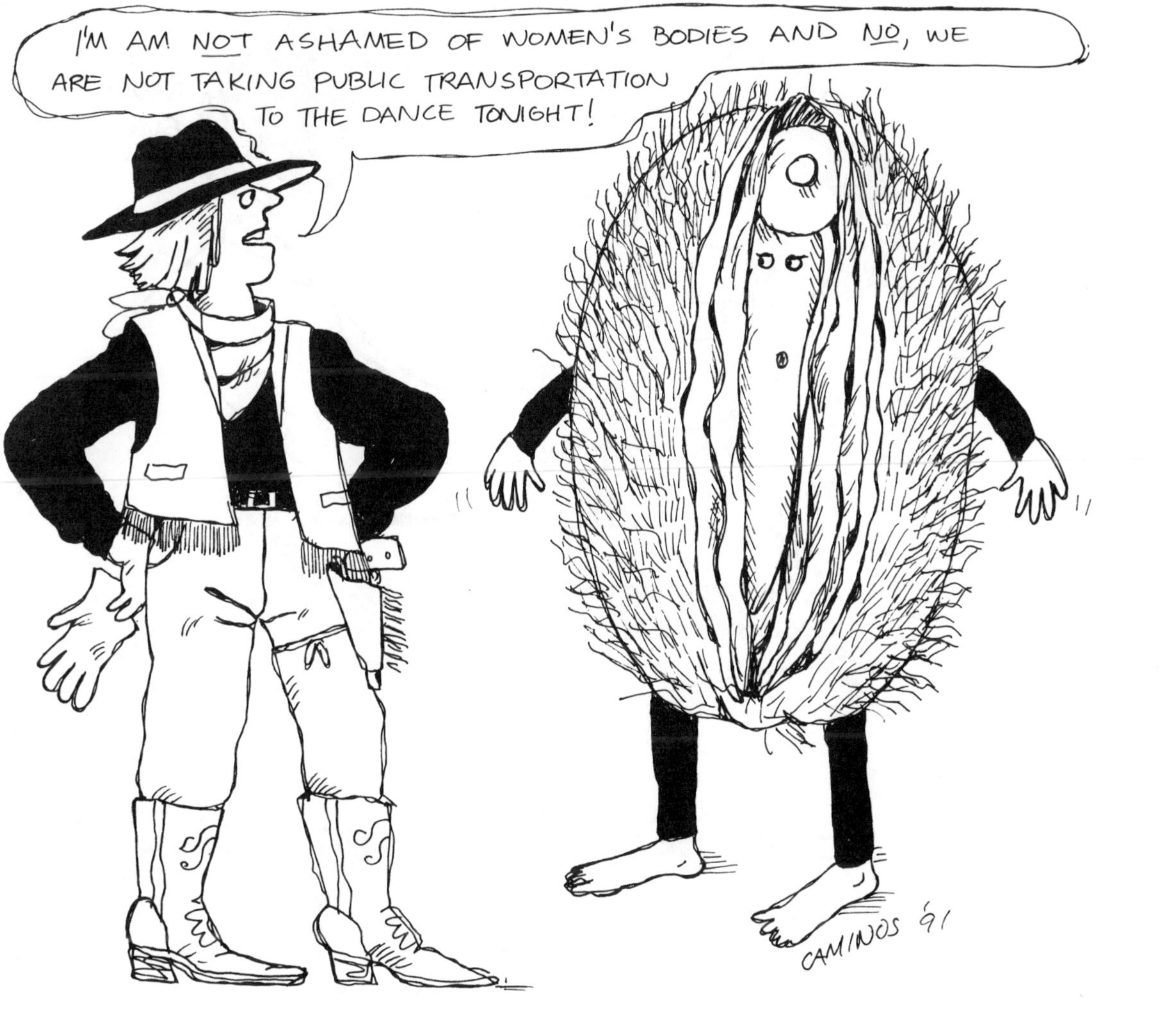
I'M AM NOT ASHAMED OF WOMEN'S BODIES AND NO, WE ARE NOT TAKING PUBLIC TRANSPORTATION TO THE DANCE TONIGHT!
CAMINOS '91

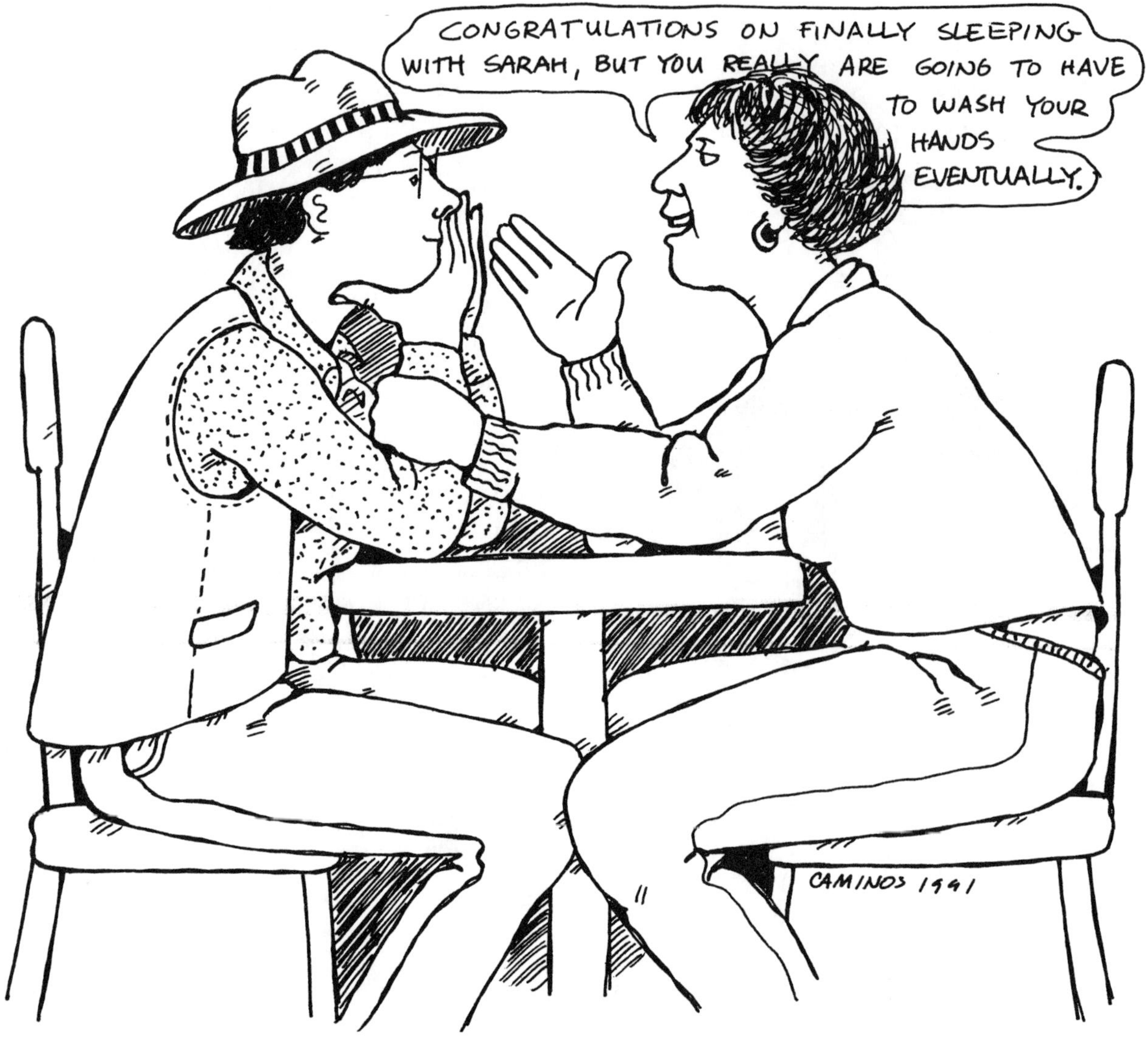
CONGRATULATIONS ON FINALLY SLEEPING WITH SARAH, BUT YOU REALLY ARE GOING TO HAVE TO WASH YOUR HANDS EVENTUALLY.
CAMINOS 1991

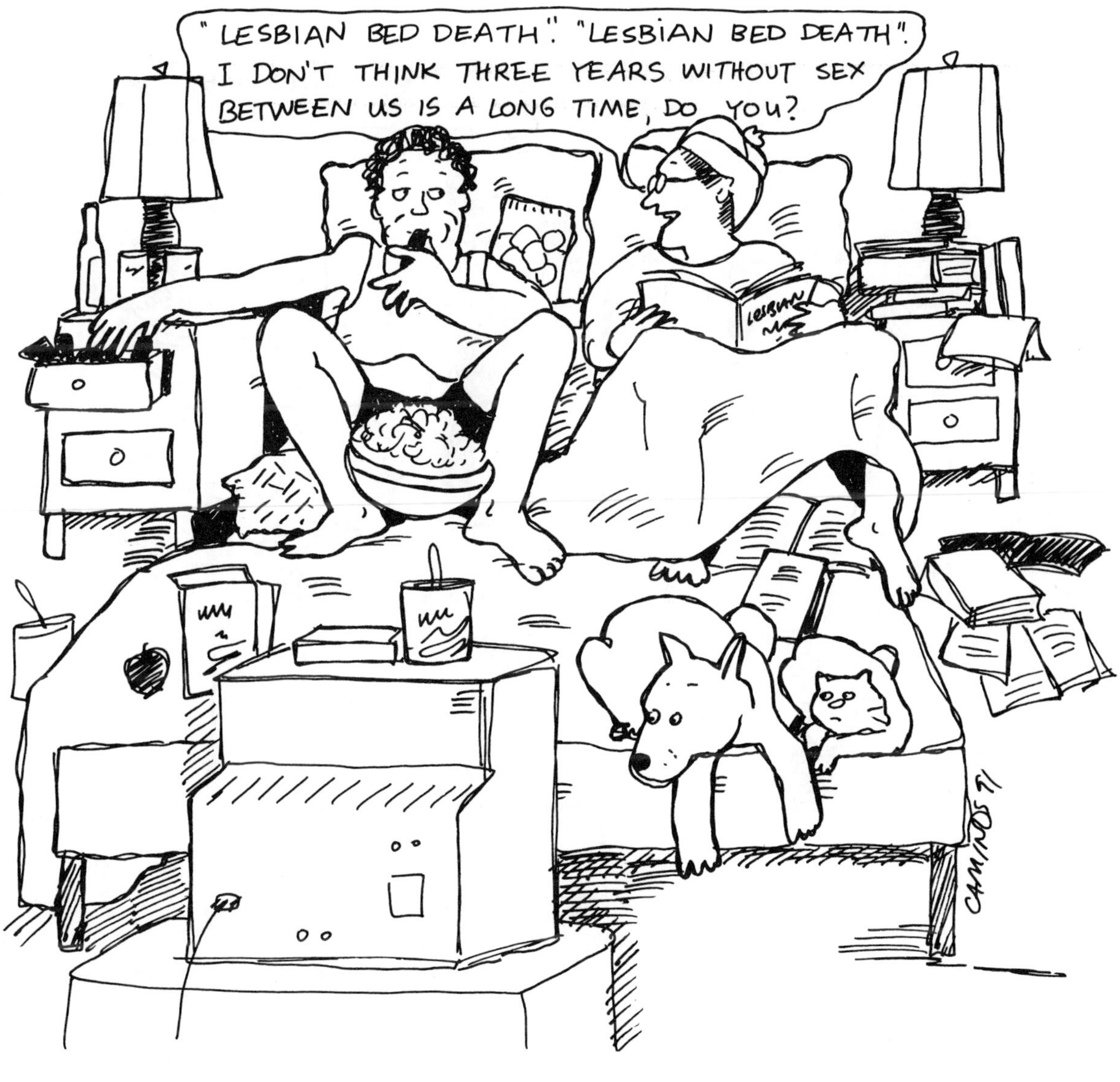
"LESBIAN BED DEATH". "LESBIAN BED DEATH". I DON'T THINK THREE YEARS WITHOUT SEX BETWEEN US IS A LONG TIME, DO YOU?

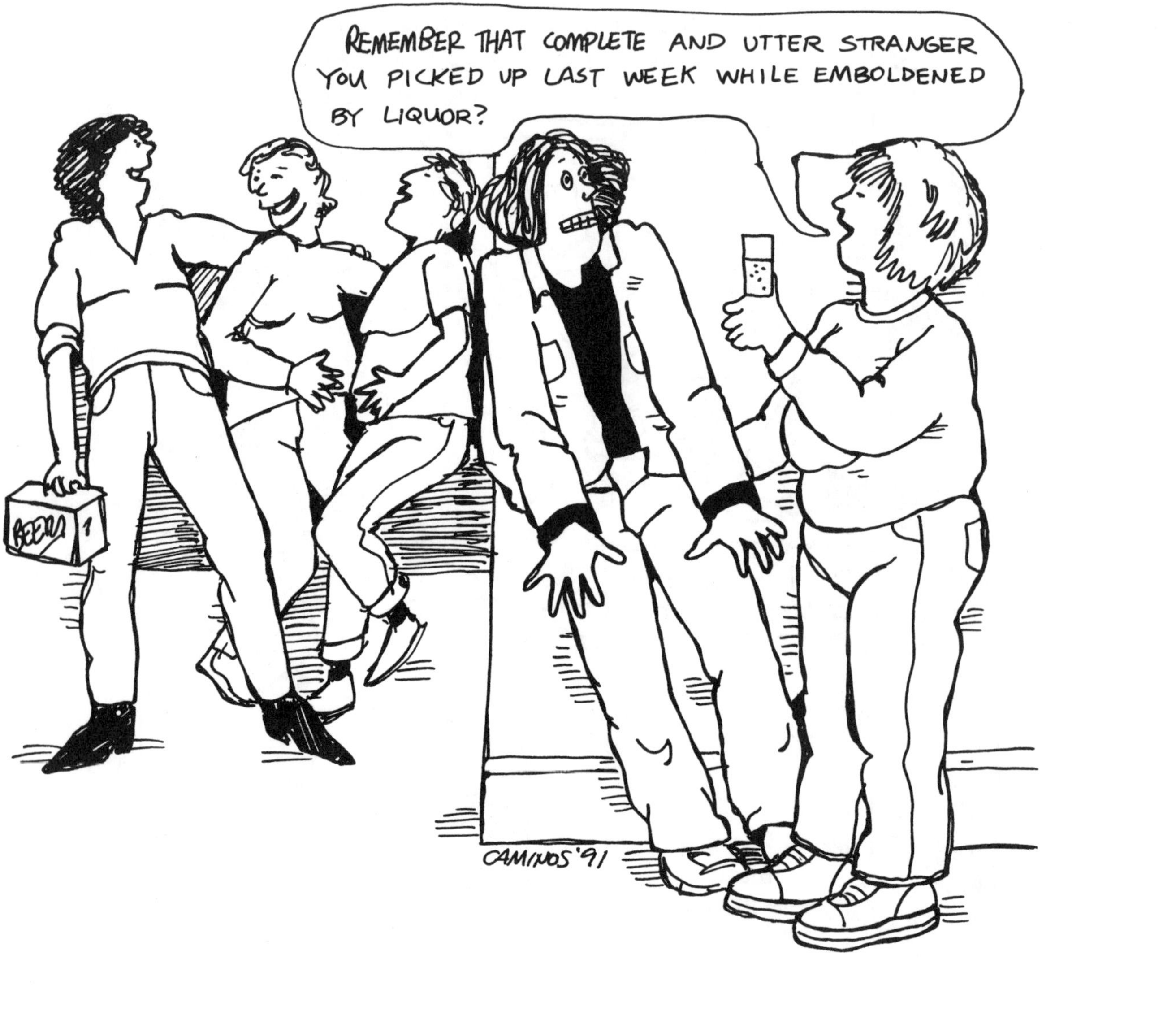
REMEMBER THAT COMPLETE AND UTTER STRANGER YOU PICKED UP LAST WEEK WHILE EMBOLDENED BY LIQUOR?
BEER
CAMINOS '91

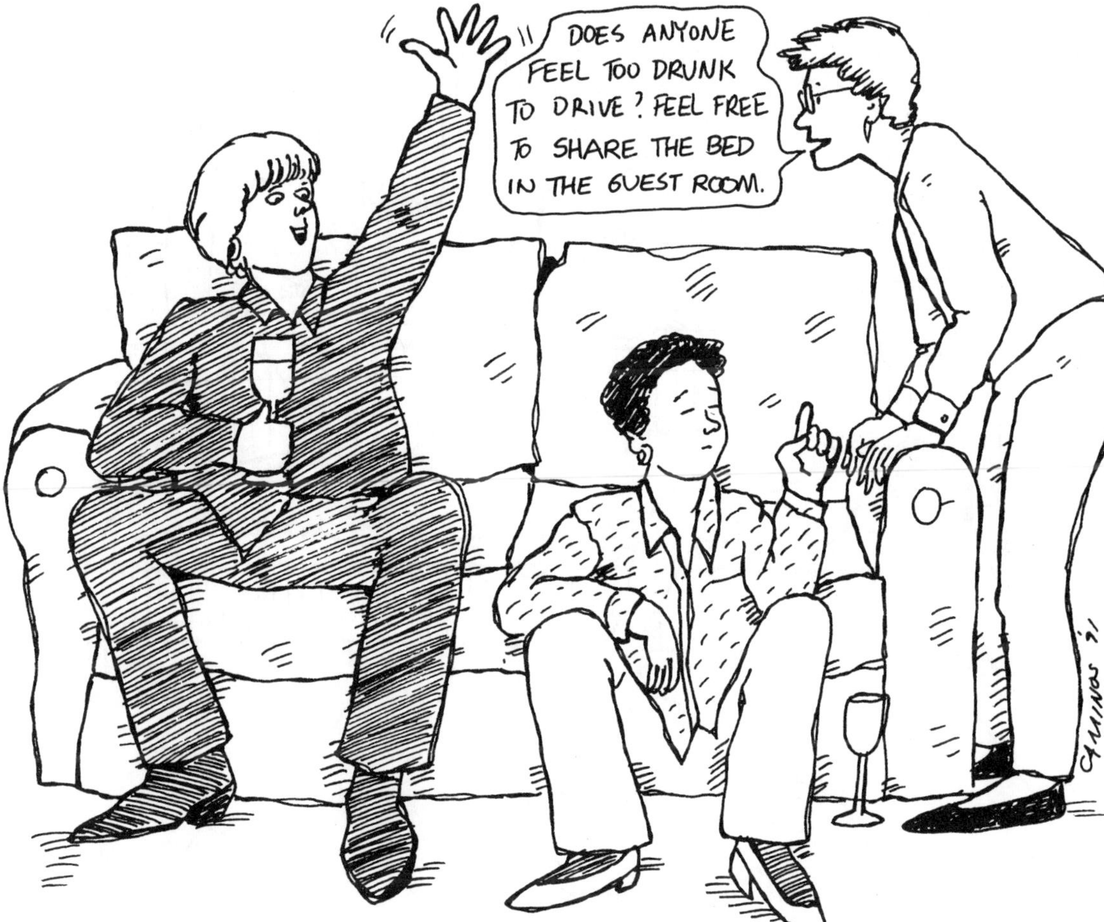
DOES ANYONE FEEL TOO DRUNK TO DRIVE? FEEL FREE TO SHARE THE BED IN THE GUEST ROOM.

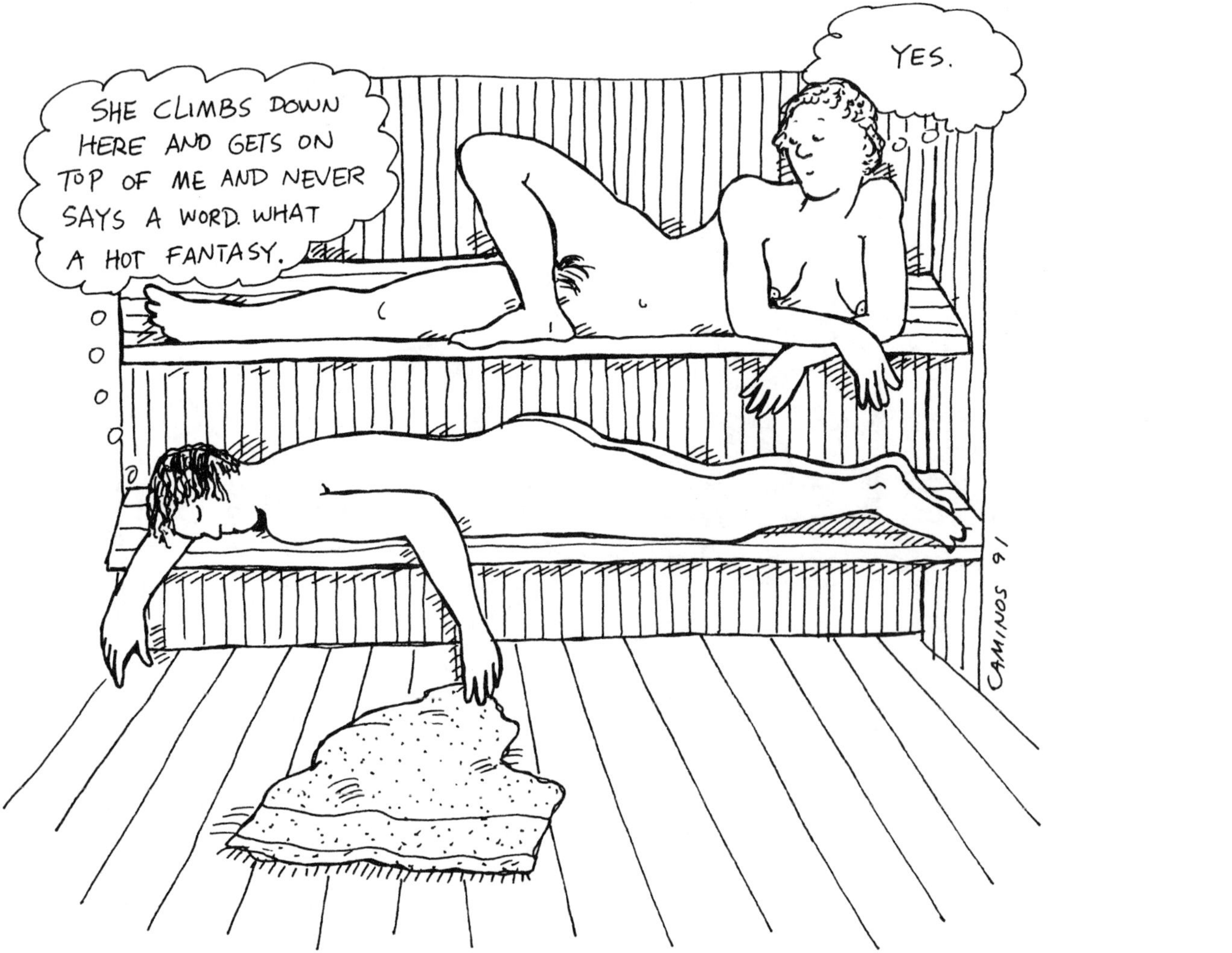
SHE CLIMBS DOWN HERE AND GETS ON TOP OF ME AND NEVER SAYS A WORD. WHAT A HOT FANTASY.
YES.
CAMINOS '91

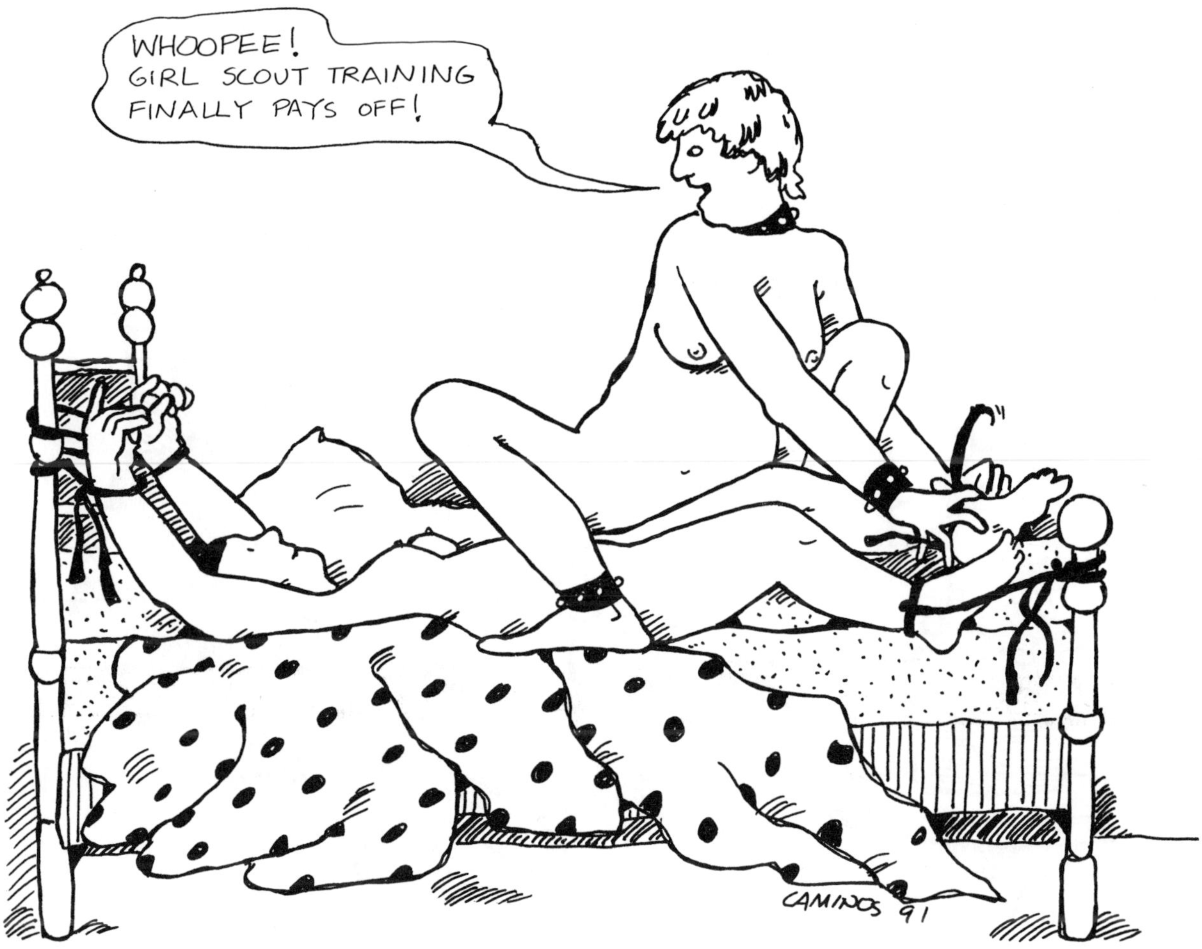
WHOOPEE!
GIRL SCOUT TRAINING
FINALLY PAYS OFF!
CAMINOS '91

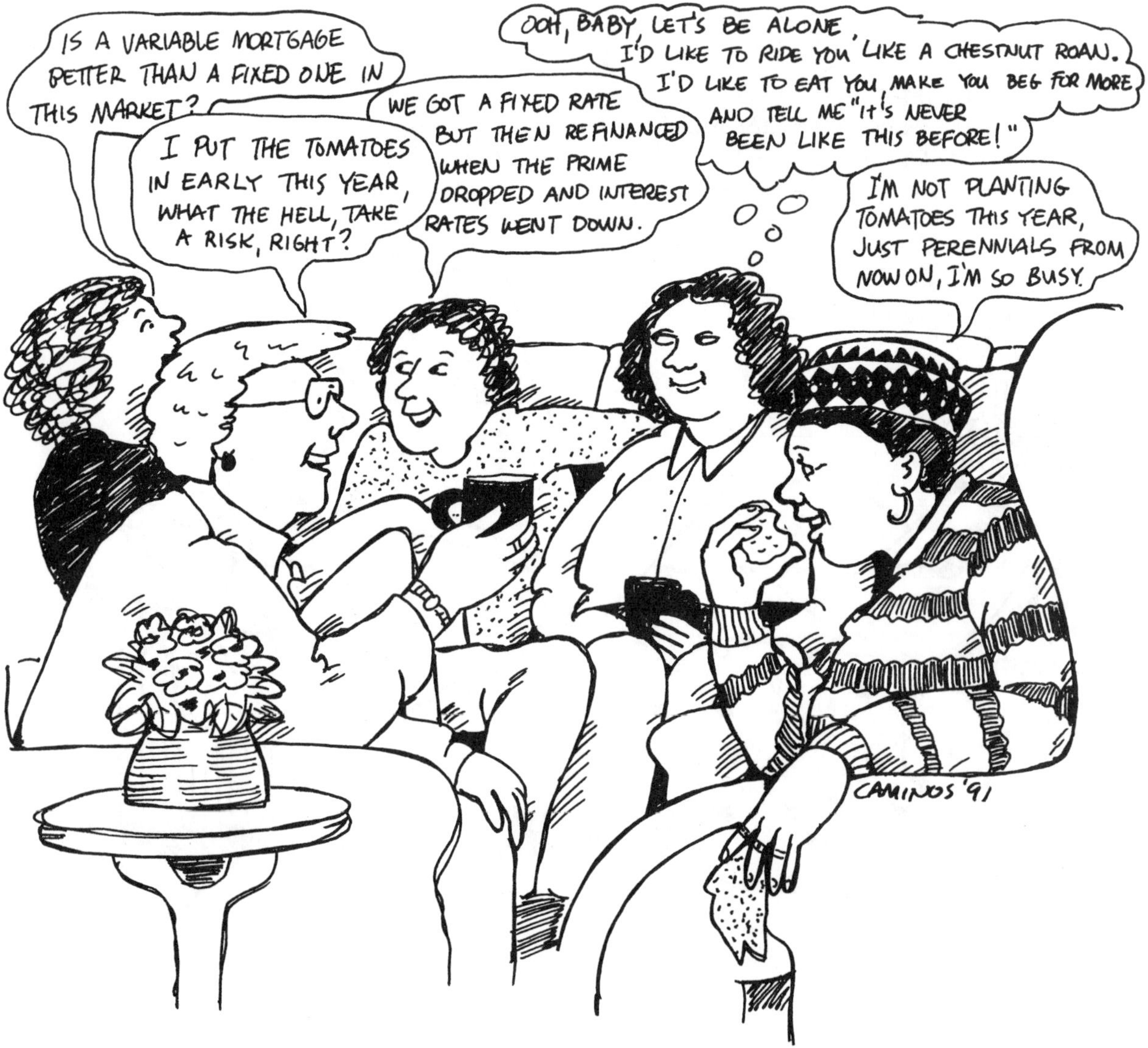
IS A VARIABLE MORTGAGE BETTER THAN A FIXED ONE IN THIS MARKET?
I PUT THE TOMATOES IN EARLY THIS YEAR, WHAT THE HELL, TAKE A RISK, RIGHT?
WE GOT A FIXED RATE BUT THEN REFINANCED WHEN THE PRIME DROPPED AND INTEREST RATES WENT DOWN.
OOH, BABY, LET'S BE ALONE, I'D LIKE TO RIDE YOU LIKE A CHESTNUT ROAN. I'D LIKE TO EAT YOU, MAKE YOU BEG FOR MORE AND TELL ME "IT'S NEVER BEEN LIKE THIS BEFORE!"
I'M NOT PLANTING TOMATOES THIS YEAR, JUST PERENNIALS FROM NOW ON, I'M SO BUSY.
CAMINOS '91

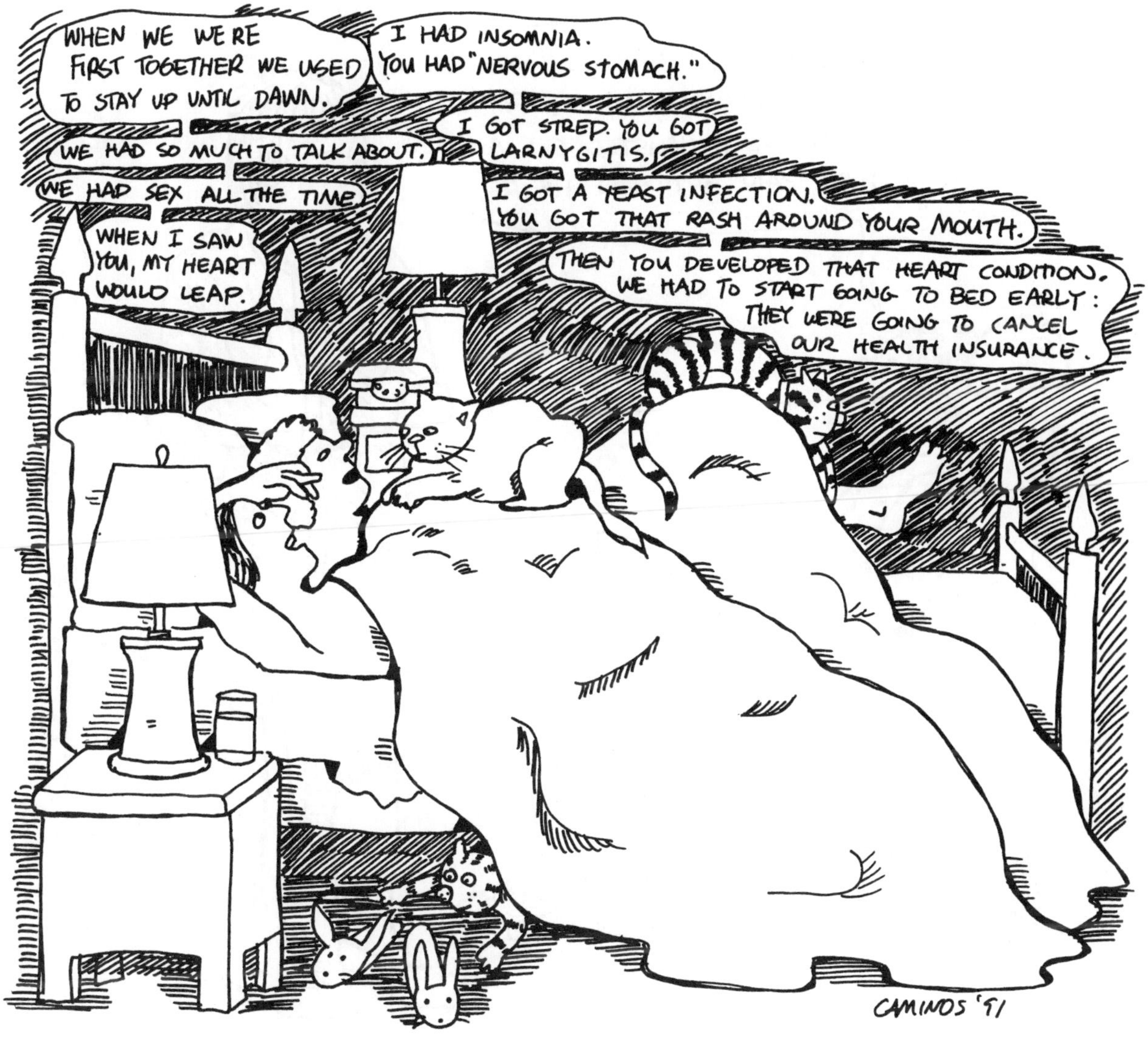

WHEN WE WERE FIRST TOGETHER WE USED TO STAY UP UNTIL DAWN.
I HAD INSOMNIA. YOU HAD "NERVOUS STOMACH."
WE HAD SO MUCH TO TALK ABOUT.
I GOT STREP. YOU GOT LARNYGITIS.
WE HAD SEX ALL THE TIME.
I GOT A YEAST INFECTION. YOU GOT THAT RASH AROUND YOUR MOUTH.
WHEN I SAW YOU, MY HEART WOULD LEAP.
THEN YOU DEVELOPED THAT HEART CONDITION. WE HAD TO START GOING TO BED EARLY: THEY WERE GOING TO CANCEL OUR HEALTH INSURANCE.
CAMINOS '91

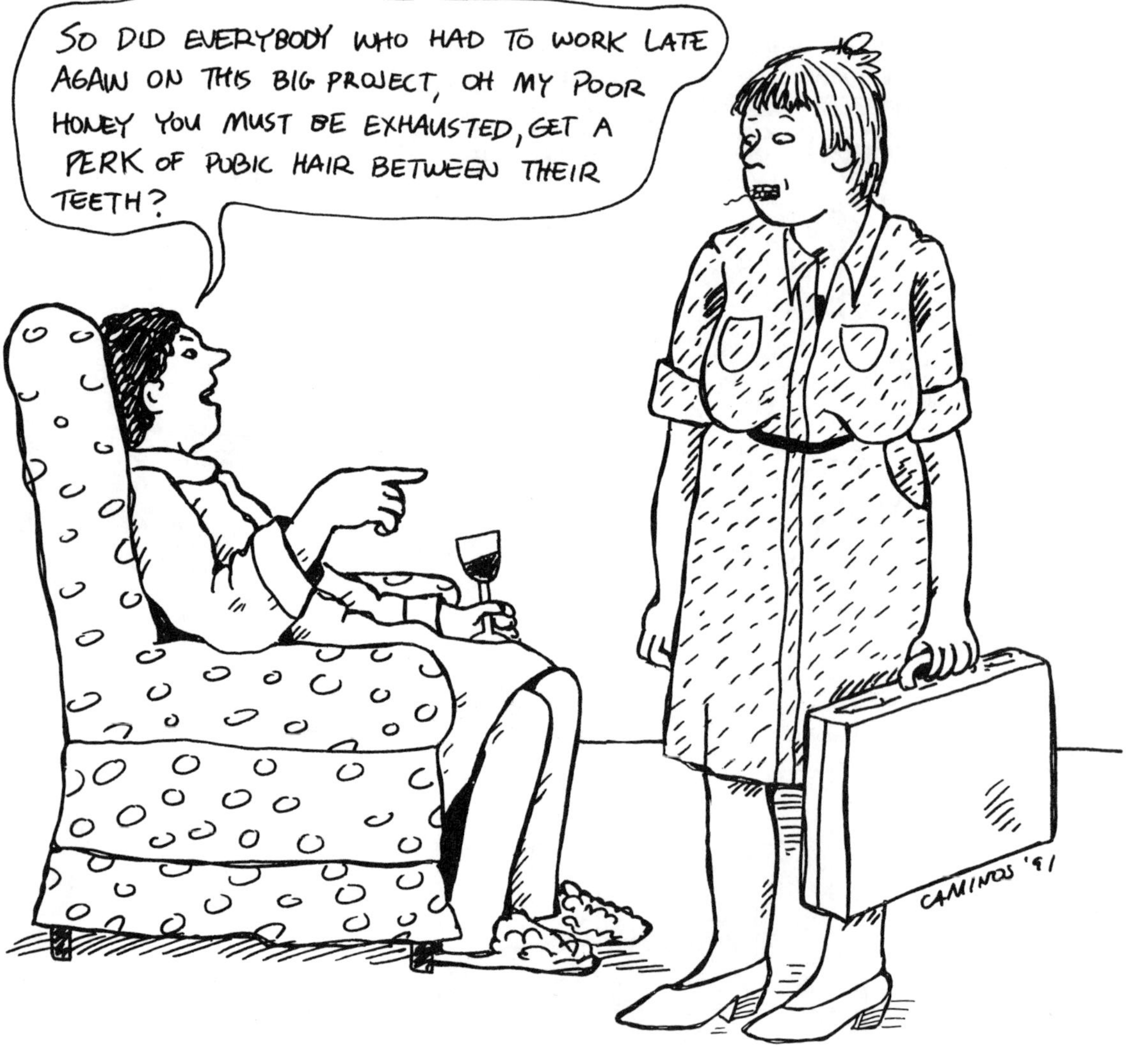
SO DID EVERYBODY WHO HAD TO WORK LATE AGAIN ON THIS BIG PROJECT, OH MY POOR HONEY YOU MUST BE EXHAUSTED, GET A PERK OF PUBIC HAIR BETWEEN THEIR TEETH?
CAMINOS '91

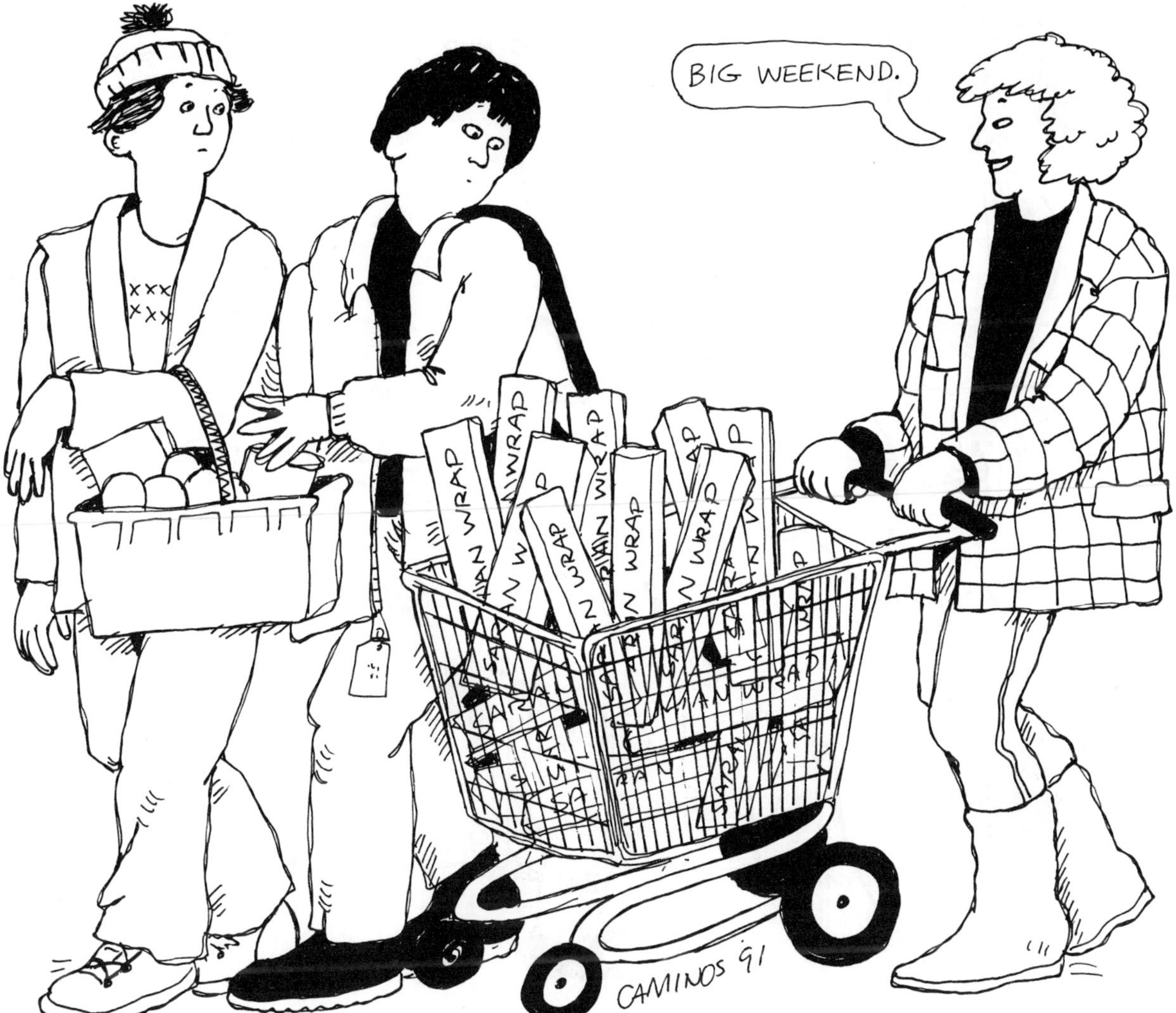
BIG WEEKEND.
CAMINOS '91

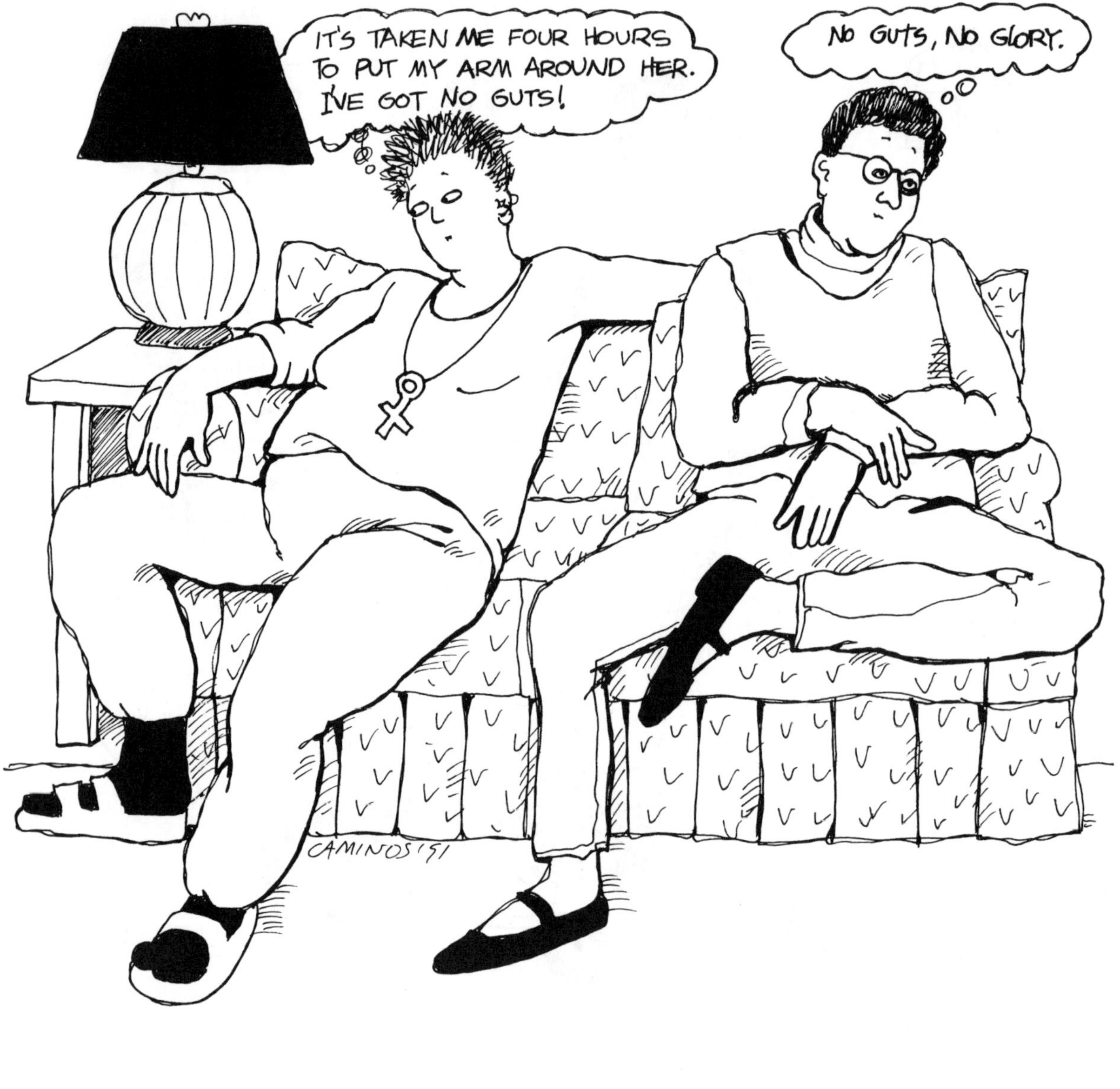
IT'S TAKEN ME FOUR HOURS
TO PUT MY ARM AROUND HER.
I'VE GOT NO GUTS!
NO GUTS, NO GLORY.
CAMINOS '91

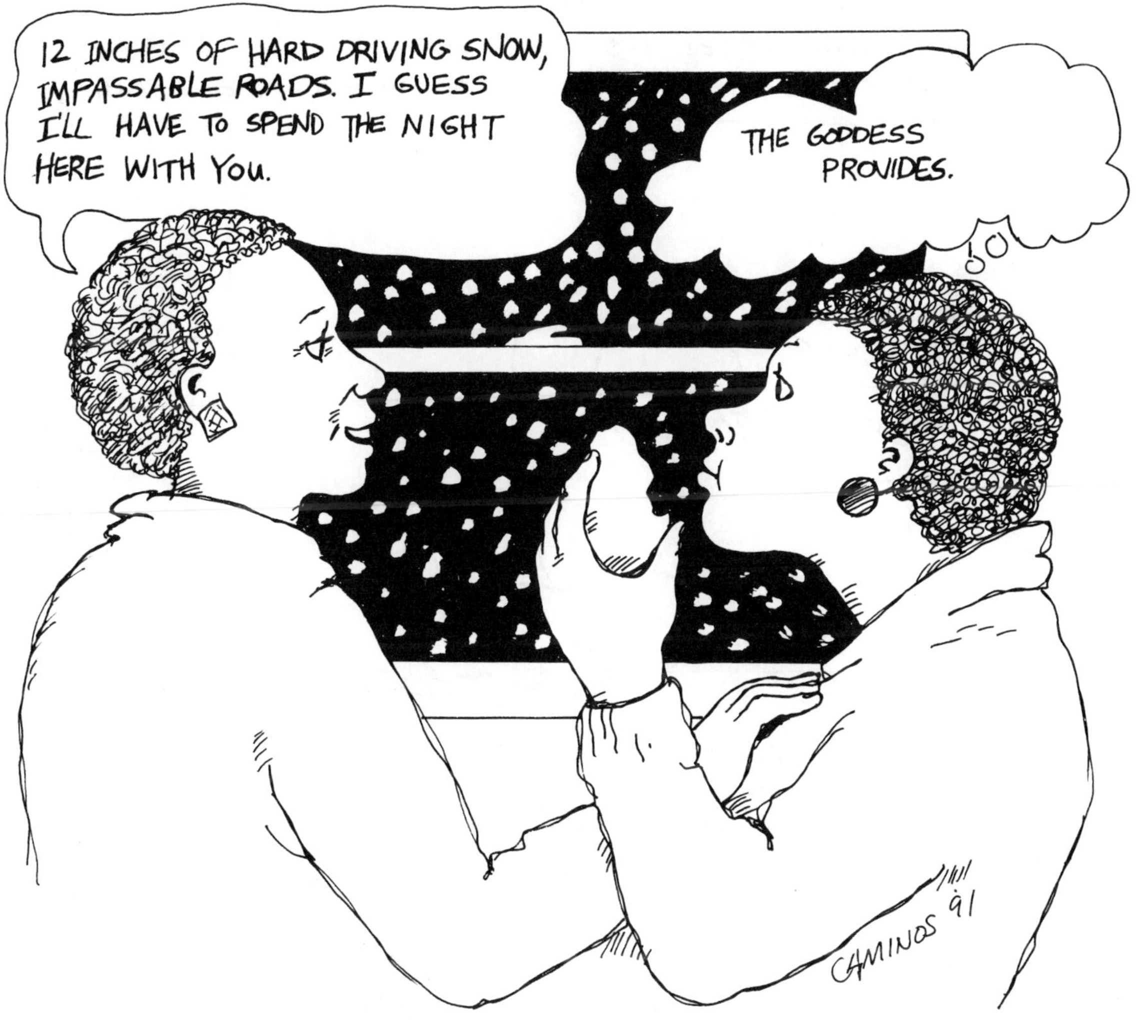
12 INCHES OF HARD DRIVING SNOW, IMPASSABLE ROADS. I GUESS I'LL HAVE TO SPEND THE NIGHT HERE WITH YOU.
THE GODDESS PROVIDES.
CAMINOS '91

SUZANNE, MAYBE IT'S TIME WE HAD A LITTLE TALK ABOUT THE RISK OF HAVING AFFAIRS AT THE OFFICE.
CAMINOS '91

IN MY DAY WE DIDN'T NEED SEX TOYS TO EXPERIENCE PLEASURE; OUR HANDS AND MOUTHS WERE SUFFICIENT, THANK YOU VERY MUCH. HOW MANY ORGASMS DID YOU SAY YOU HAD WHILE USING THAT STATE OF THE ART VIBRATOR?

"...AND LEAD ME NOT INTO TEMPTATION, BUT DELIVER ME FROM EVIL." SINS OF THE FLESH. CARNAL KNOWLEDGE. CARDINAL SIN OF LUST, THE WORST ONE. DEAR GOD, LET ME NOT BE CATHOLIC JUST THIS ONCE.
MY ROOM #IS 952
CAMINOS '91

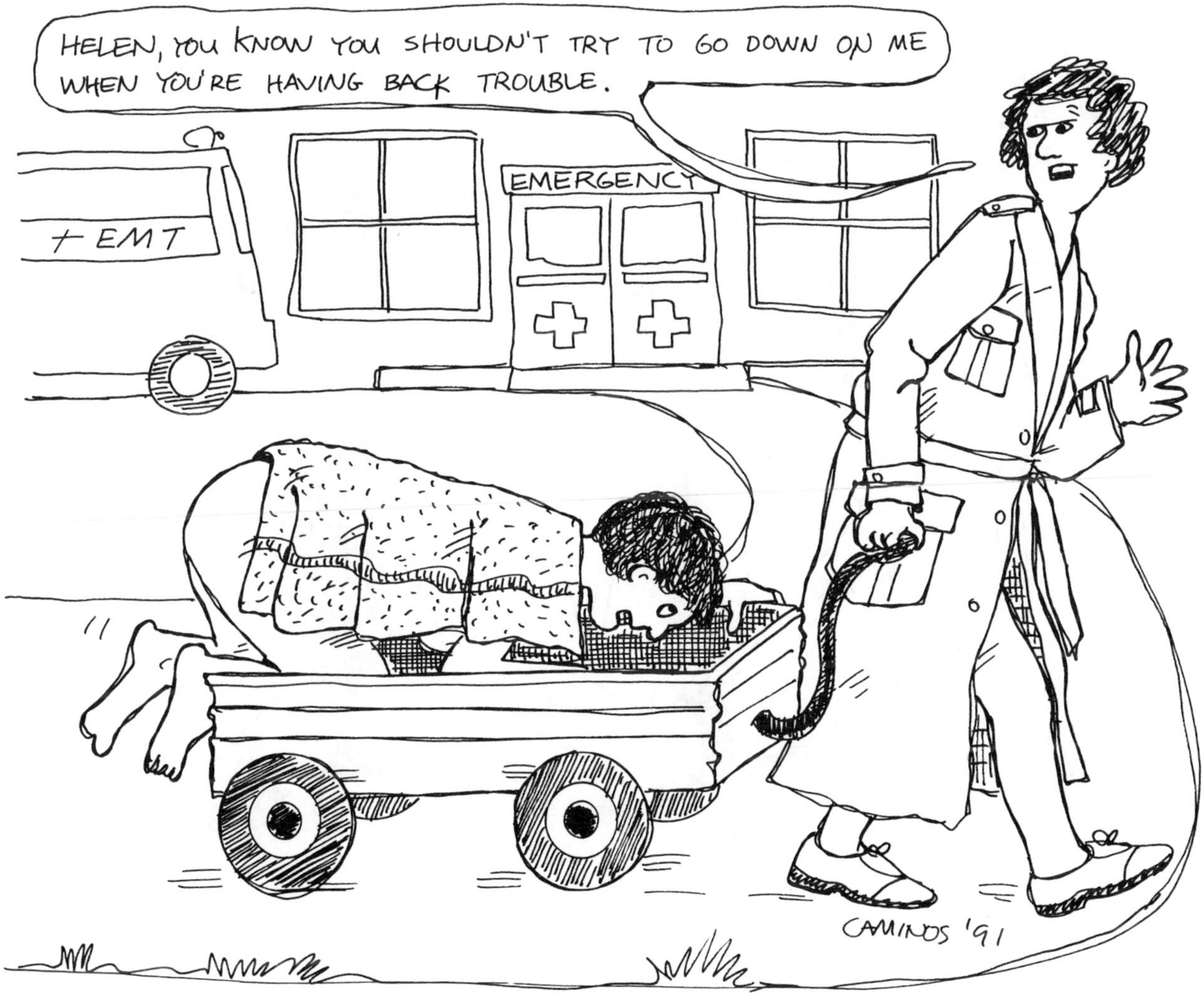
HELEN, YOU KNOW YOU SHOULDN'T TRY TO GO DOWN ON ME WHEN YOU'RE HAVING BACK TROUBLE.
EMERGENCY
+ EMT
CAMINOS '91

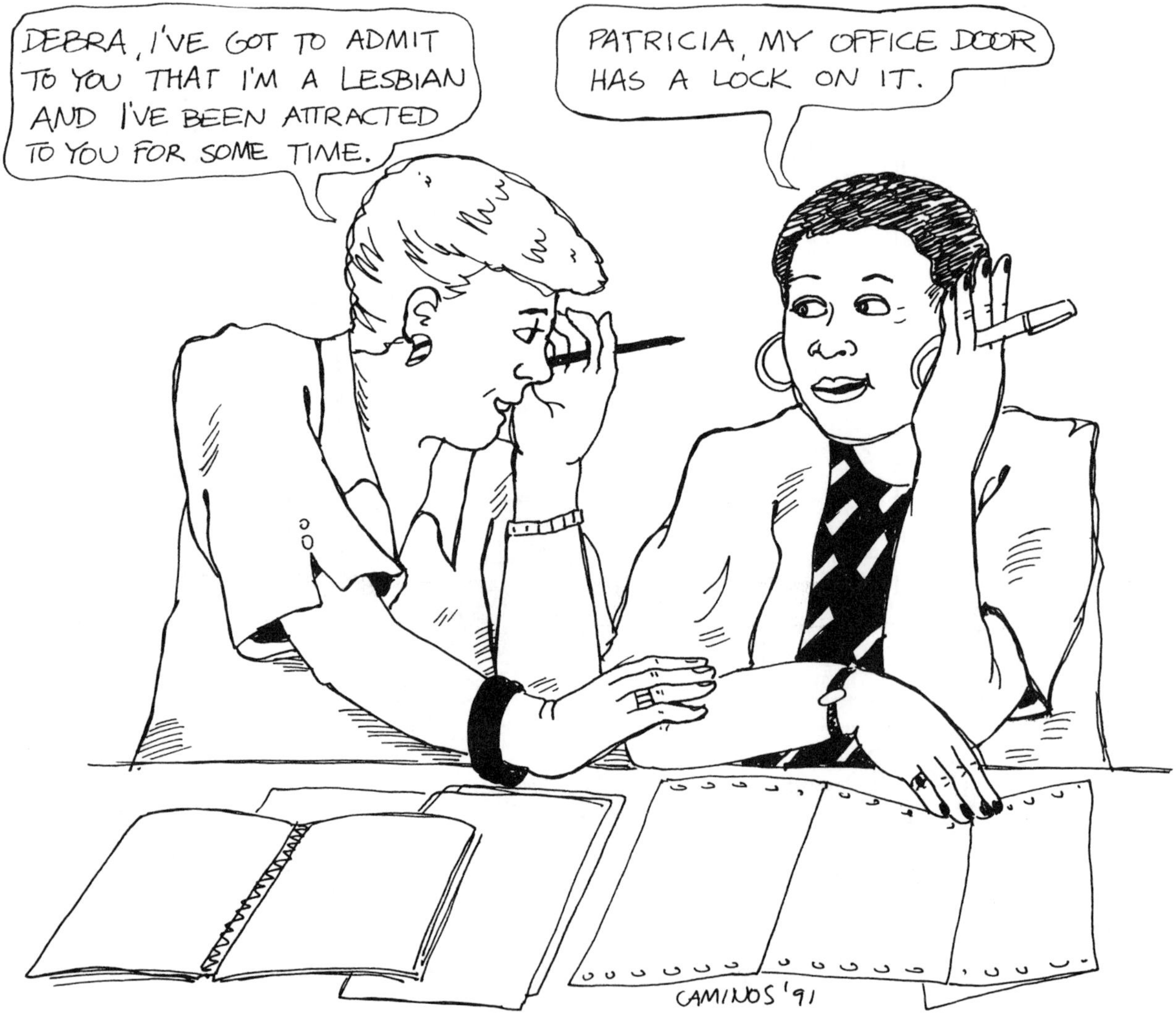
DEBRA, I'VE GOT TO ADMIT TO YOU THAT I'M A LESBIAN AND I'VE BEEN ATTRACTED TO YOU FOR SOME TIME.
PATRICIA, MY OFFICE DOOR HAS A LOCK ON IT.
CAMINOS '91

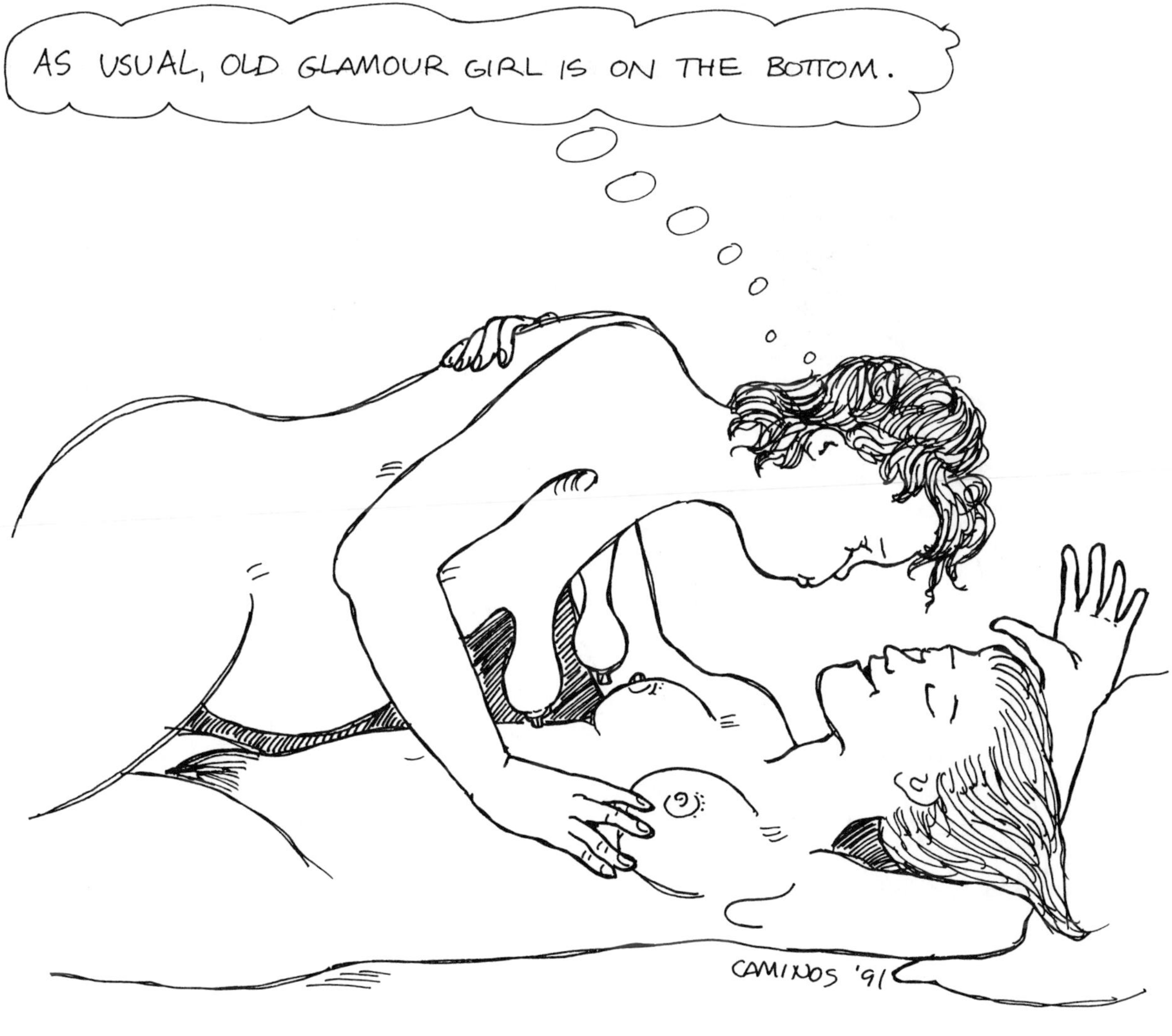
AS USUAL, OLD GLAMOUR GIRL IS ON THE BOTTOM.
CAMINOS '91

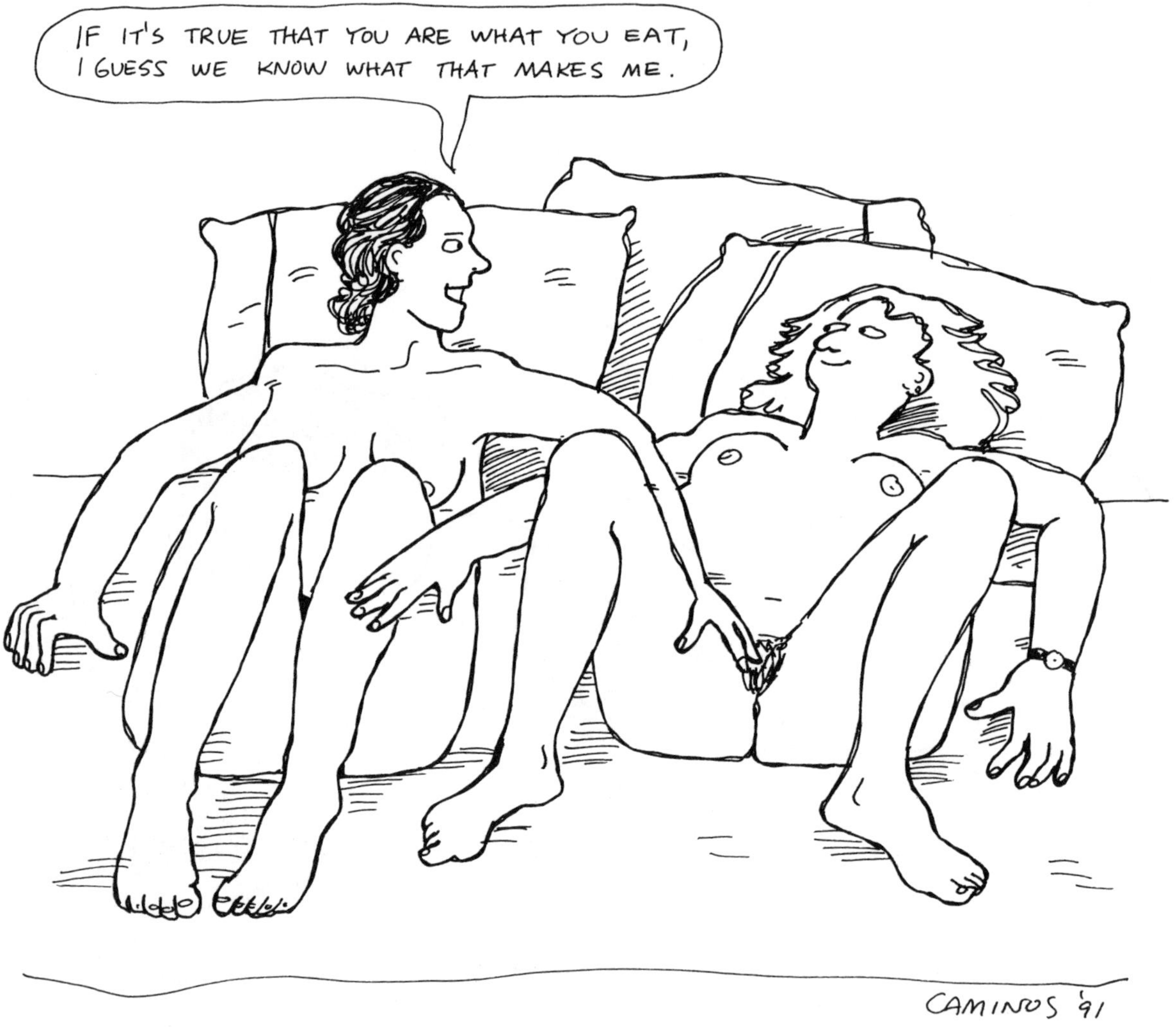
IF IT'S TRUE THAT YOU ARE WHAT YOU EAT, I GUESS WE KNOW WHAT THAT MAKES ME.
CAMINOS '91

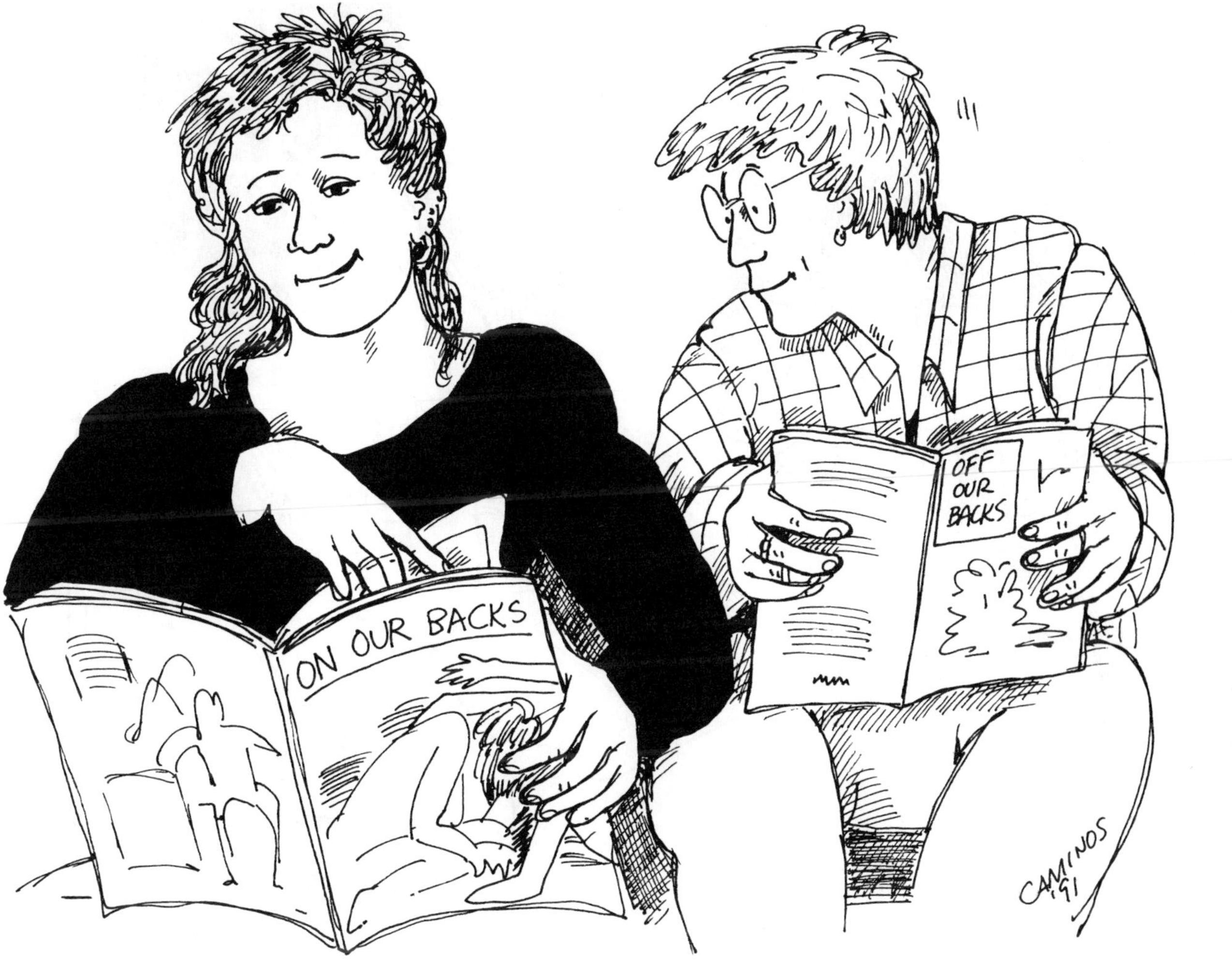
ON OUR BACKS
OFF OUR BACKS
CAMINOS '91

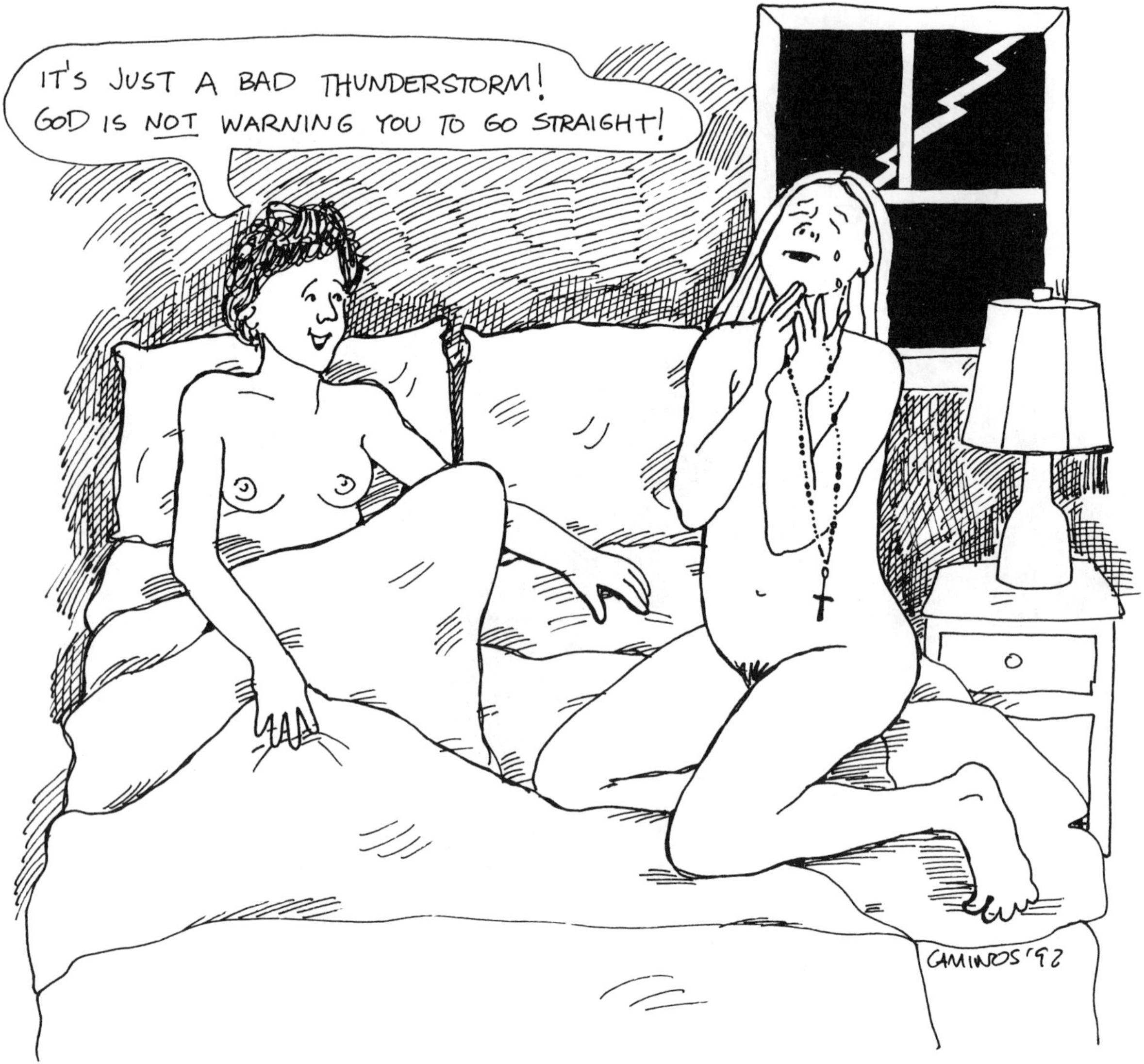
IT'S JUST A BAD THUNDERSTORM! GOD IS NOT WARNING YOU TO GO STRAIGHT!
CAMINOS '92

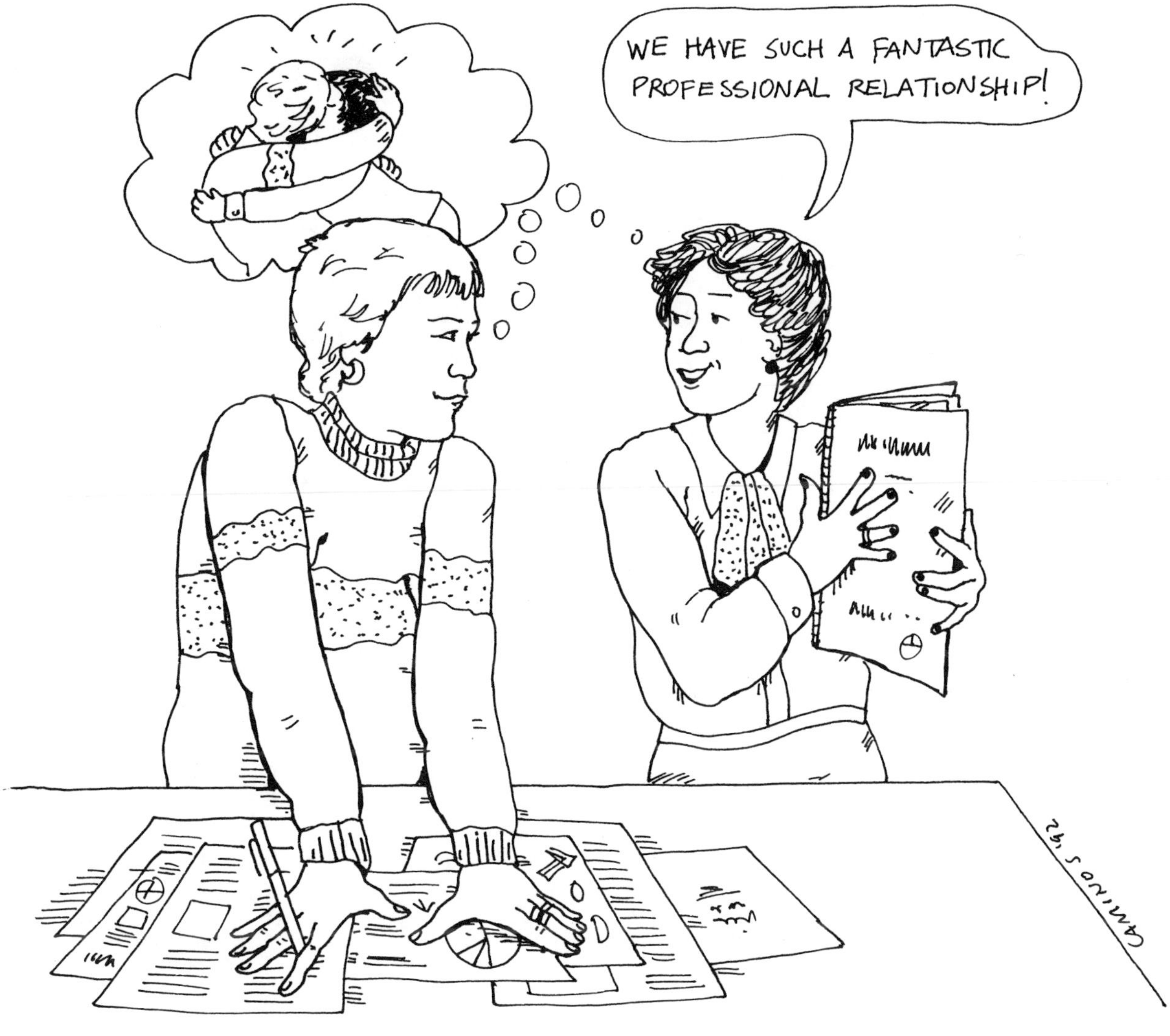
WE HAVE SUCH A FANTASTIC PROFESSIONAL RELATIONSHIP!
CAMINOS '92

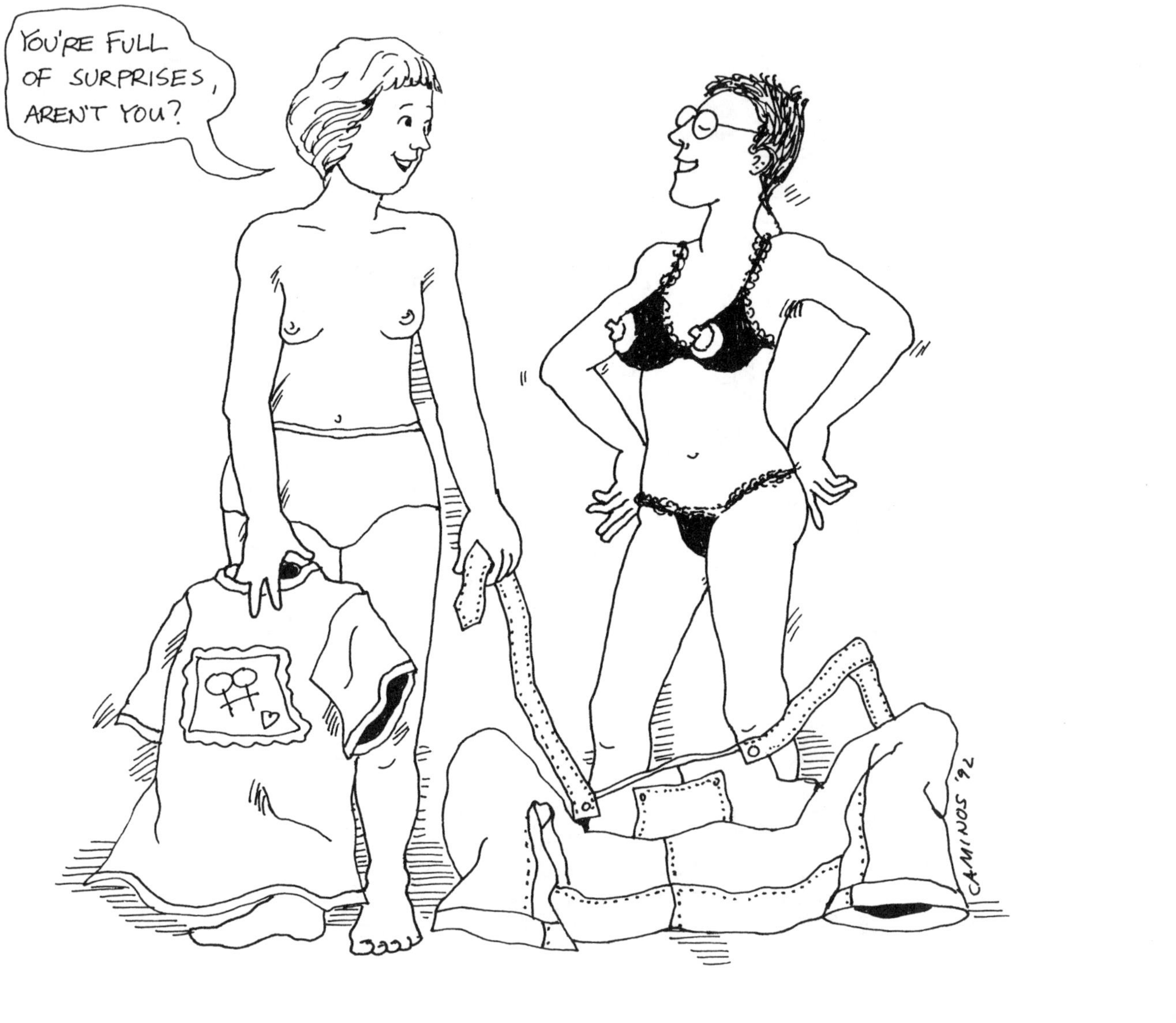
YOU'RE FULL OF SURPRISES, AREN'T YOU?
CAMINOS '92

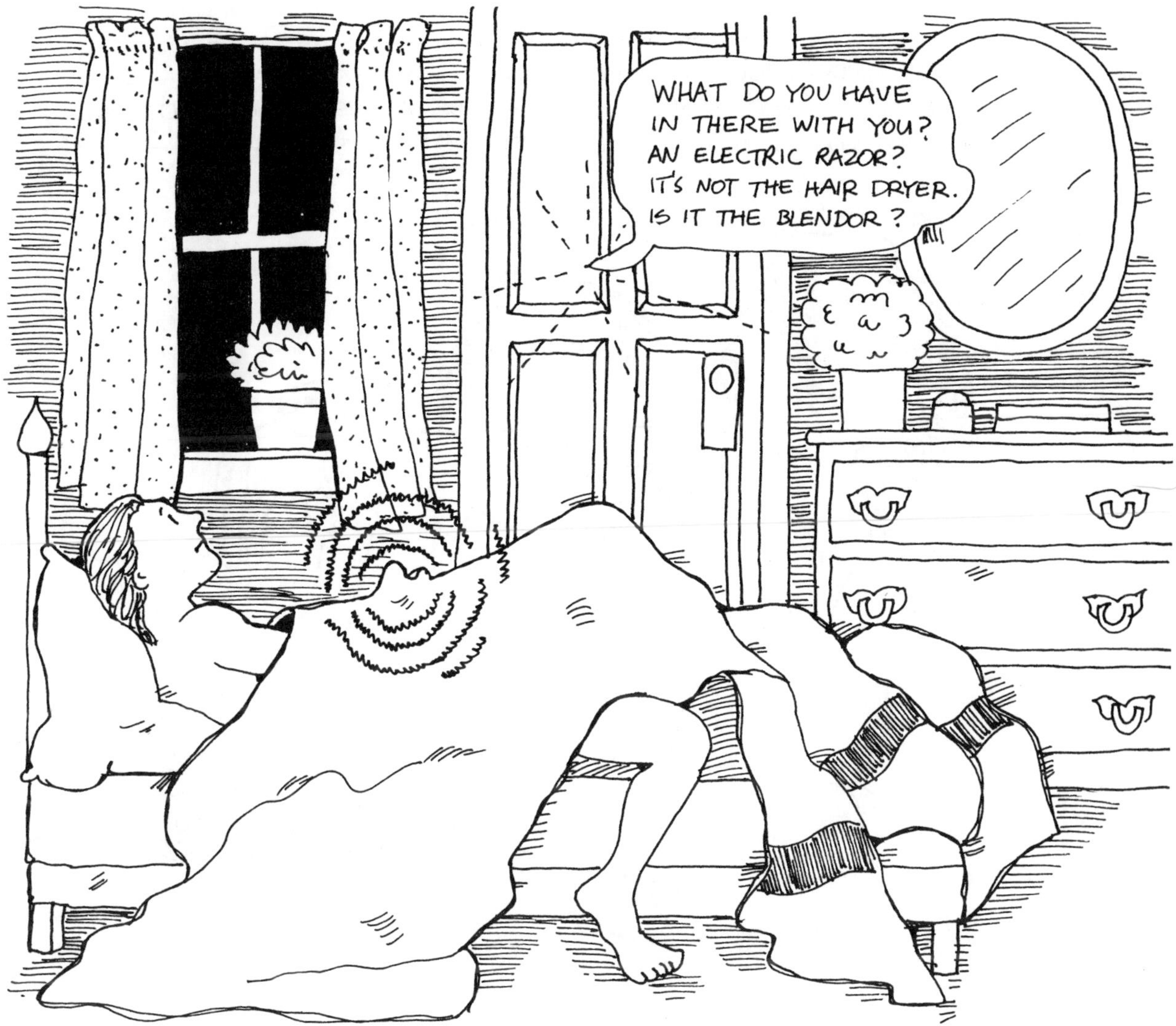
WHAT DO YOU HAVE IN THERE WITH YOU? AN ELECTRIC RAZOR? IT'S NOT THE HAIR DRYER. IS IT THE BLENDOR?

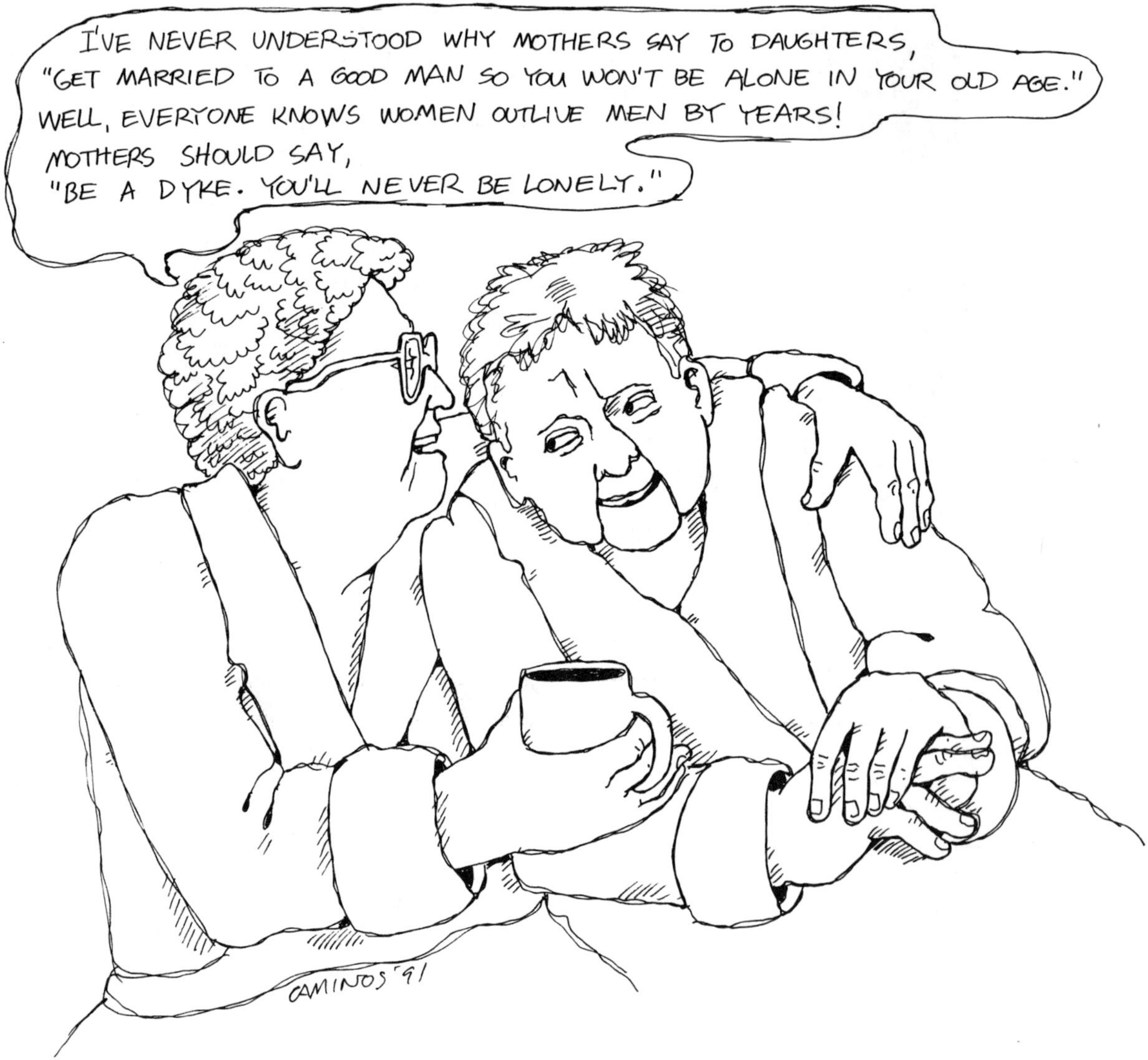
I'VE NEVER UNDERSTOOD WHY MOTHERS SAY TO DAUGHTERS, "GET MARRIED TO A GOOD MAN SO YOU WON'T BE ALONE IN YOUR OLD AGE." WELL, EVERYONE KNOWS WOMEN OUTLIVE MEN BY YEARS! MOTHERS SHOULD SAY, "BE A DYKE. YOU'LL NEVER BE LONELY."
CAMINOS '91

I KNOW "OLD IS BEAUTIFUL". I KNOW ABOUT "LINES OF EXPERIENCE", "YOU'RE NOT GETTING OLDER, YOU'RE GETTING BETTER", "AGE BRINGS WISDOM". WELL, I'M GOOD ENOUGH, OLD ENOUGH, AND SMART ENOUGH TO KNOW THIS SUCKS.
CAMINOS '91

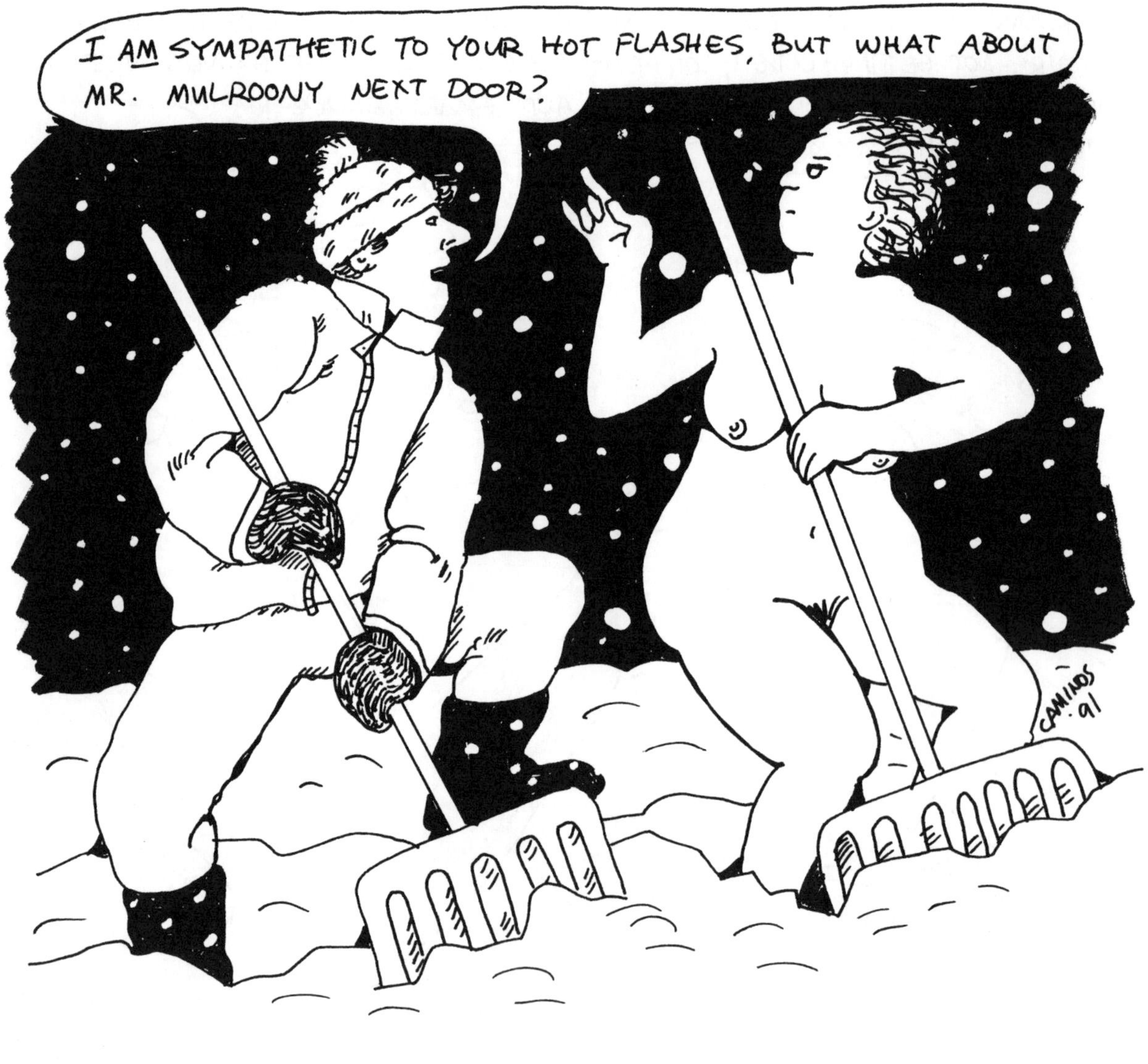
I AM SYMPATHETIC TO YOUR HOT FLASHES, BUT WHAT ABOUT MR. MULROONY NEXT DOOR?
CAMINOS '91

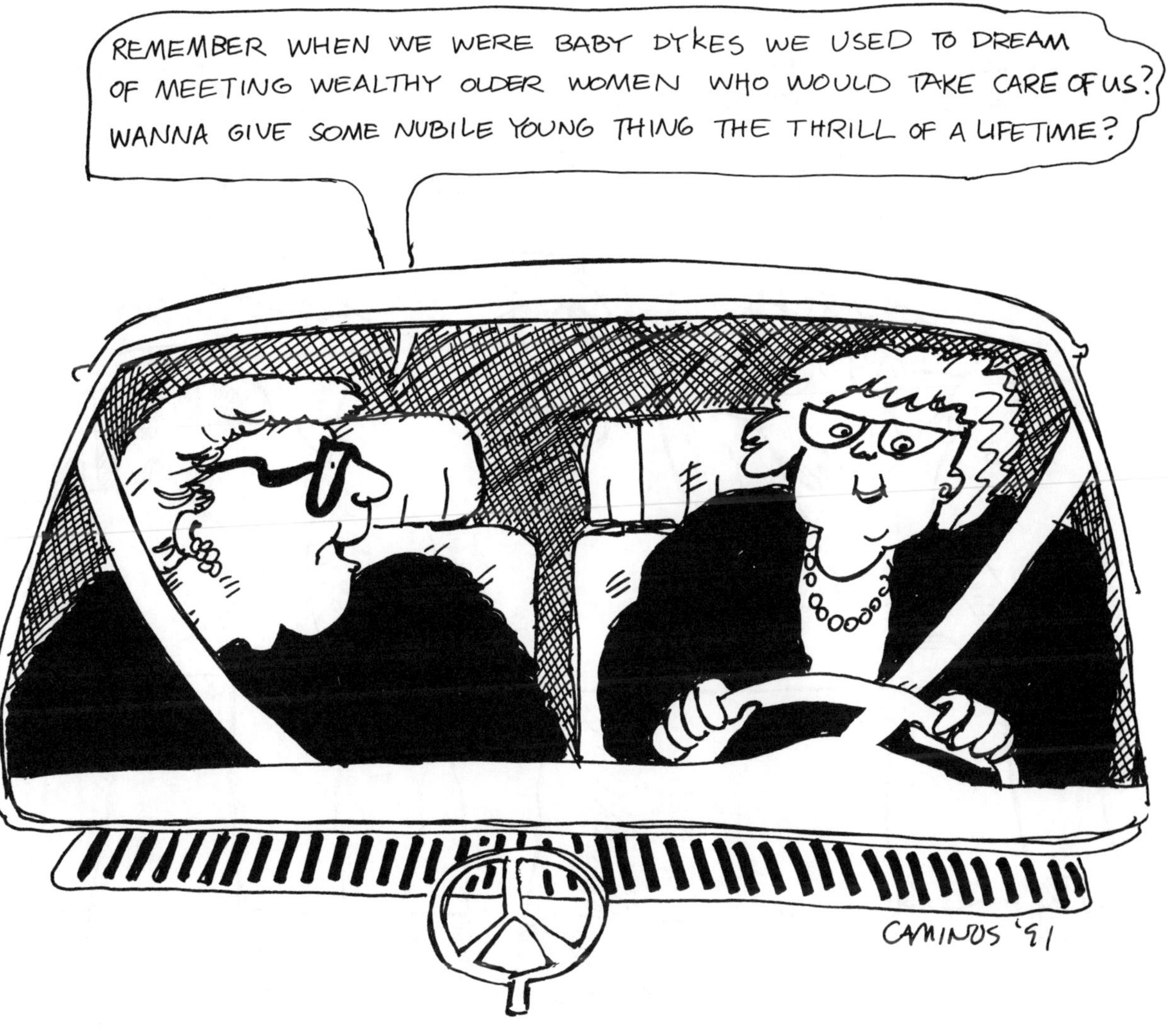
REMEMBER WHEN WE WERE BABY DYKES WE USED TO DREAM OF MEETING WEALTHY OLDER WOMEN WHO WOULD TAKE CARE OF US? WANNA GIVE SOME NUBILE YOUNG THING THE THRILL OF A LIFETIME?
CAMINOS '91

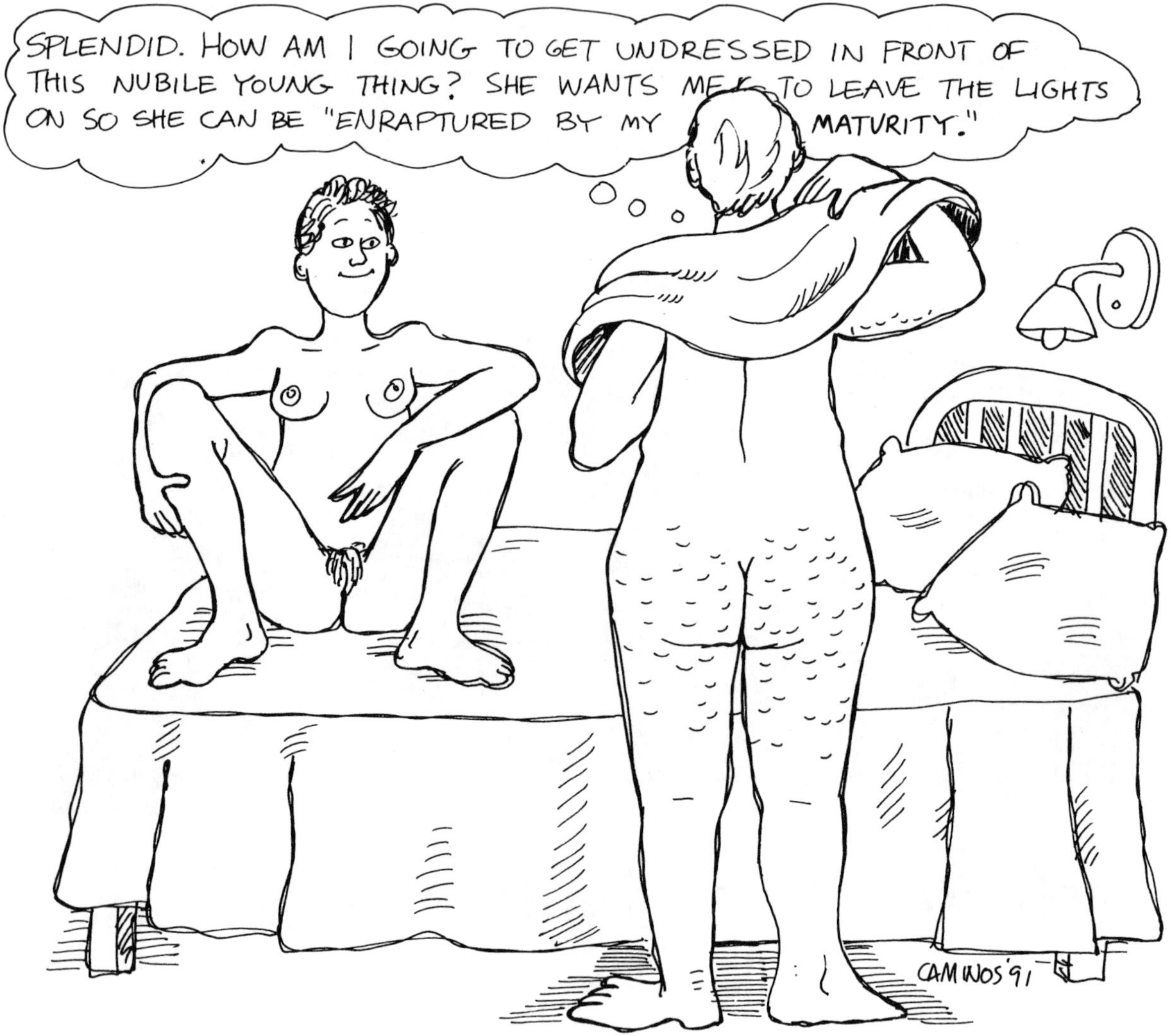
SPLENDID. HOW AM I GOING TO GET UNDRESSED IN FRONT OF THIS NUBILE YOUNG THING? SHE WANTS ME TO LEAVE THE LIGHTS ON SO SHE CAN BE "ENRAPTURED BY MY MATURITY."
CAMINOS '91

SHIT, GOING OUT WITH THIS SUAVE OLDER WOMAN WAS A BIG MISTAKE. SHE PROBABLY THINKS I'M VAPID AND NAÏVE IN BED, WHICH I'M AFRAID IS TRUE, ESPECIALLY WHEN COMPARED WITH HER. WHAT IF I'M SO NERVOUS I HAVE DIARRHEA?
SHIT, GOING OUT WITH THIS TRENDY YOUNGER WOMAN WAS A MISTAKE. SHE PROBABLY FINDS ME BORING, AND NOT WITH IT, WHICH IS TRUE. I'M RUN OF THE MILL IN BED. WHAT IF I'M SO NERVOUS I HAVE DIARRHEA?
CAMINOS '91

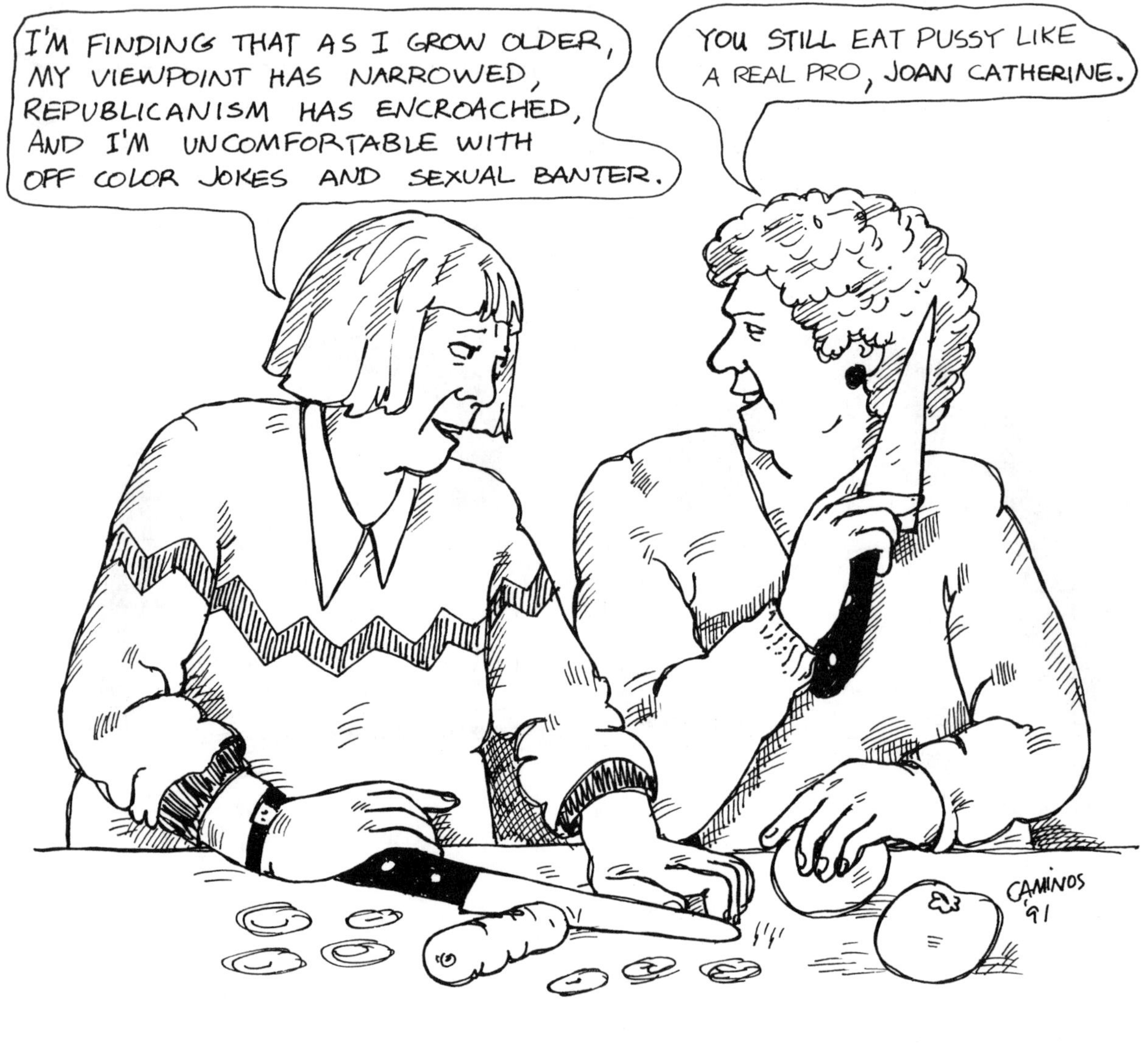
I'M FINDING THAT AS I GROW OLDER, MY VIEWPOINT HAS NARROWED, REPUBLICANISM HAS ENCROACHED, AND I'M UNCOMFORTABLE WITH OFF COLOR JOKES AND SEXUAL BANTER.
YOU STILL EAT PUSSY LIKE A REAL PRO, JOAN CATHERINE.
CAMINOS '91

MOM, DID IT EVER OCCUR TO YOU THAT YOUR AUNT FLORENCE AND HER TRAVELING COMPANION GRACE WERE MORE THAN GREAT FRIENDS?
CAMINOS '91

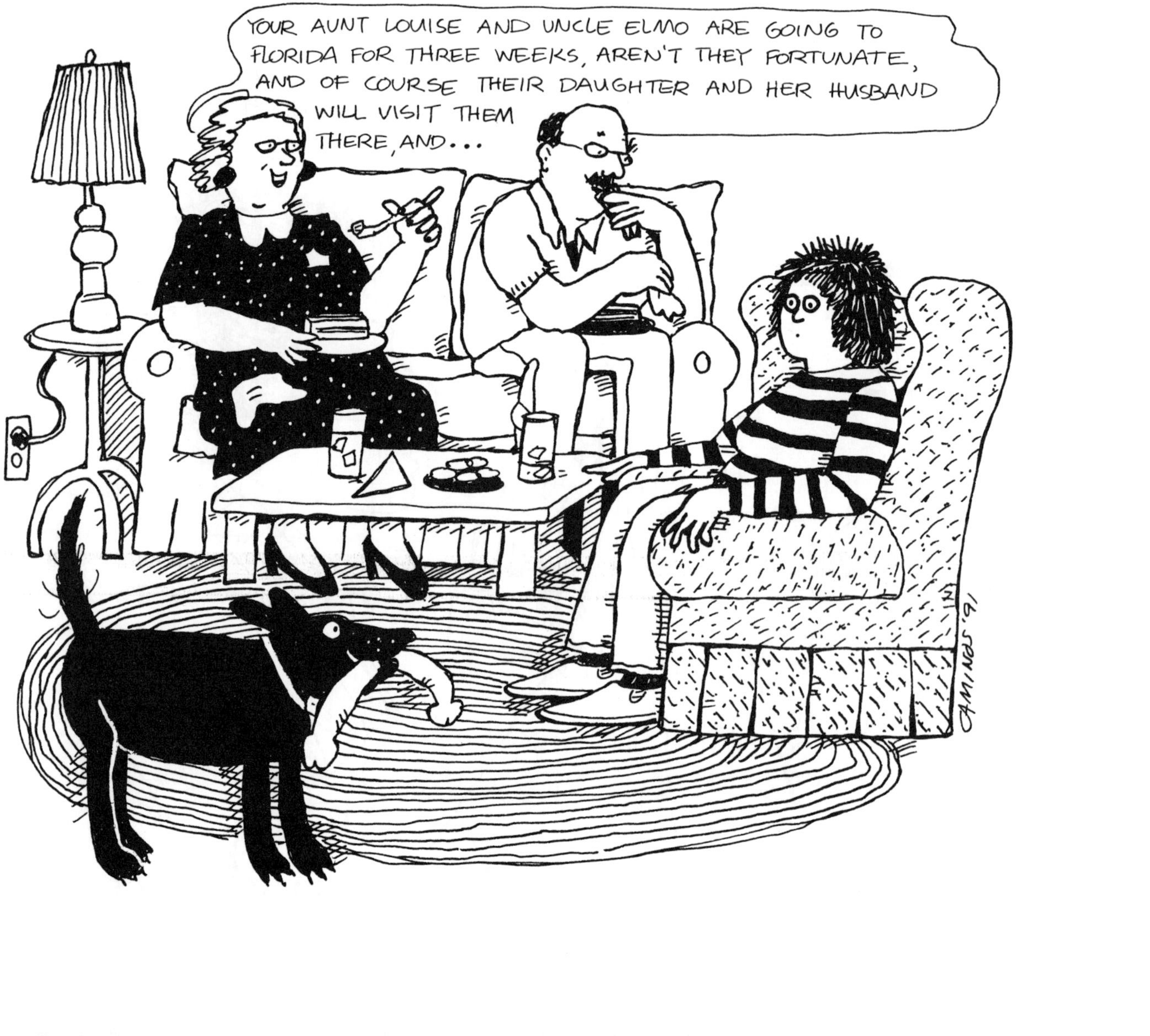
YOUR AUNT LOUISE AND UNCLE ELMO ARE GOING TO FLORIDA FOR THREE WEEKS, AREN'T THEY FORTUNATE, AND OF COURSE THEIR DAUGHTER AND HER HUSBAND WILL VISIT THEM THERE, AND...
CAMINOS '91

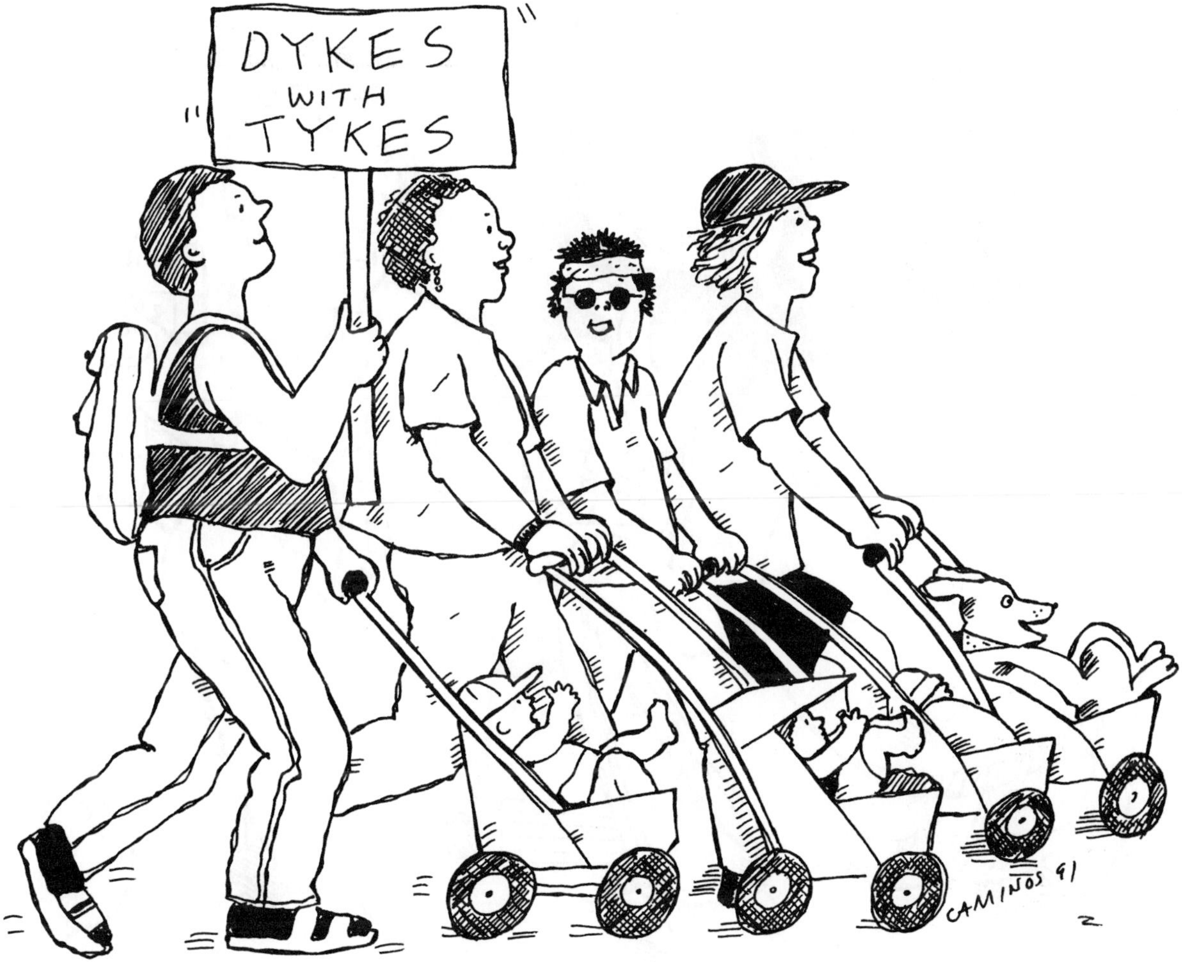
DYKES
WITH
TYKES
CAMINOS 91

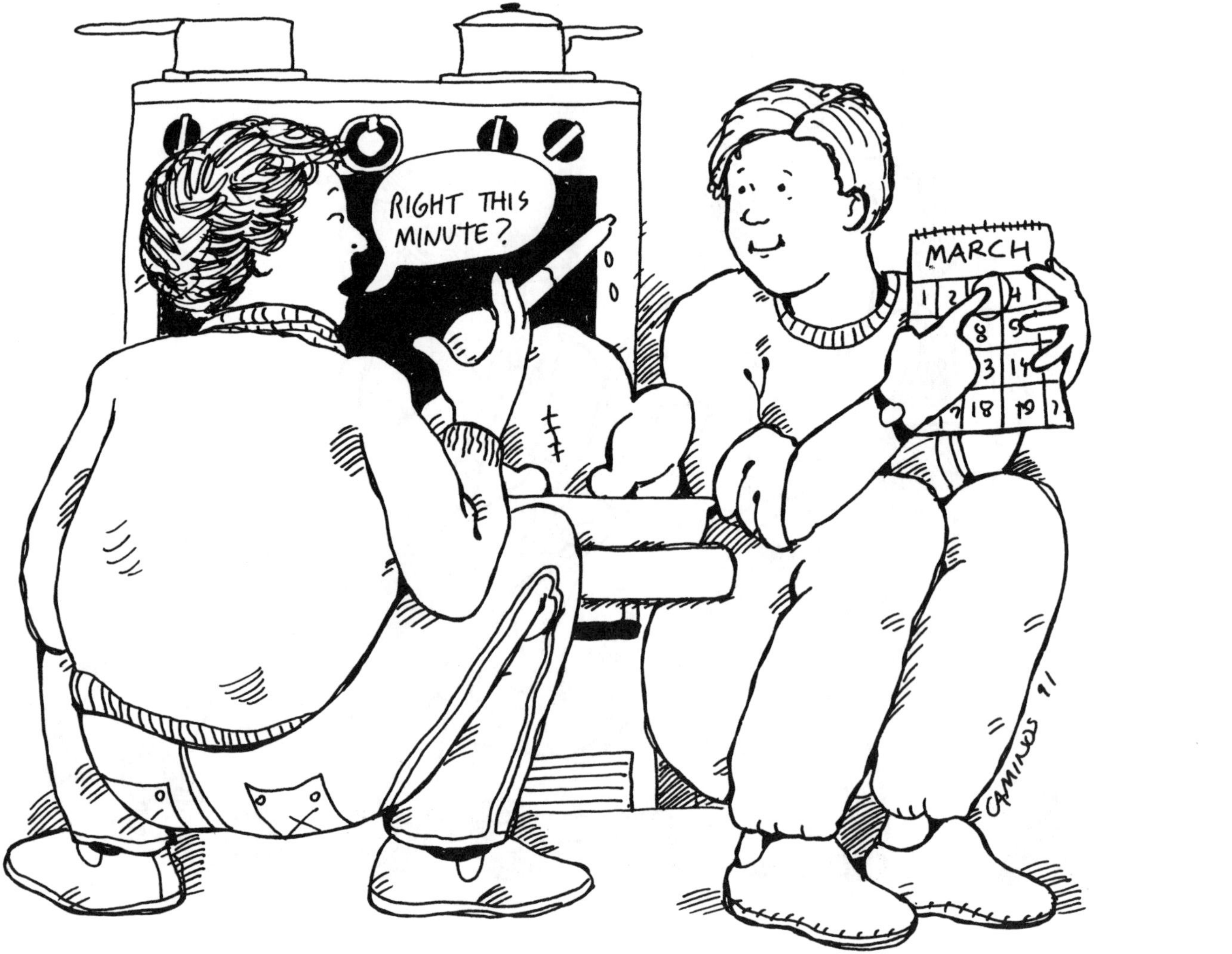
RIGHT THIS MINUTE?
MARCH

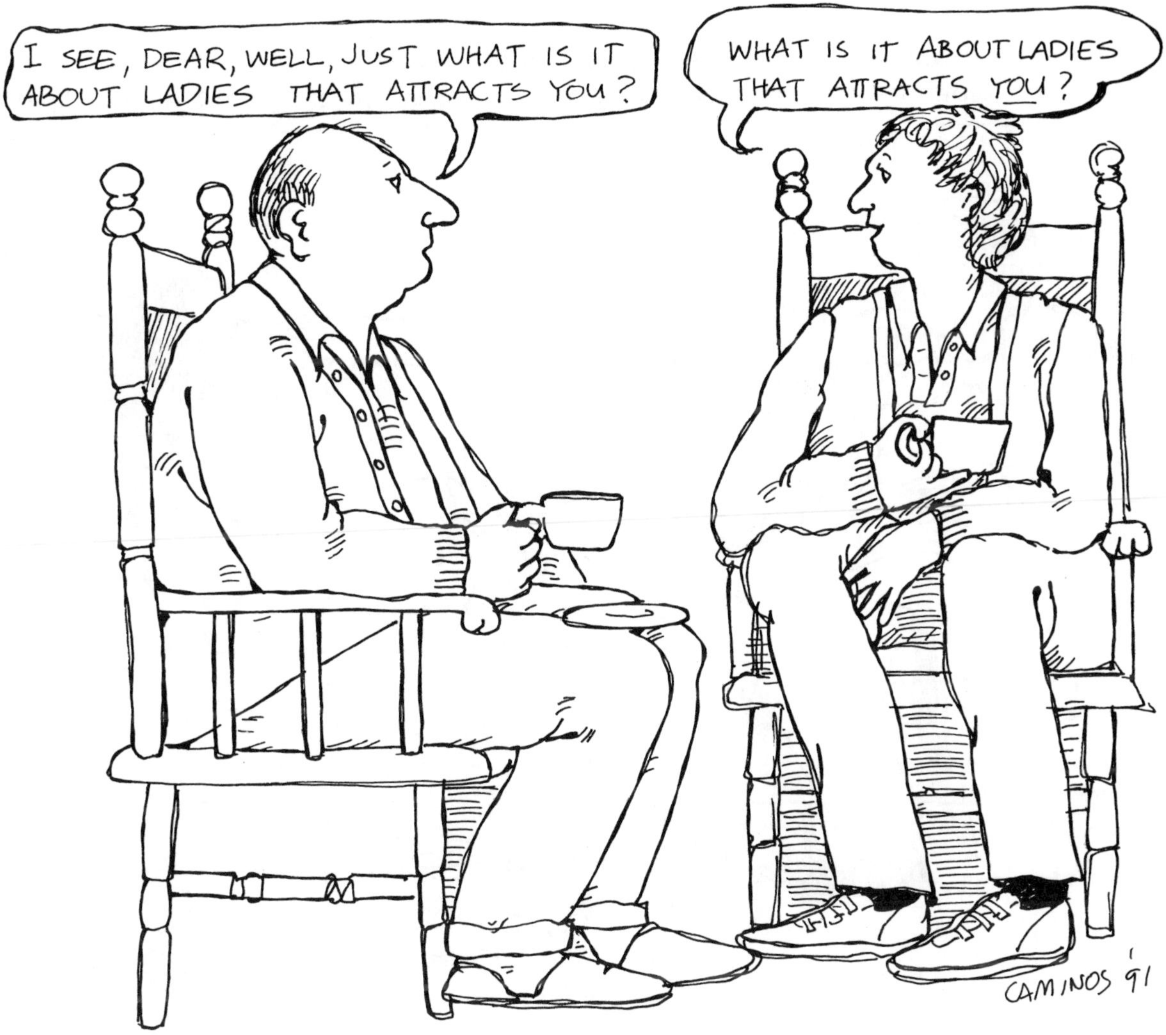
I SEE, DEAR, WELL, JUST WHAT IS IT ABOUT LADIES THAT ATTRACTS YOU?
WHAT IS IT ABOUT LADIES THAT ATTRACTS YOU?
CAMINOS '91

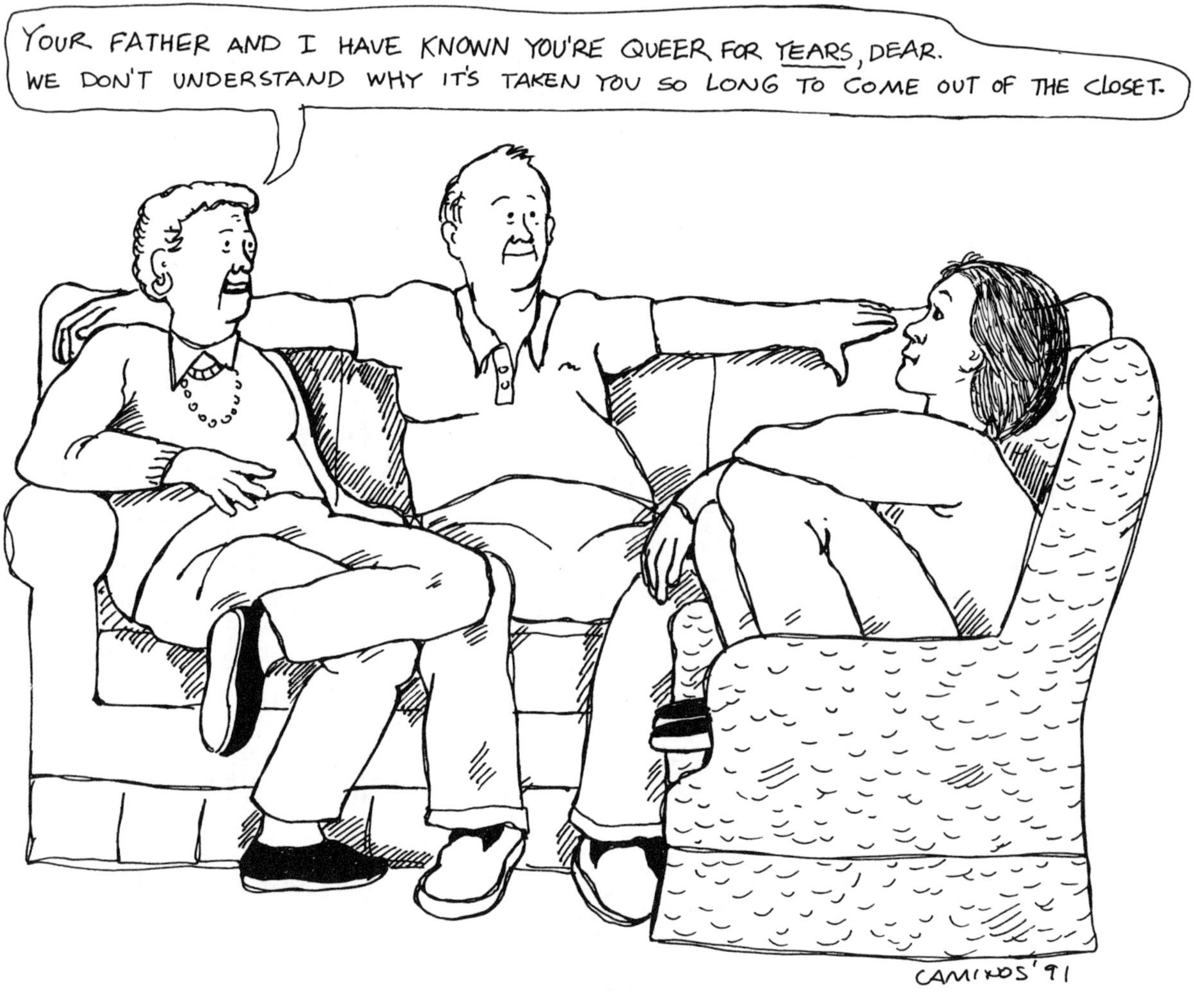
YOUR FATHER AND I HAVE KNOWN YOU'RE QUEER FOR YEARS, DEAR.
WE DON'T UNDERSTAND WHY IT'S TAKEN YOU SO LONG TO COME OUT OF THE CLOSET.
CAMINOS '91

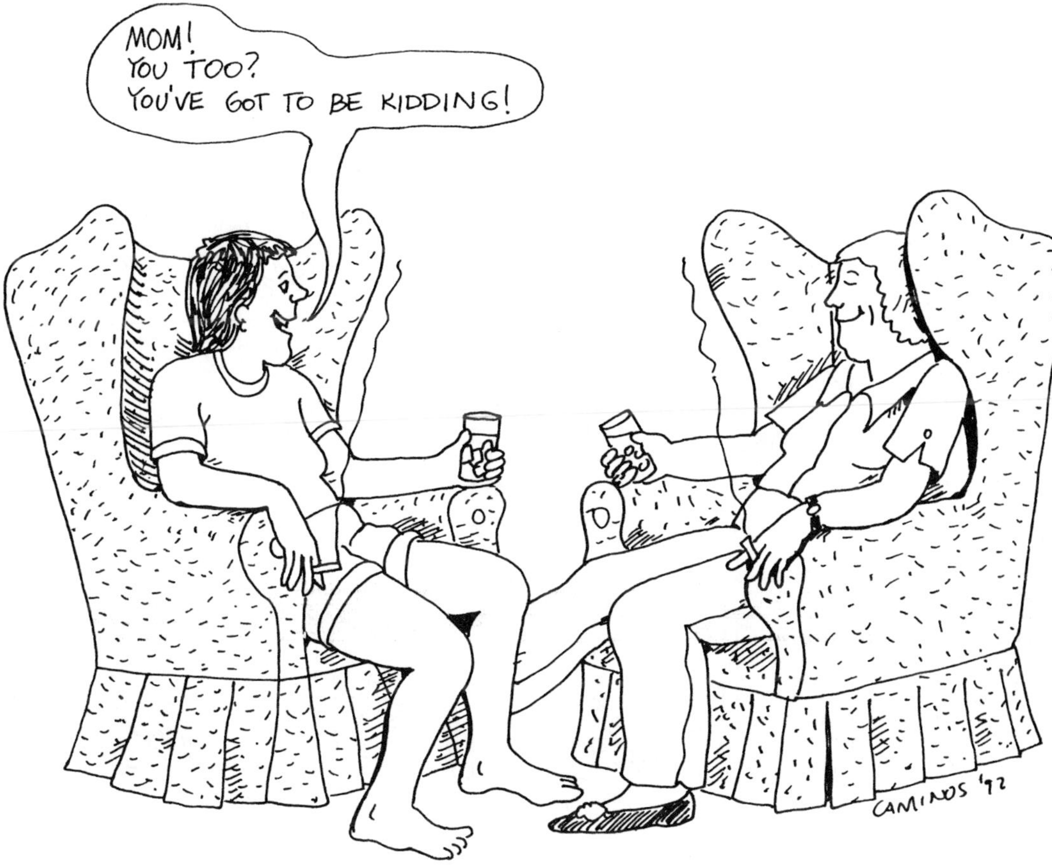
MOM!
YOU TOO?
YOU'VE GOT TO BE KIDDING!
CAMINOS '92

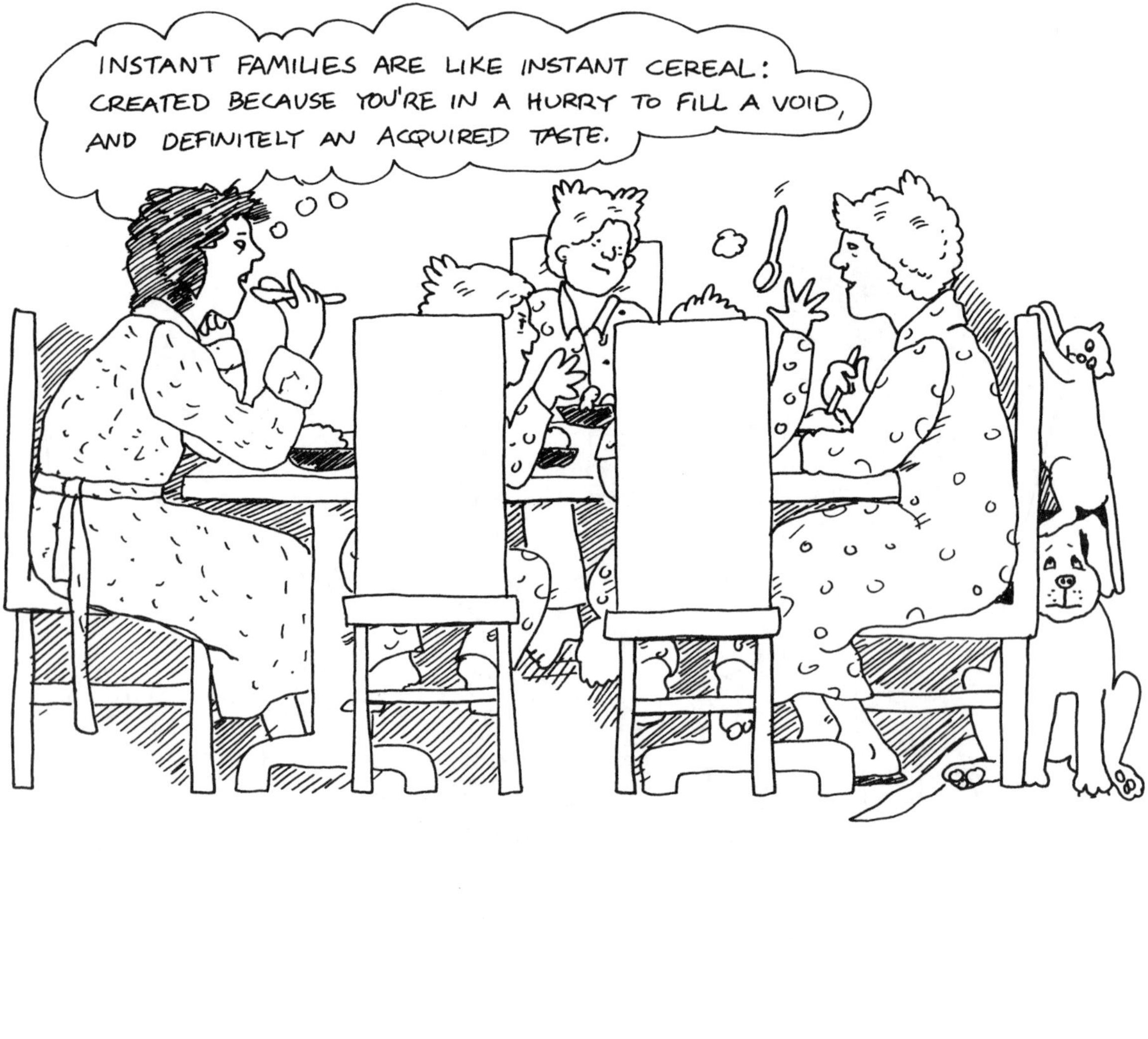
INSTANT FAMILIES ARE LIKE INSTANT CEREAL: CREATED BECAUSE YOU'RE IN A HURRY TO FILL A VOID, AND DEFINITELY AN ACQUIRED TASTE.

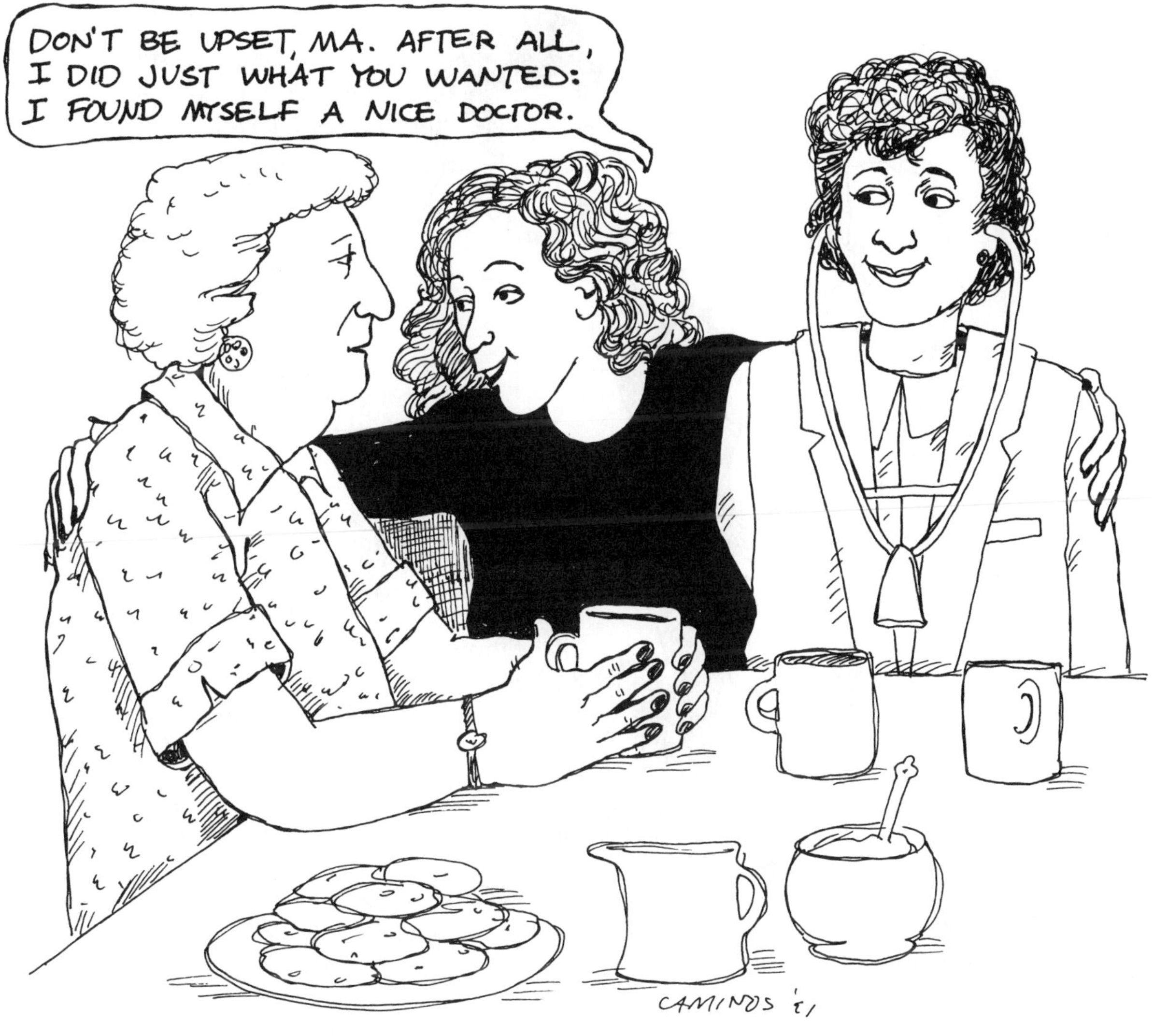
DON'T BE UPSET, MA. AFTER ALL, I DID JUST WHAT YOU WANTED: I FOUND MYSELF A NICE DOCTOR.
CAMINOS '81

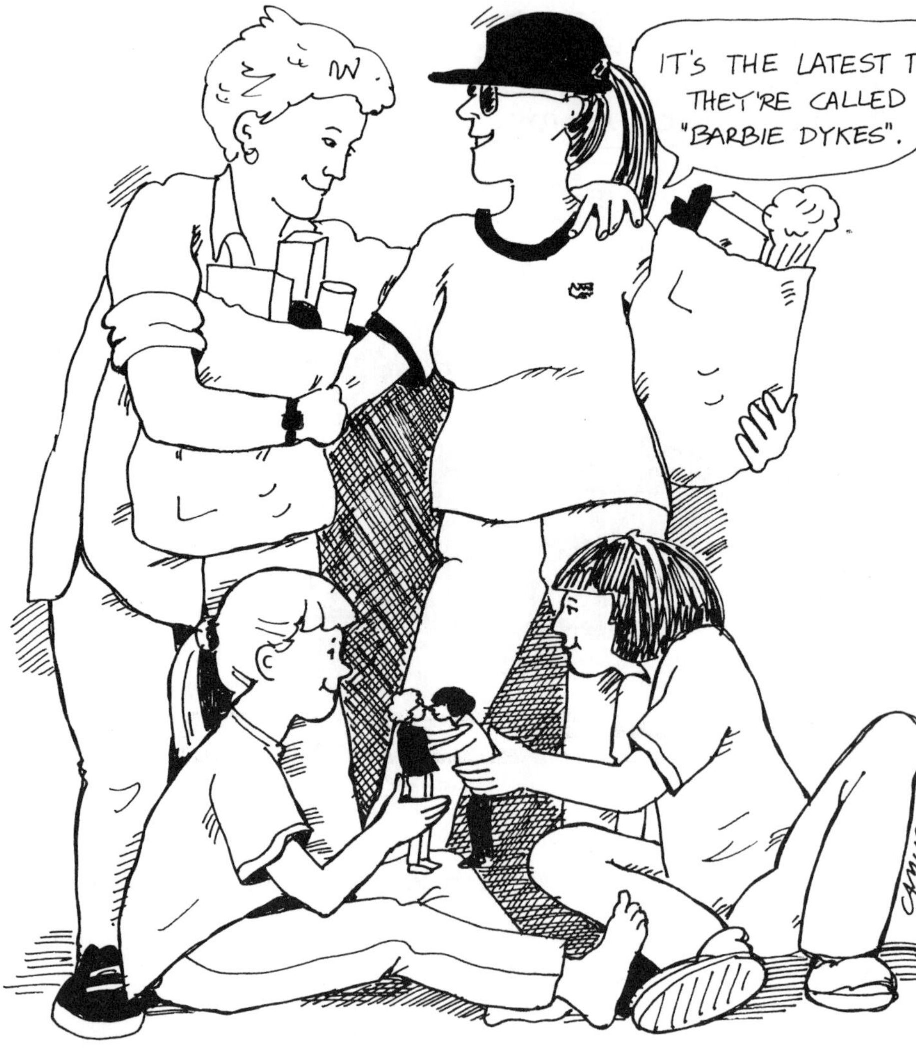
IT'S THE LATEST THING. THEY'RE CALLED "BARBIE DYKES".
CAMINOS '92

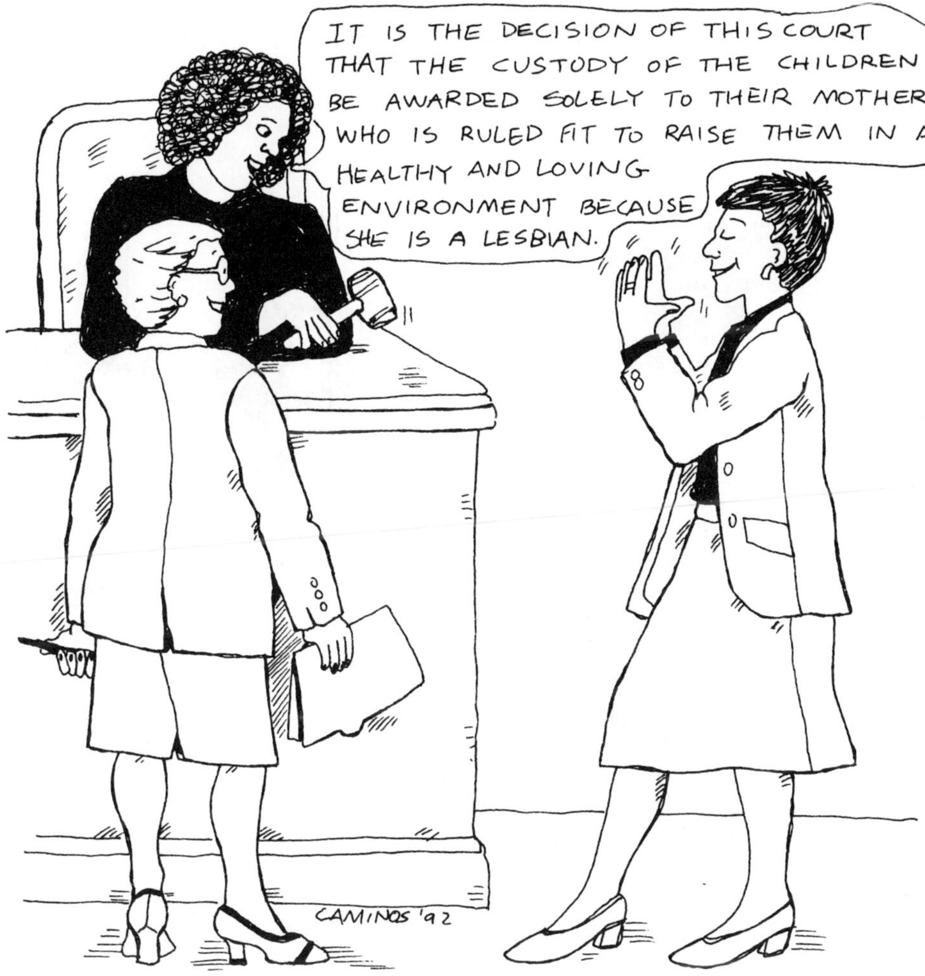
IT IS THE DECISION OF THIS COURT THAT THE CUSTODY OF THE CHILDREN BE AWARDED SOLELY TO THEIR MOTHER, WHO IS RULED FIT TO RAISE THEM IN A HEALTHY AND LOVING ENVIRONMENT BECAUSE SHE IS A LESBIAN.
CAMINOS '92

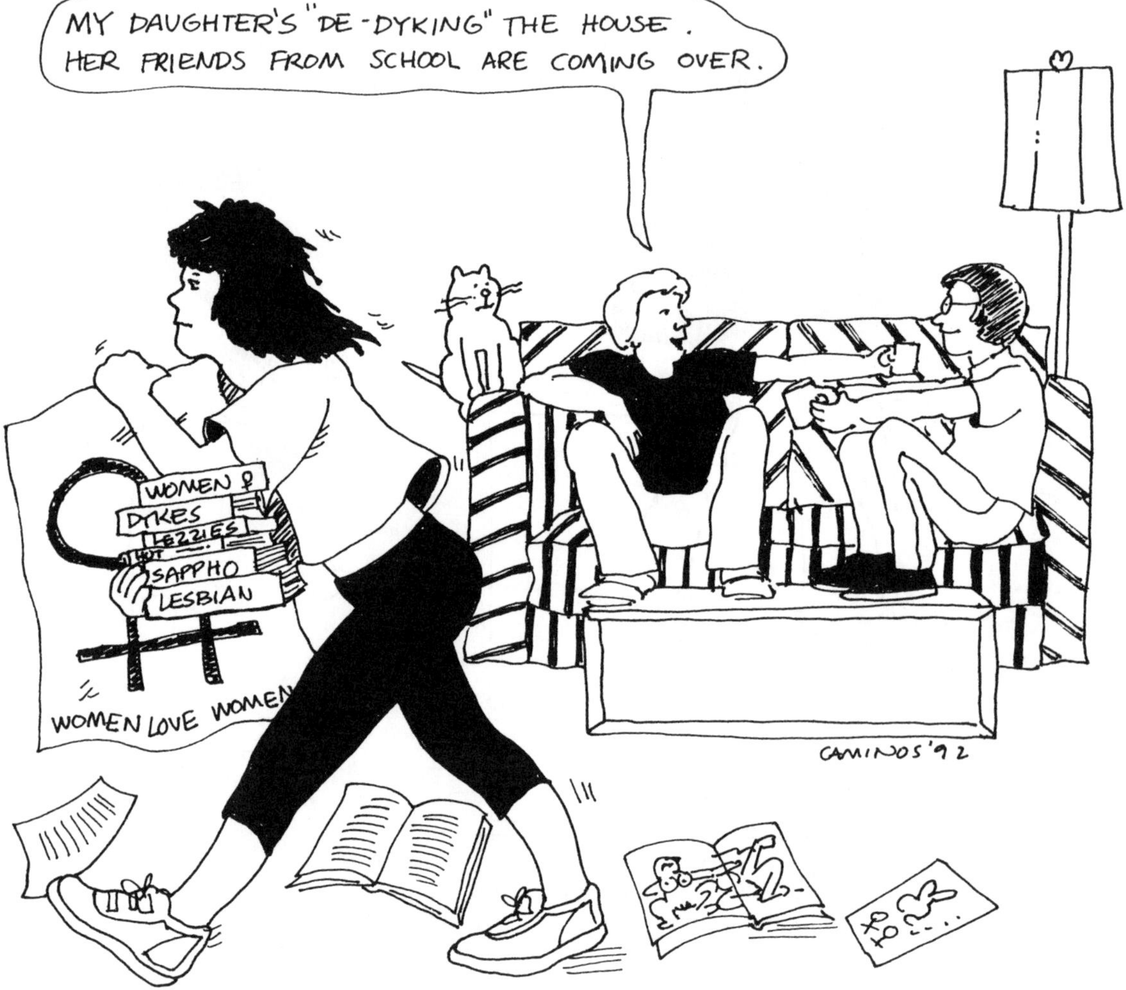
MY DAUGHTER'S "DE-DYKING" THE HOUSE. HER FRIENDS FROM SCHOOL ARE COMING OVER.
WOMEN
DYKES
LEZZIES
HOT
SAPPHO
LESBIAN
WOMEN LOVE WOMEN
CAMINOS '92

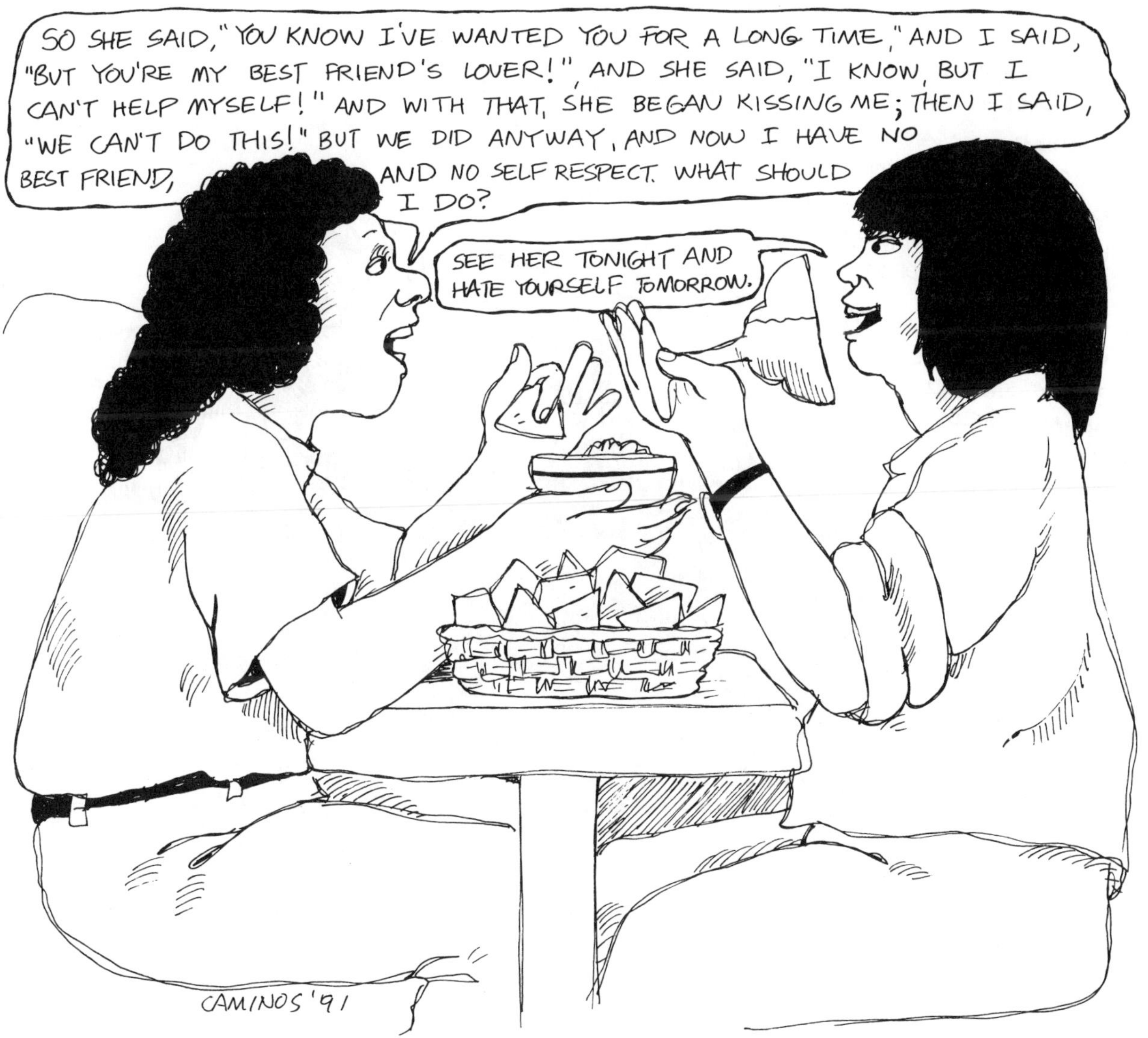

SO SHE SAID, "YOU KNOW I'VE WANTED YOU FOR A LONG TIME," AND I SAID, "BUT YOU'RE MY BEST FRIEND'S LOVER!", AND SHE SAID, "I KNOW, BUT I CAN'T HELP MYSELF!" AND WITH THAT, SHE BEGAN KISSING ME; THEN I SAID, "WE CAN'T DO THIS!" BUT WE DID ANYWAY, AND NOW I HAVE NO BEST FRIEND, AND NO SELF RESPECT. WHAT SHOULD I DO?
SEE HER TONIGHT AND HATE YOURSELF TOMORROW.
CAMINOS '91

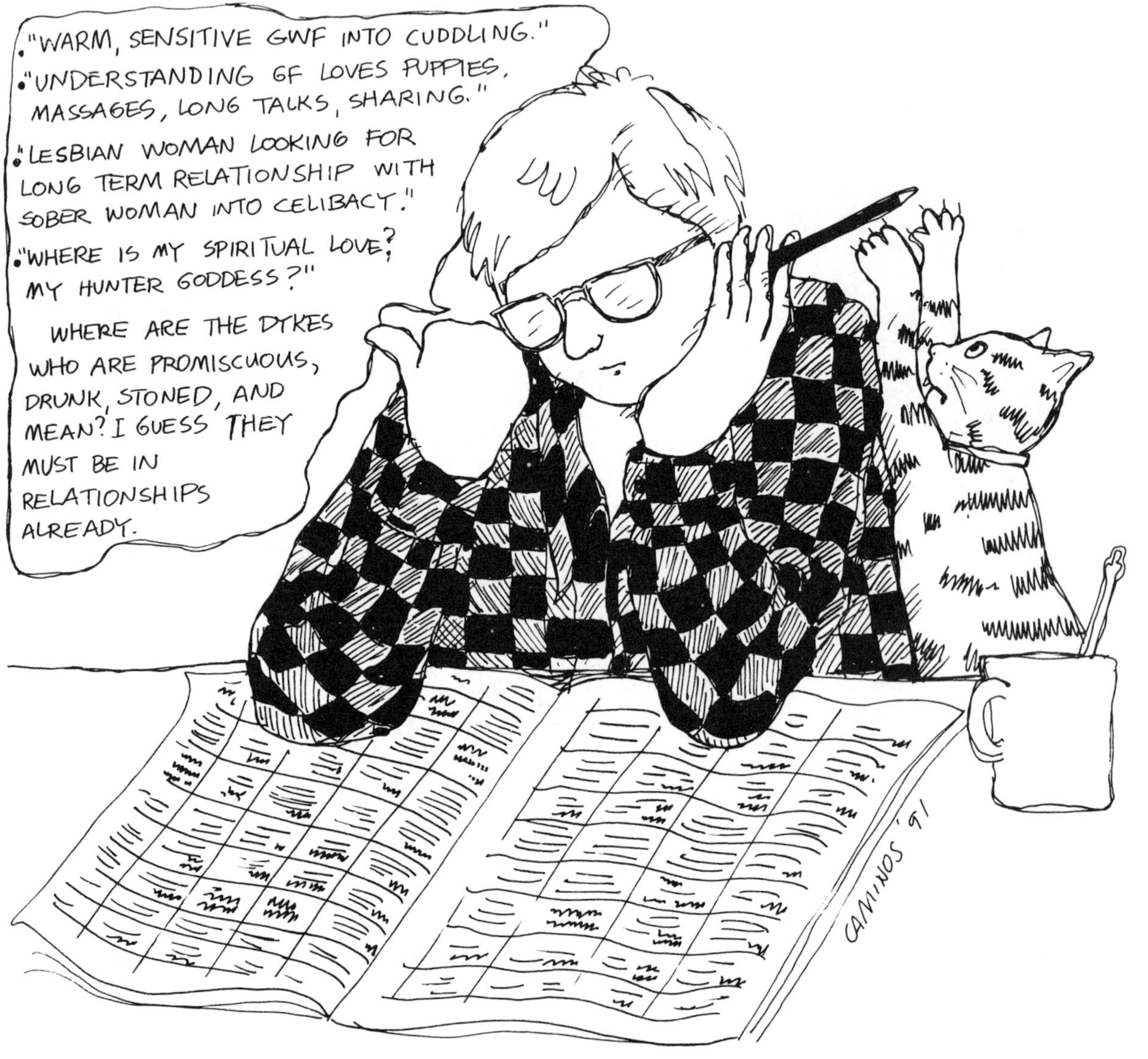
• "WARM, SENSITIVE GWF INTO CUDDLING."
• "UNDERSTANDING GF LOVES PUPPIES, MASSAGES, LONG TALKS, SHARING."
• "LESBIAN WOMAN LOOKING FOR LONG TERM RELATIONSHIP WITH SOBER WOMAN INTO CELIBACY."
• "WHERE IS MY SPIRITUAL LOVE? MY HUNTER GODDESS?"
WHERE ARE THE DYKES WHO ARE PROMISCUOUS, DRUNK, STONED, AND MEAN? I GUESS THEY MUST BE IN RELATIONSHIPS ALREADY.
CAMINOS '91

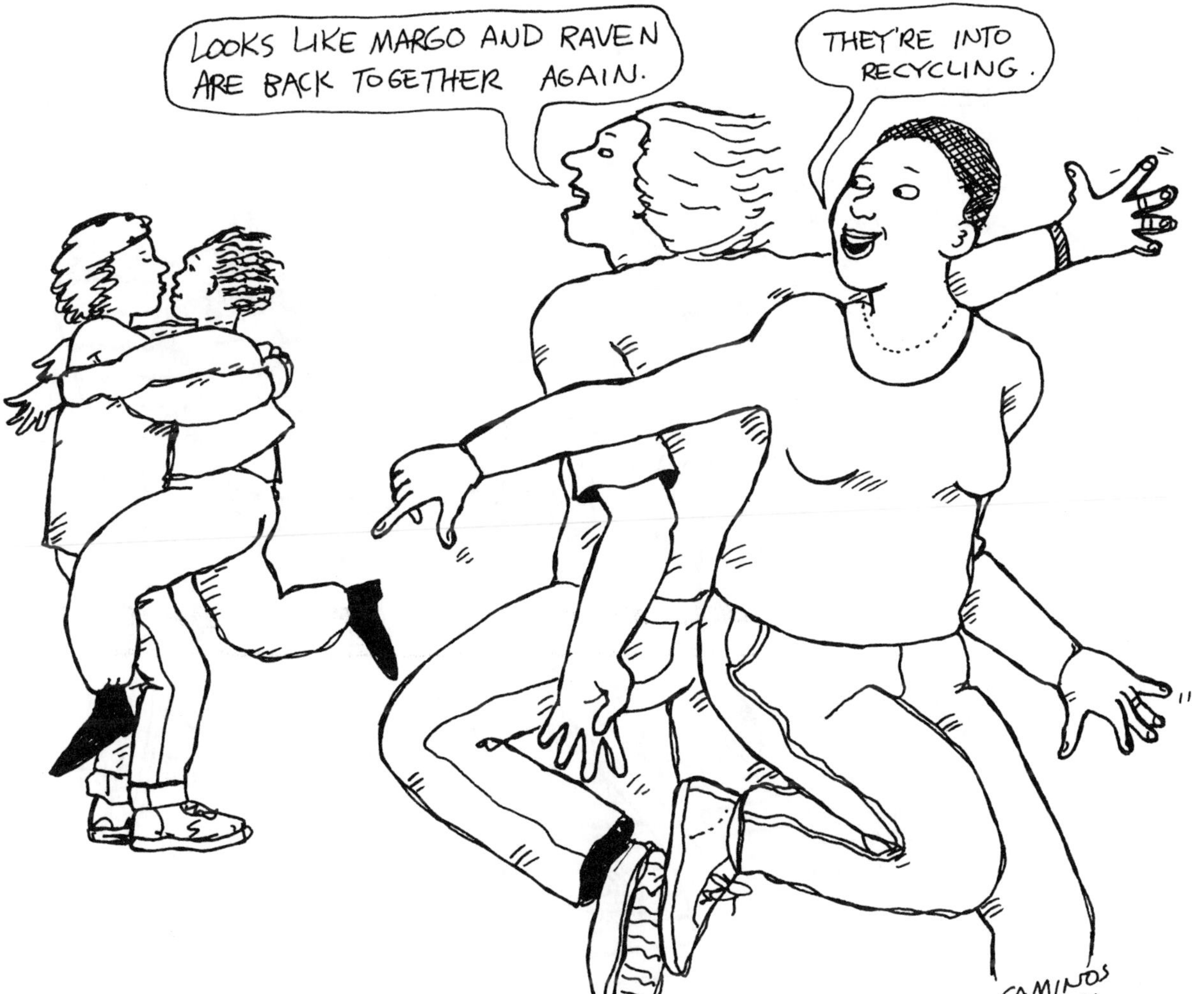
LOOKS LIKE MARGO AND RAVEN ARE BACK TOGETHER AGAIN.
THEY'RE INTO RECYCLING.
CAMINOS '91

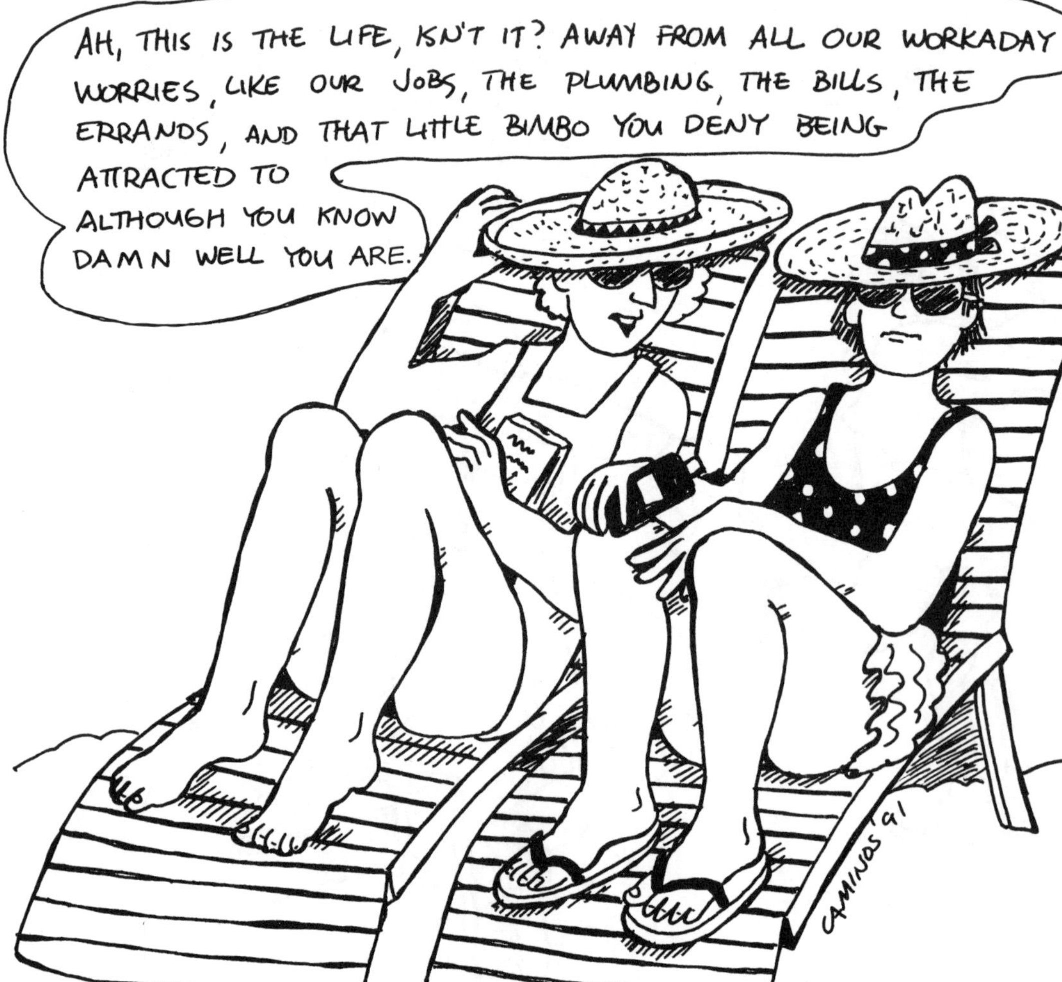
AH, THIS IS THE LIFE, ISN'T IT? AWAY FROM ALL OUR WORKADAY WORRIES, LIKE OUR JOBS, THE PLUMBING, THE BILLS, THE ERRANDS, AND THAT LITTLE BIMBO YOU DENY BEING ATTRACTED TO ALTHOUGH YOU KNOW DAMN WELL YOU ARE.
CAMINOS '91

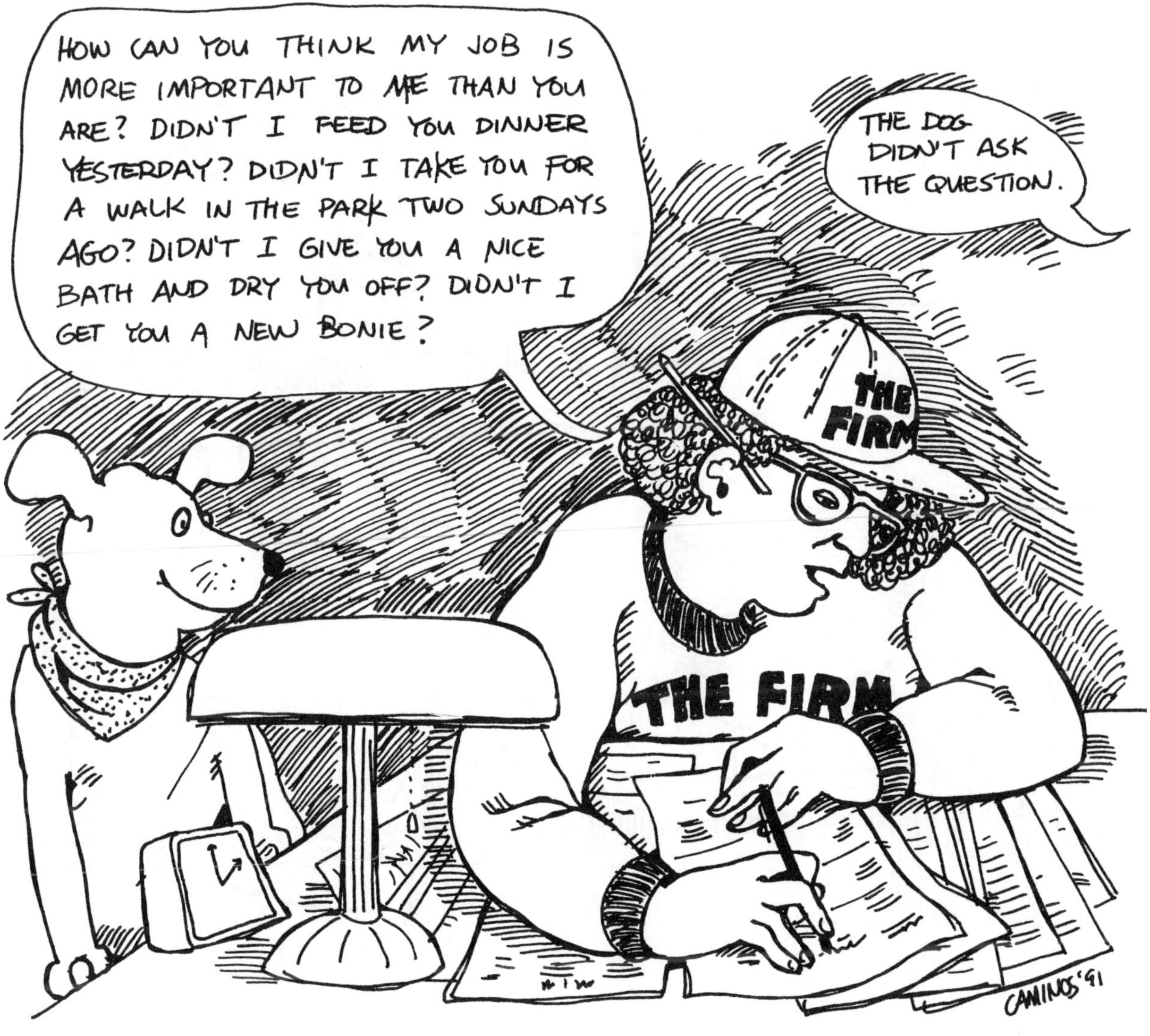
HOW CAN YOU THINK MY JOB IS MORE IMPORTANT TO ME THAN YOU ARE? DIDN'T I FEED YOU DINNER YESTERDAY? DIDN'T I TAKE YOU FOR A WALK IN THE PARK TWO SUNDAYS AGO? DIDN'T I GIVE YOU A NICE BATH AND DRY YOU OFF? DIDN'T I GET YOU A NEW BONIE?
THE DOG DIDN'T ASK THE QUESTION.
THE FIRM
THE FIRM
CAMINOS '91

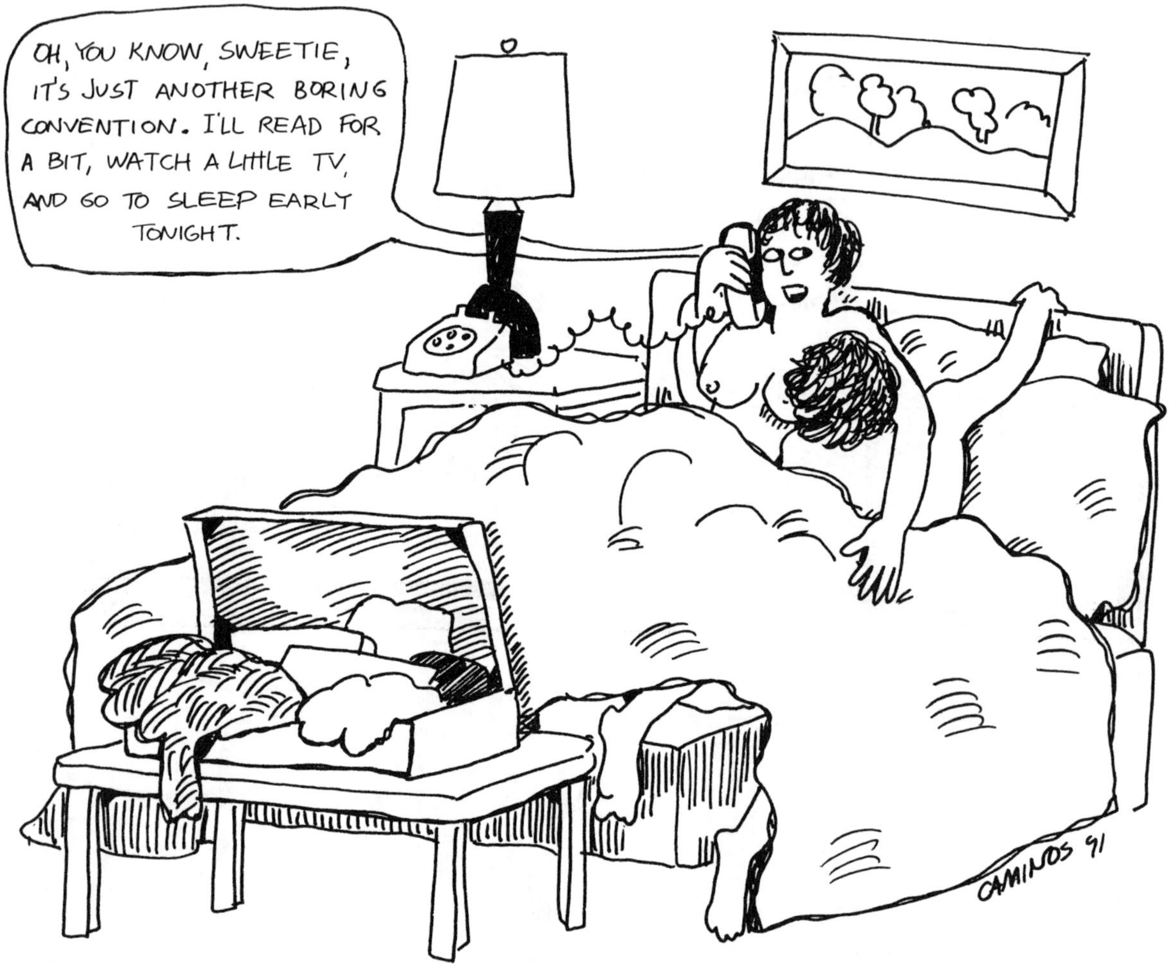
OH, YOU KNOW, SWEETIE, IT'S JUST ANOTHER BORING CONVENTION. I'LL READ FOR A BIT, WATCH A LITTLE TV, AND GO TO SLEEP EARLY TONIGHT.
CAMINOS '91

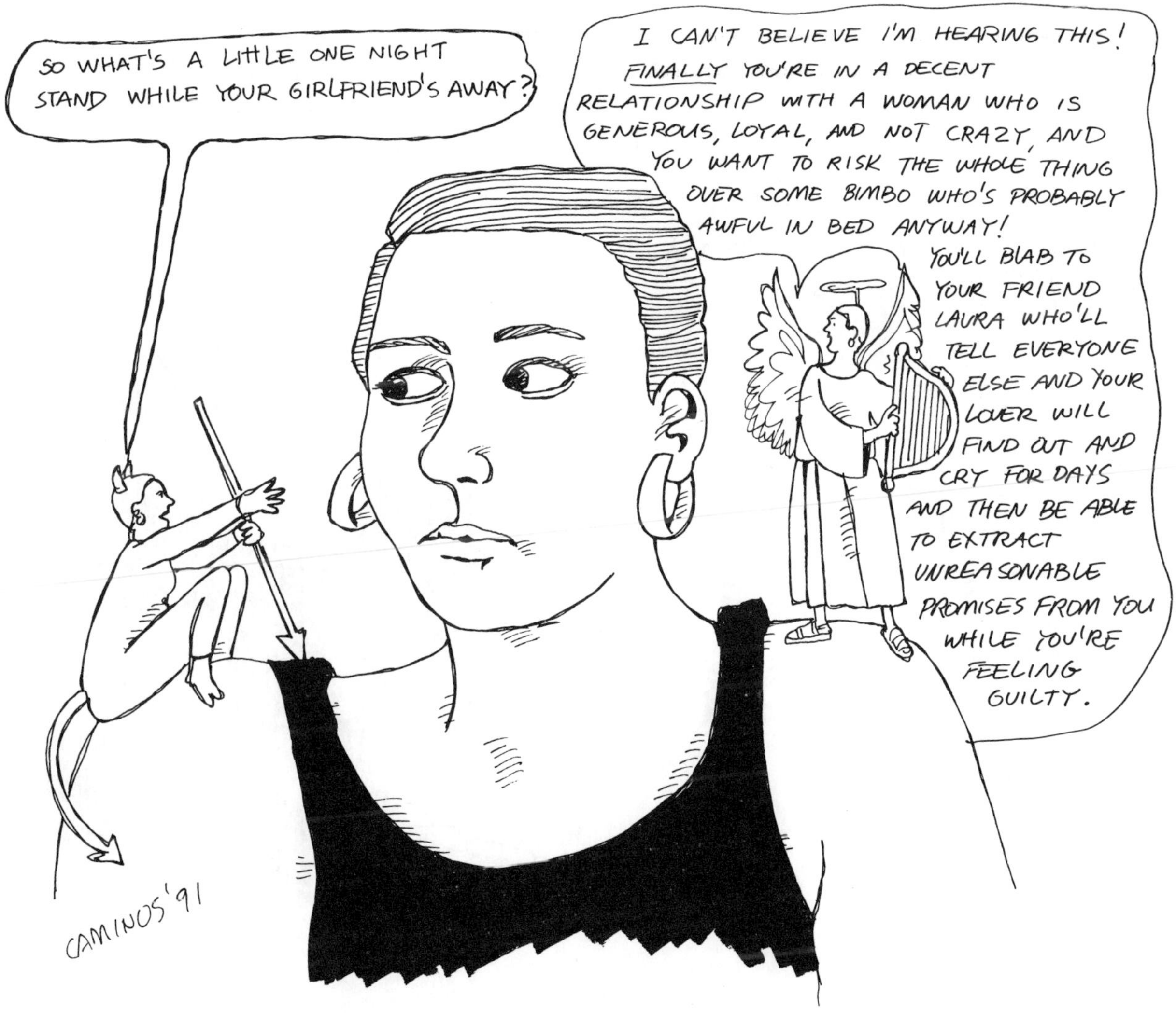
SO WHAT'S A LITTLE ONE NIGHT STAND WHILE YOUR GIRLFRIEND'S AWAY?
I CAN'T BELIEVE I'M HEARING THIS! FINALLY YOU'RE IN A DECENT RELATIONSHIP WITH A WOMAN WHO IS GENEROUS, LOYAL, AND NOT CRAZY, AND YOU WANT TO RISK THE WHOLE THING OVER SOME BIMBO WHO'S PROBABLY AWFUL IN BED ANYWAY! YOU'LL BLAB TO YOUR FRIEND LAURA WHO'LL TELL EVERYONE ELSE AND YOUR LOVER WILL FIND OUT AND CRY FOR DAYS AND THEN BE ABLE TO EXTRACT UNREASONABLE PROMISES FROM YOU WHILE YOU'RE FEELING GUILTY.
CAMINOS '91

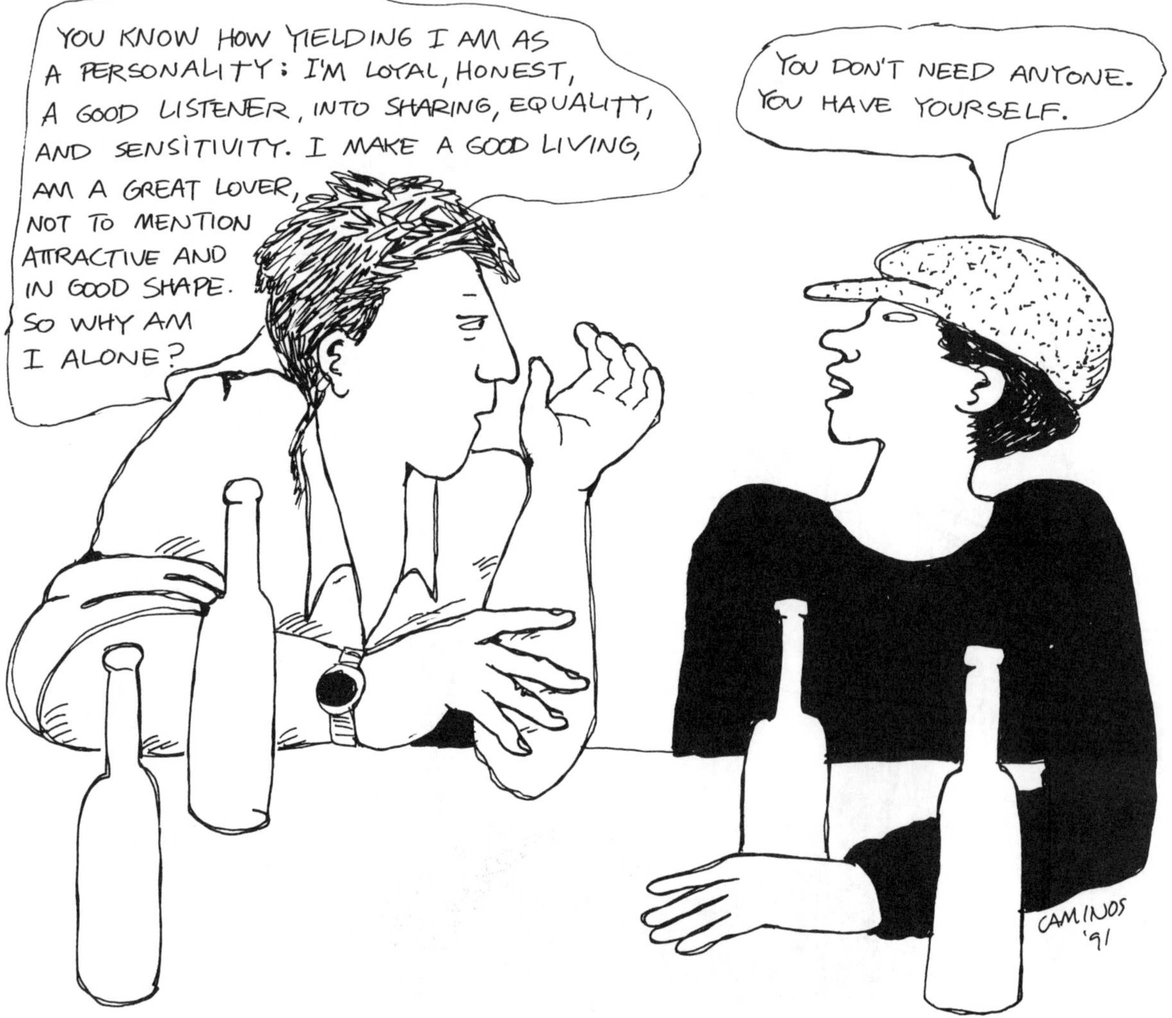
YOU KNOW HOW YIELDING I AM AS A PERSONALITY: I'M LOYAL, HONEST, A GOOD LISTENER, INTO SHARING, EQUALITY, AND SENSITIVITY. I MAKE A GOOD LIVING, AM A GREAT LOVER, NOT TO MENTION ATTRACTIVE AND IN GOOD SHAPE. SO WHY AM I ALONE?
YOU DON'T NEED ANYONE. YOU HAVE YOURSELF.
CAMINOS '91

GOD, I'VE GOT A ROTTEN SINUS HEADACHE, MY EARS ARE CLOGGED, I'VE GOT POST NASAL DRIP THAT GIVING ME TERRIBLE BREATH! DINNER'S GIVEN ME AWFUL GAS, AND I THINK MY YEAST INFECTION'S COME BACK.
LOOK, RELAX. I DON'T WANT TO MAKE LOVE, EITHER.
CAMINOS '91

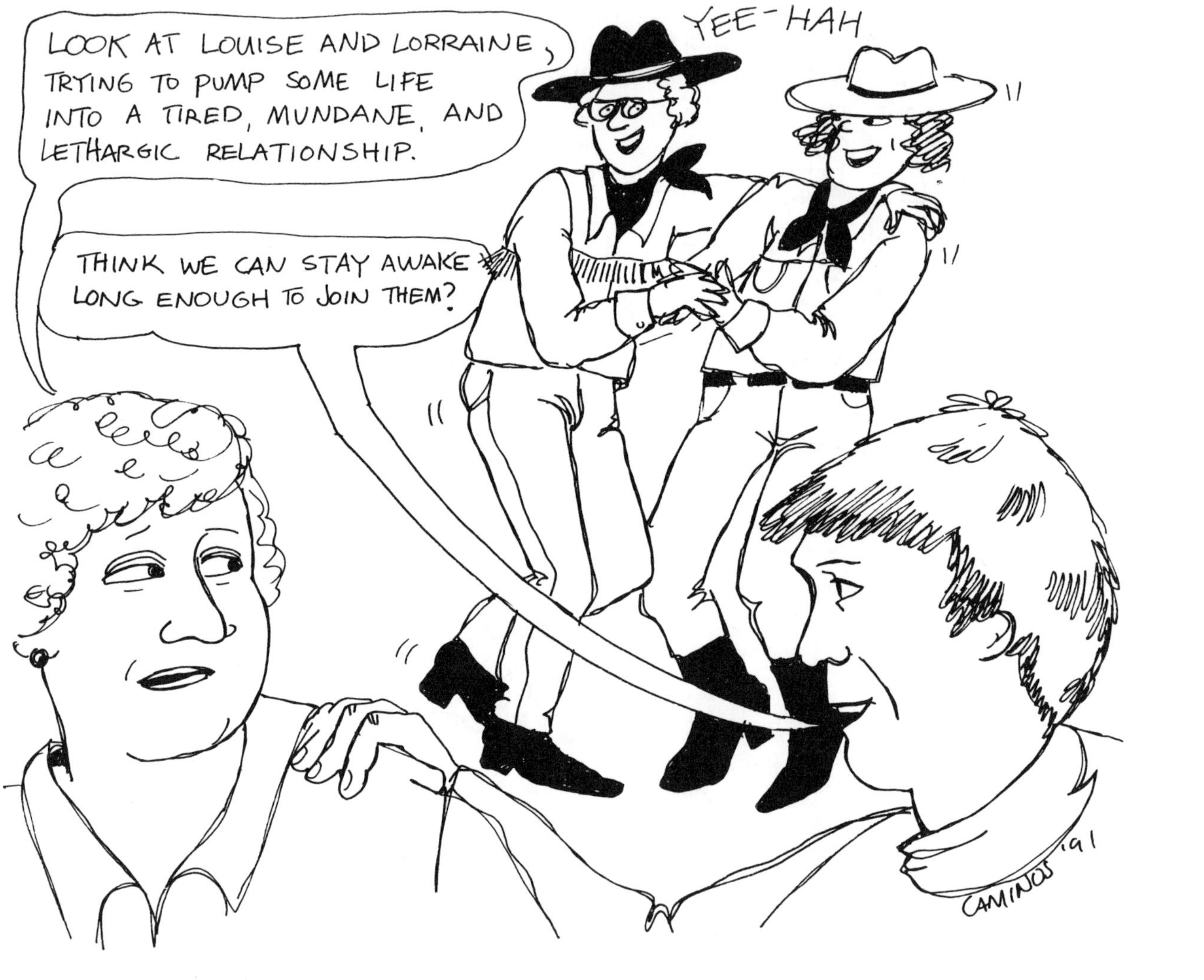
LOOK AT LOUISE AND LORRAINE, TRYING TO PUMP SOME LIFE INTO A TIRED, MUNDANE, AND LETHARGIC RELATIONSHIP.
THINK WE CAN STAY AWAKE LONG ENOUGH TO JOIN THEM?
YEE-HAH
CAMINOS '91

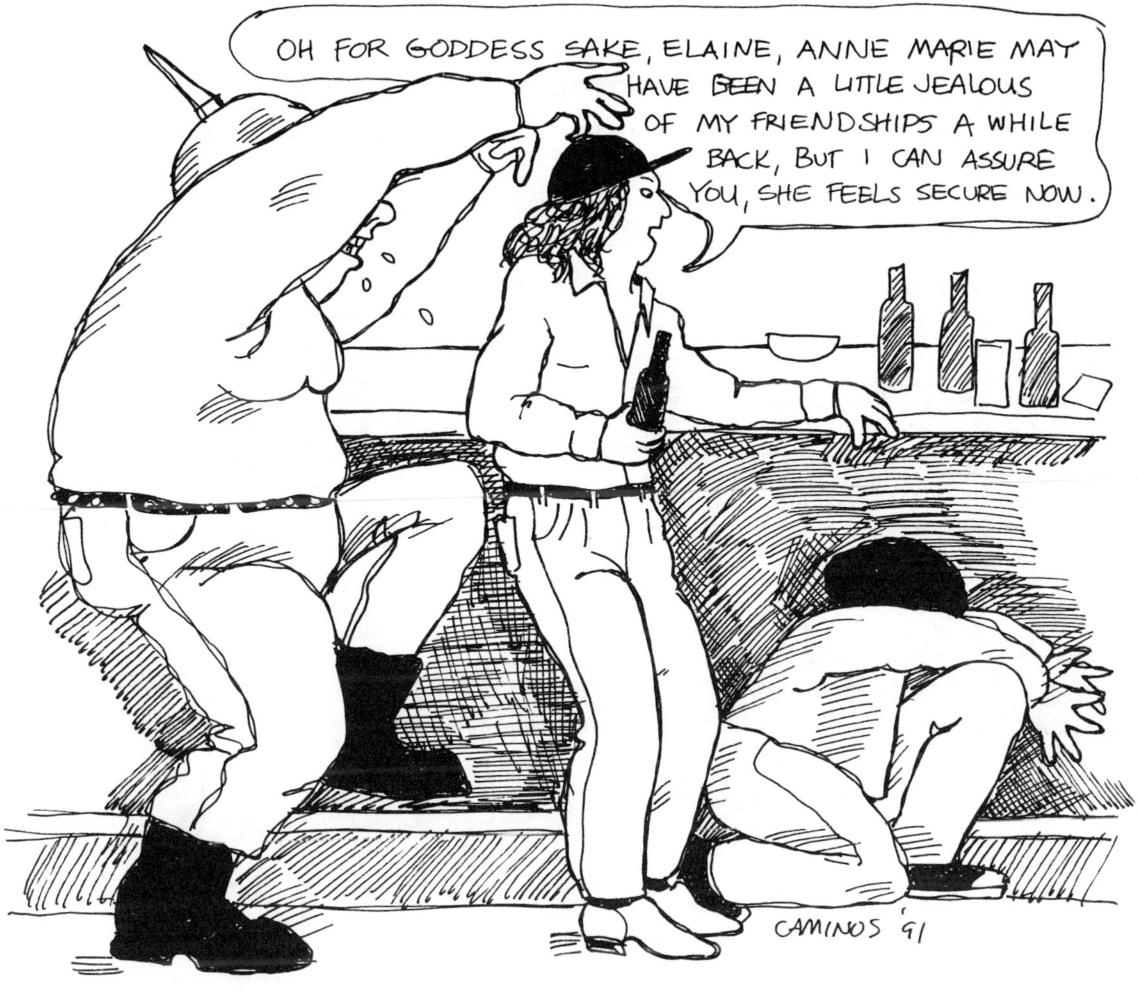
OH FOR GODDESS SAKE, ELAINE, ANNE MARIE MAY HAVE BEEN A LITTLE JEALOUS OF MY FRIENDSHIPS A WHILE BACK, BUT I CAN ASSURE YOU, SHE FEELS SECURE NOW.
CAMINOS '91

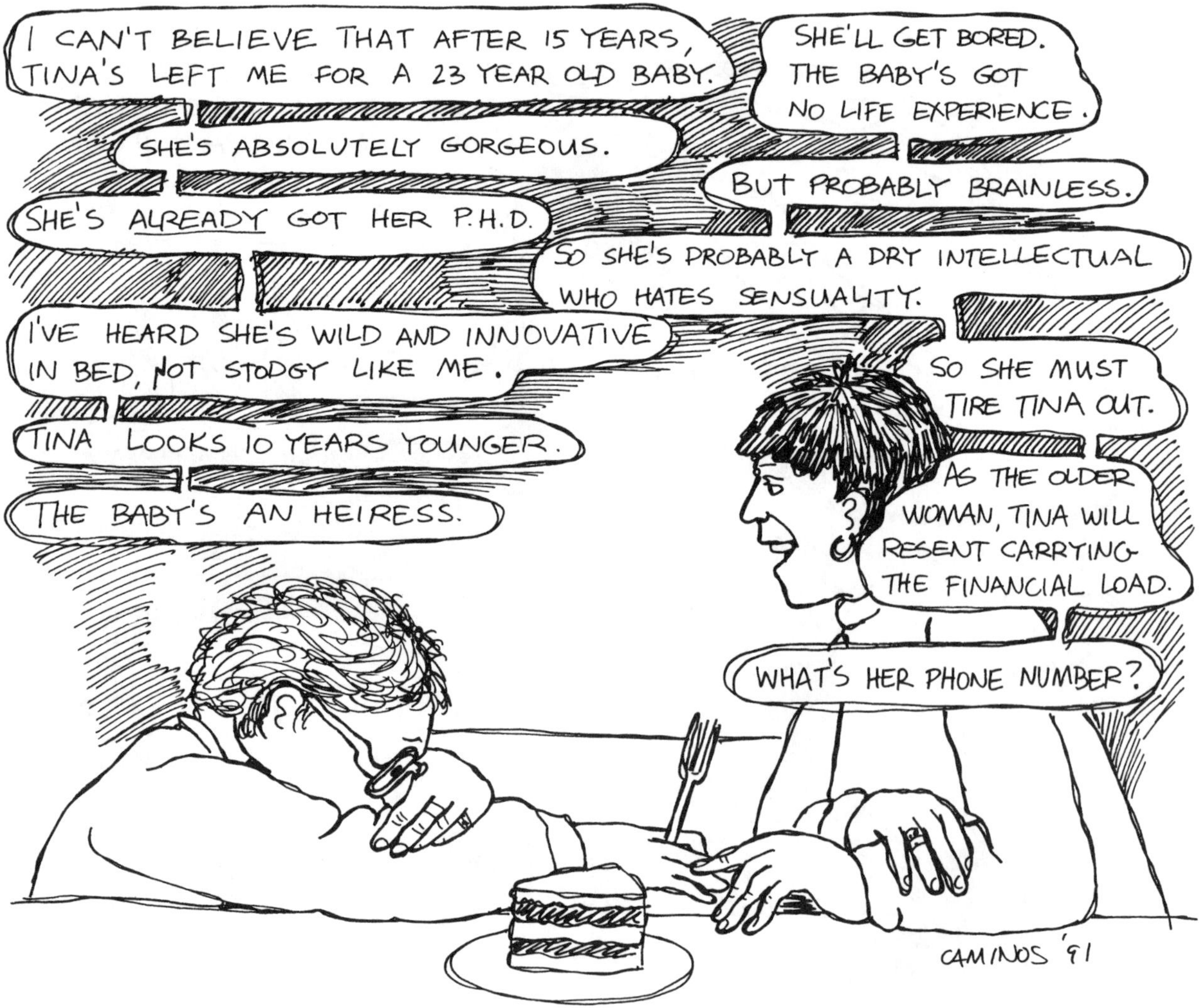
I CAN'T BELIEVE THAT AFTER 15 YEARS, TINA'S LEFT ME FOR A 23 YEAR OLD BABY.
SHE'LL GET BORED. THE BABY'S GOT NO LIFE EXPERIENCE.
SHE'S ABSOLUTELY GORGEOUS.
BUT PROBABLY BRAINLESS.
SHE'S ALREADY GOT HER P.H.D.
SO SHE'S PROBABLY A DRY INTELLECTUAL WHO HATES SENSUALITY.
I'VE HEARD SHE'S WILD AND INNOVATIVE IN BED, NOT STODGY LIKE ME.
SO SHE MUST TIRE TINA OUT.
TINA LOOKS 10 YEARS YOUNGER.
AS THE OLDER WOMAN, TINA WILL RESENT CARRYING THE FINANCIAL LOAD.
THE BABY'S AN HEIRESS.
WHAT'S HER PHONE NUMBER?
CAMINOS '91

SWEETHEART, YOUR FURRY FRIENDS ARE PART OF YOUR KIND AND GENEROUS NATURE. I'M SURE MY LIFE THREATENING ALLERGY WILL SUBSIDE AND WE'LL BE ABLE TO KISS IN DUE TIME.
CAMINOS '91

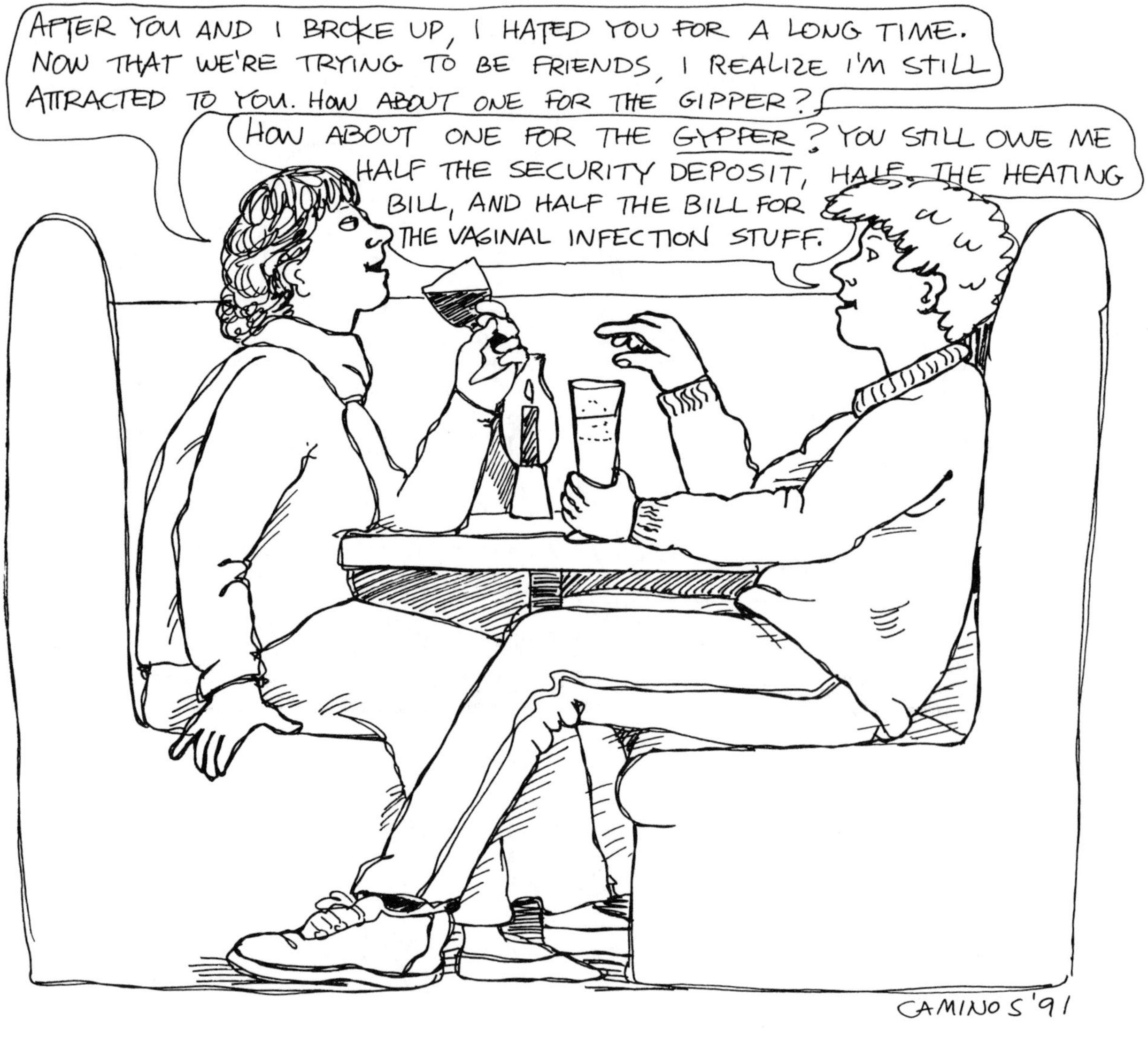
AFTER YOU AND I BROKE UP, I HATED YOU FOR A LONG TIME. NOW THAT WE'RE TRYING TO BE FRIENDS, I REALIZE I'M STILL ATTRACTED TO YOU. HOW ABOUT ONE FOR THE GIPPER?
HOW ABOUT ONE FOR THE GYPPER? YOU STILL OWE ME HALF THE SECURITY DEPOSIT, HALF THE HEATING BILL, AND HALF THE BILL FOR THE VAGINAL INFECTION STUFF.
CAMINOS '91

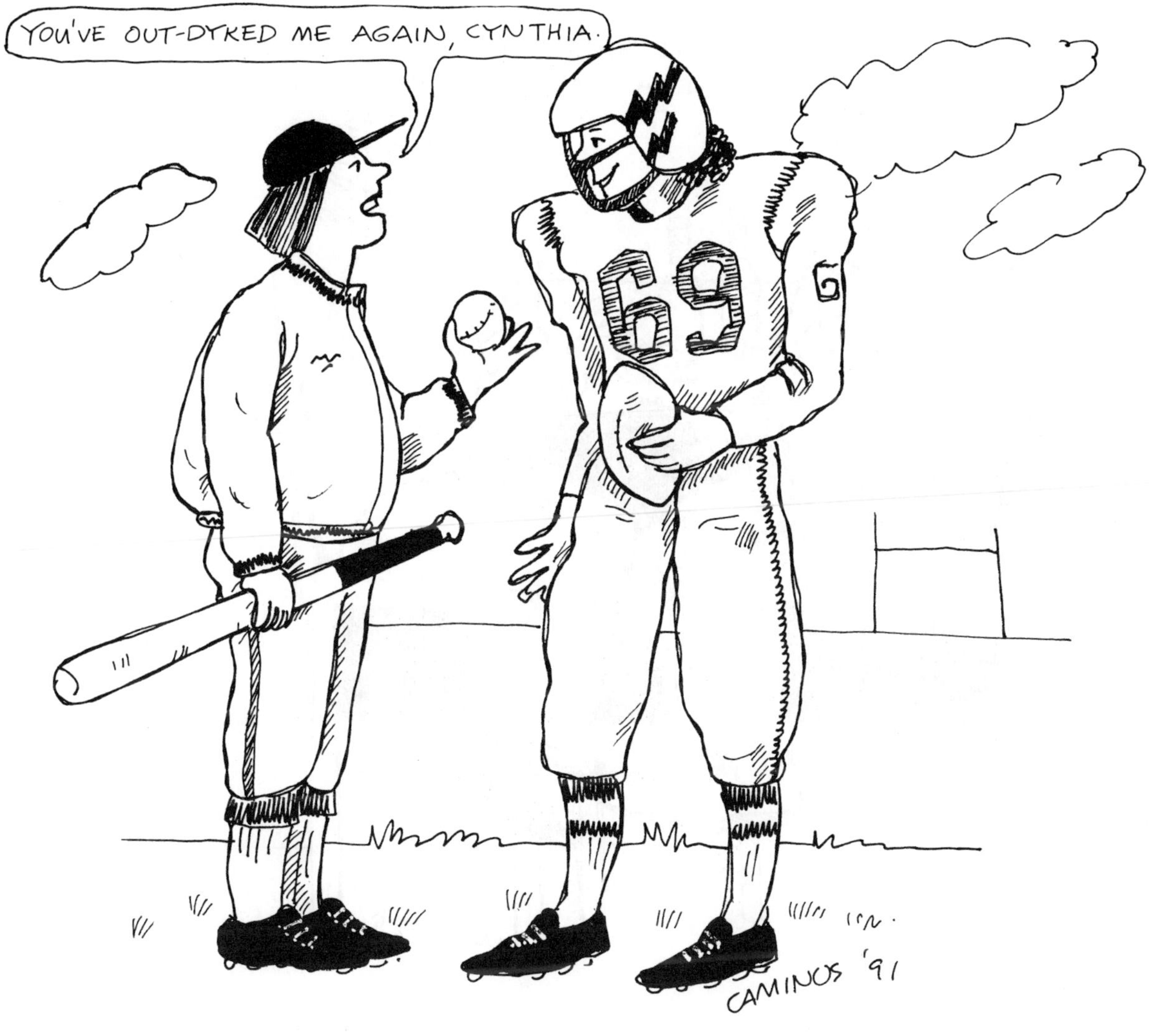
YOU'VE OUT-DYKED ME AGAIN, CYNTHIA.
69
CAMINOS '91

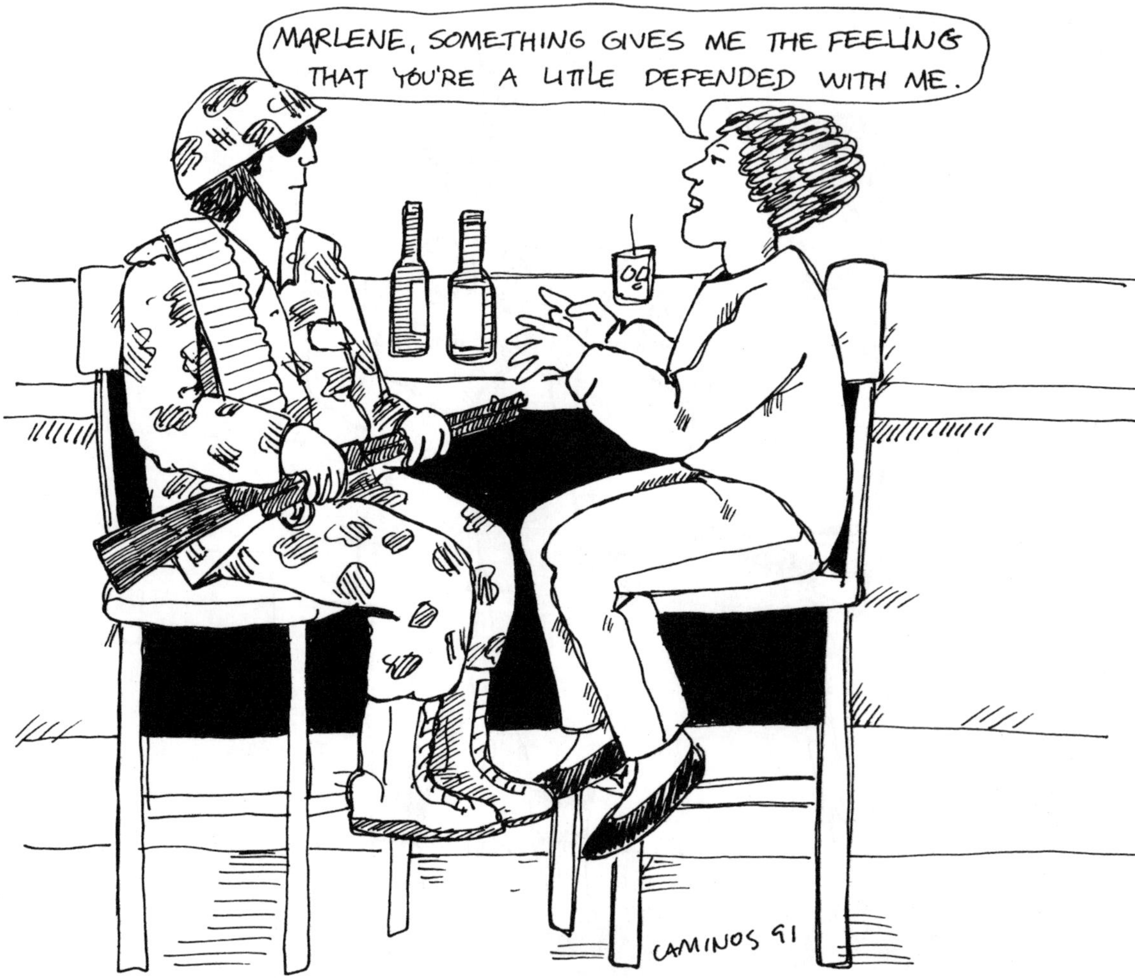
MARLENE, SOMETHING GIVES ME THE FEELING THAT YOU'RE A LITTLE DEFENDED WITH ME.
CAMINOS 91

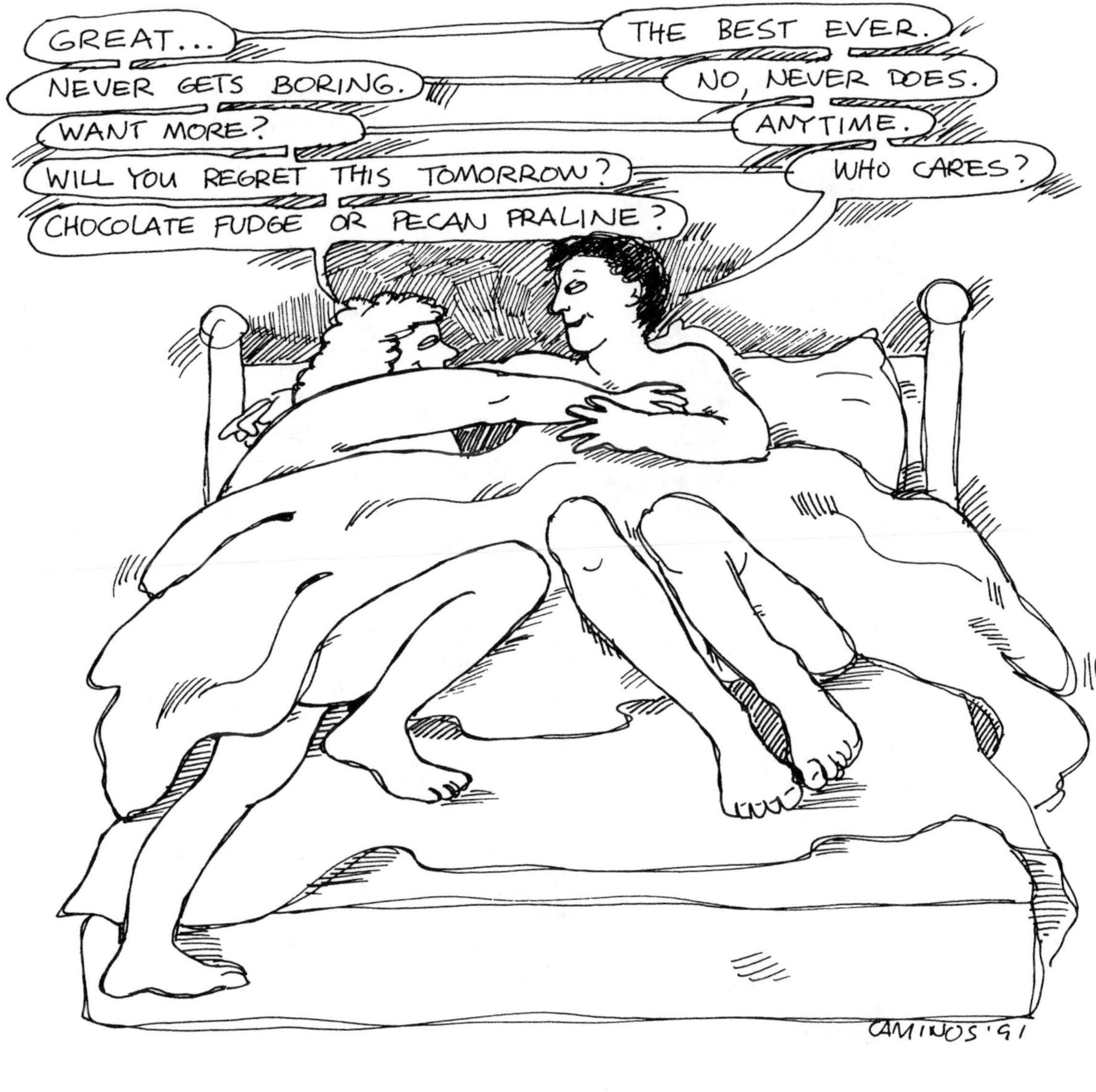
GREAT...
THE BEST EVER.
NEVER GETS BORING.
NO, NEVER DOES.
WANT MORE?
ANYTIME.
WILL YOU REGRET THIS TOMORROW?
WHO CARES?
CHOCOLATE FUDGE OR PECAN PRALINE?
CAMINOS '91

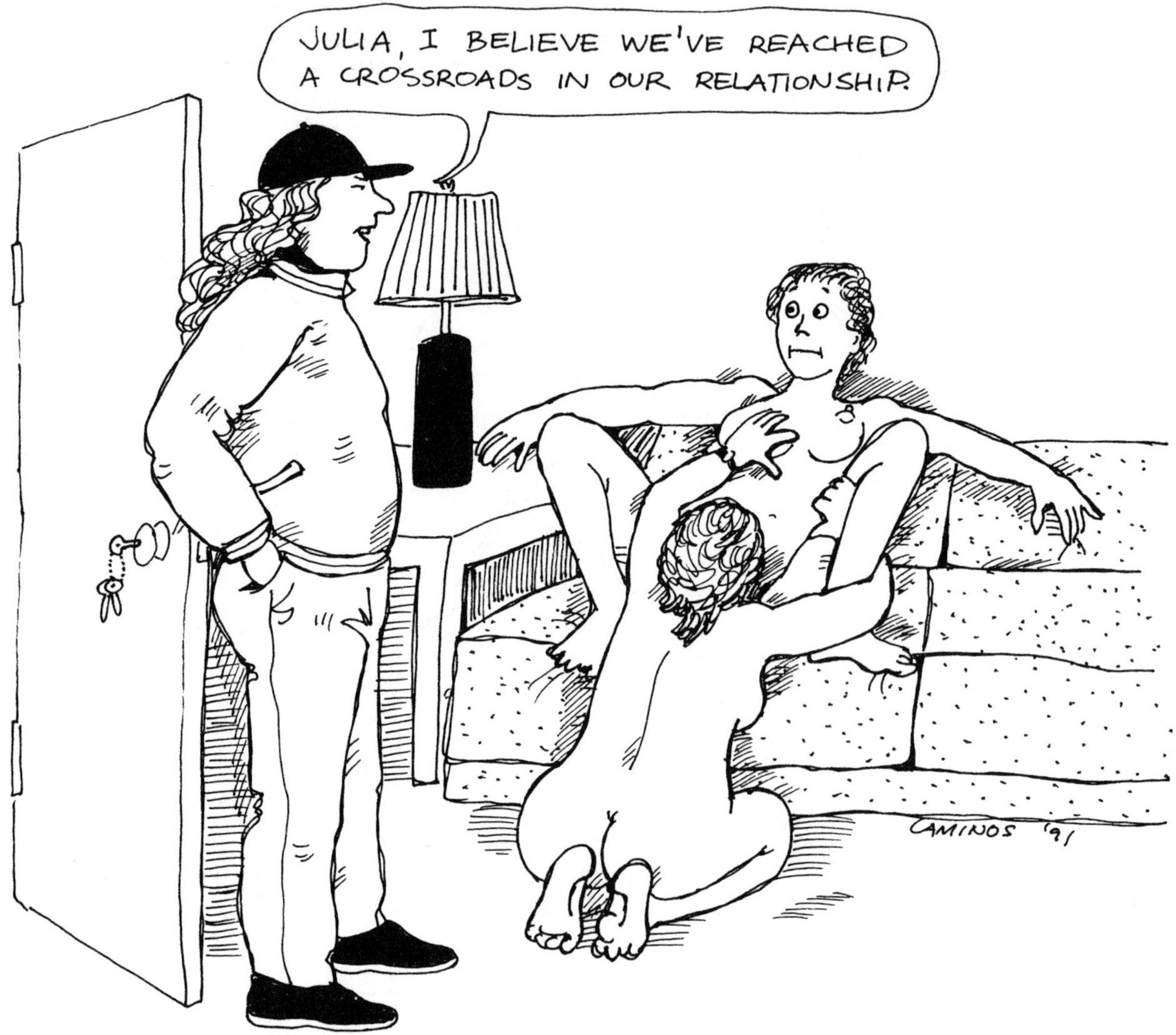
JULIA, I BELIEVE WE'VE REACHED A CROSSROADS IN OUR RELATIONSHIP.
CAMINOS '91

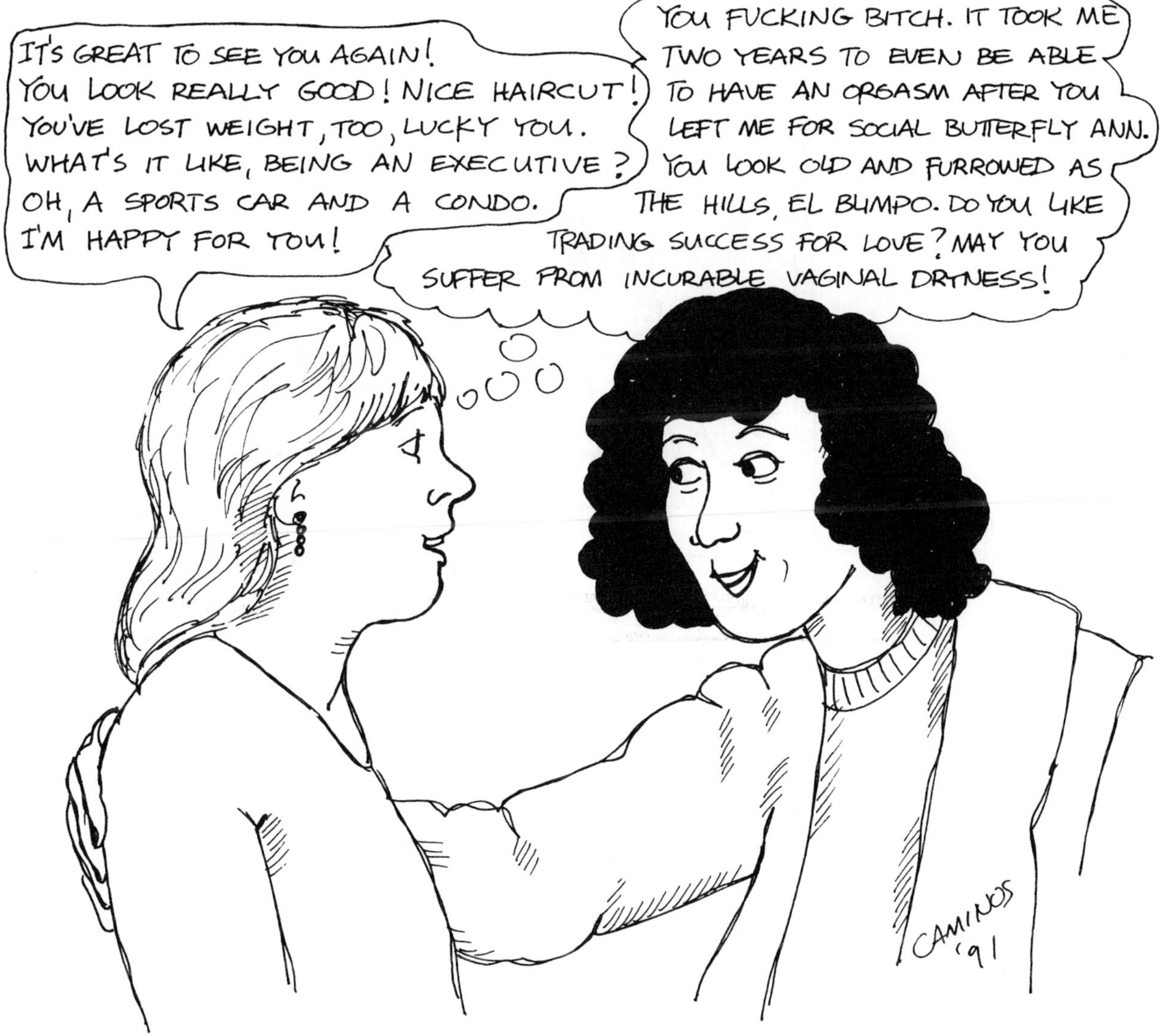
IT'S GREAT TO SEE YOU AGAIN! YOU LOOK REALLY GOOD! NICE HAIRCUT! YOU'VE LOST WEIGHT, TOO, LUCKY YOU. WHAT'S IT LIKE, BEING AN EXECUTIVE? OH, A SPORTS CAR AND A CONDO. I'M HAPPY FOR YOU!
YOU FUCKING BITCH. IT TOOK ME TWO YEARS TO EVEN BE ABLE TO HAVE AN ORGASM AFTER YOU LEFT ME FOR SOCIAL BUTTERFLY ANN. YOU LOOK OLD AND FURROWED AS THE HILLS, EL BUMPO. DO YOU LIKE TRADING SUCCESS FOR LOVE? MAY YOU SUFFER FROM INCURABLE VAGINAL DRYNESS!
CAMINOS '91

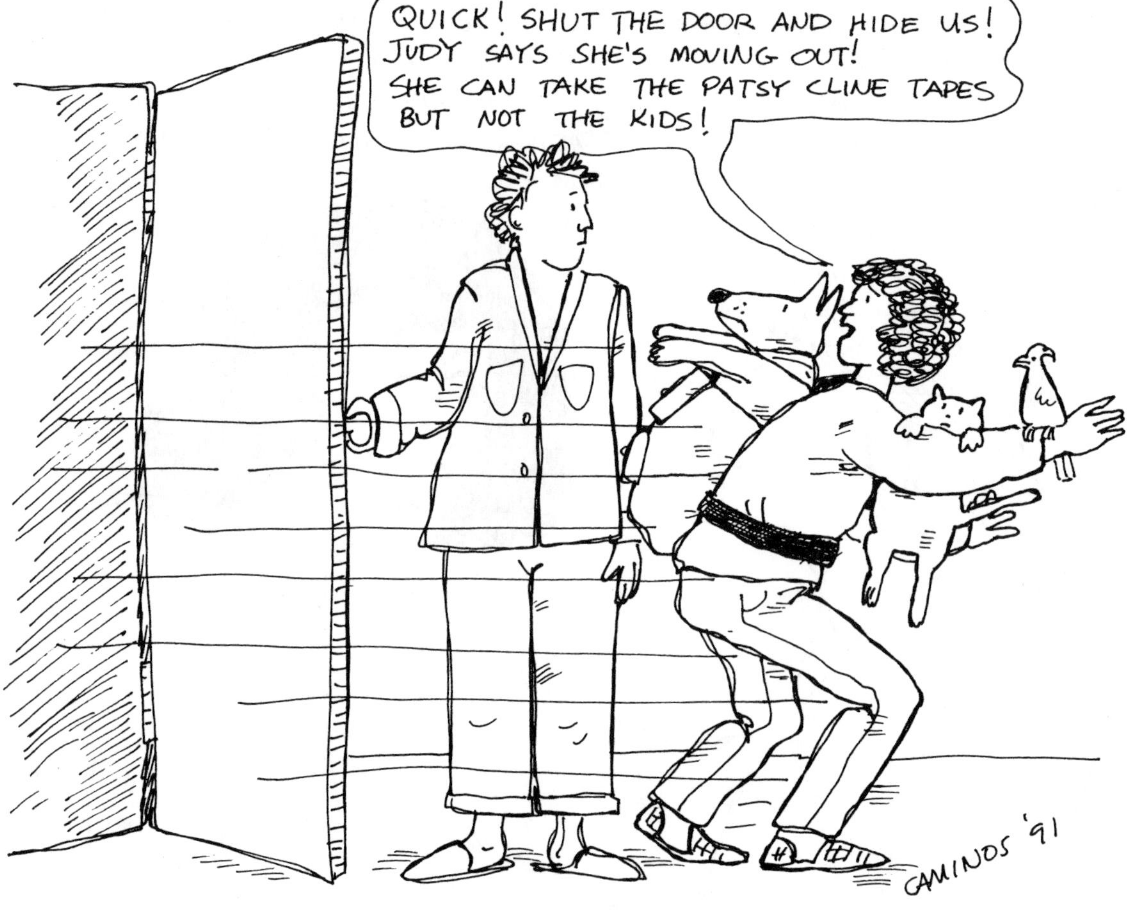
QUICK! SHUT THE DOOR AND HIDE US! JUDY SAYS SHE'S MOVING OUT! SHE CAN TAKE THE PATSY CLINE TAPES BUT NOT THE KIDS!
CAMINOS '91

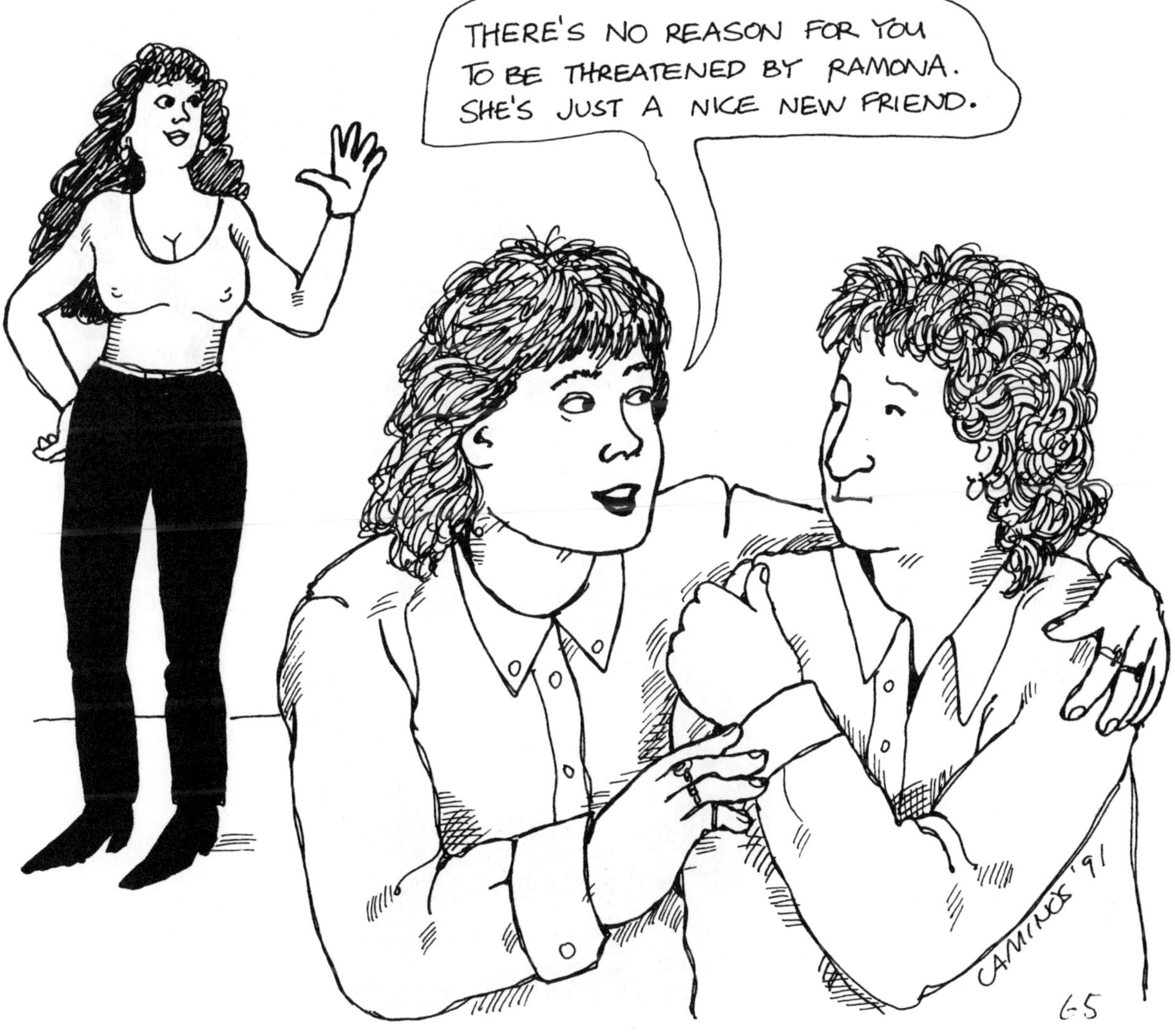
THERE'S NO REASON FOR YOU TO BE THREATENED BY RAMONA. SHE'S JUST A NICE NEW FRIEND.

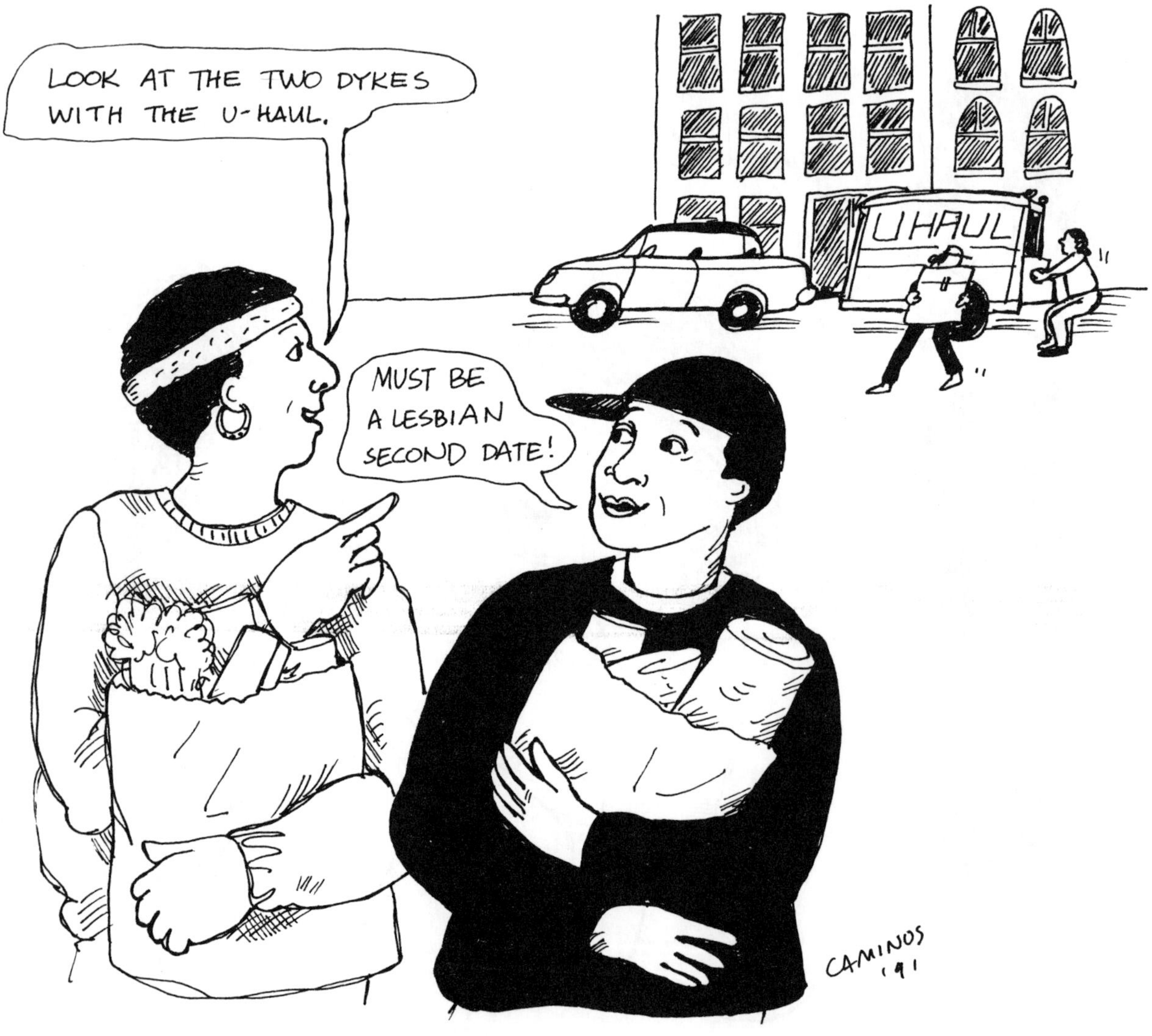
LOOK AT THE TWO DYKES WITH THE U-HAUL.
MUST BE A LESBIAN SECOND DATE!
UHAUL
CAMINOS '91

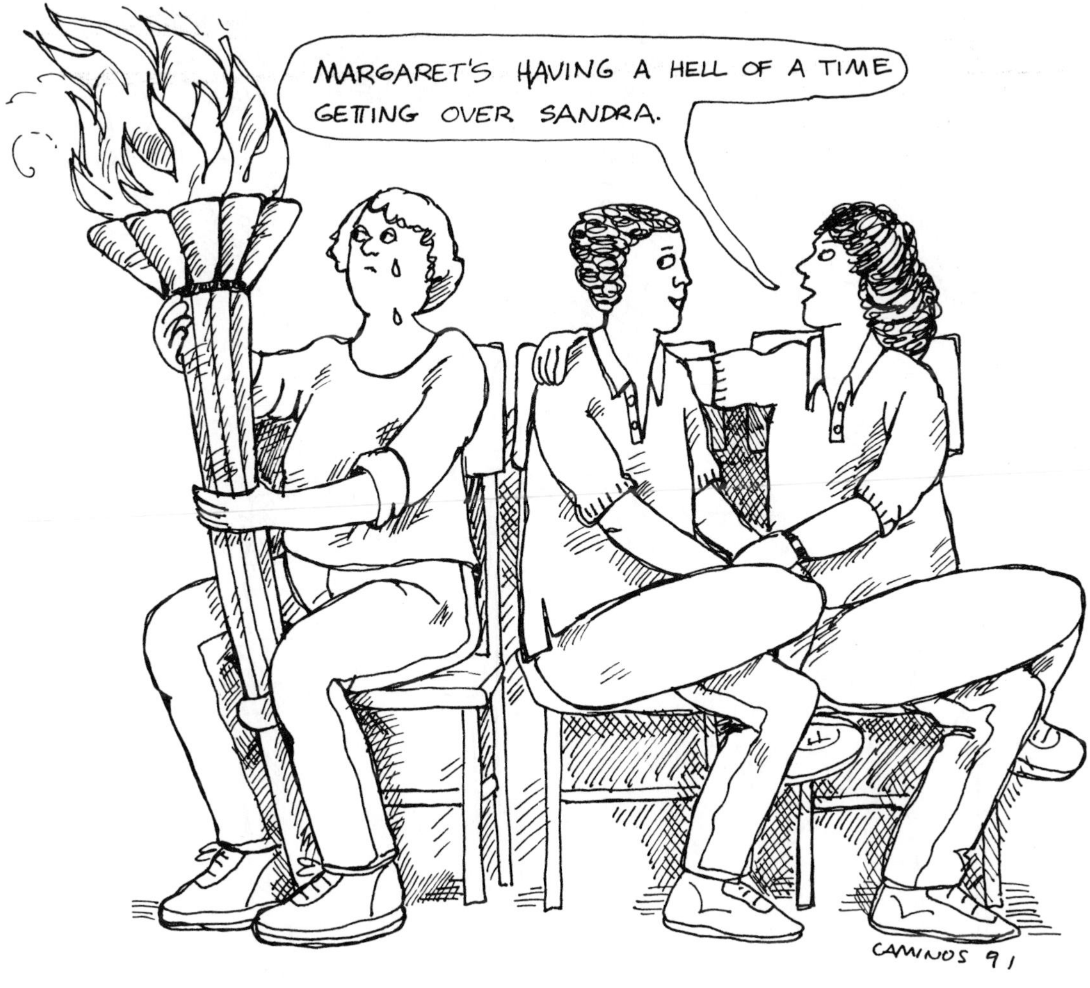
MARGARET'S HAVING A HELL OF A TIME GETTING OVER SANDRA.
CAMINOS 91

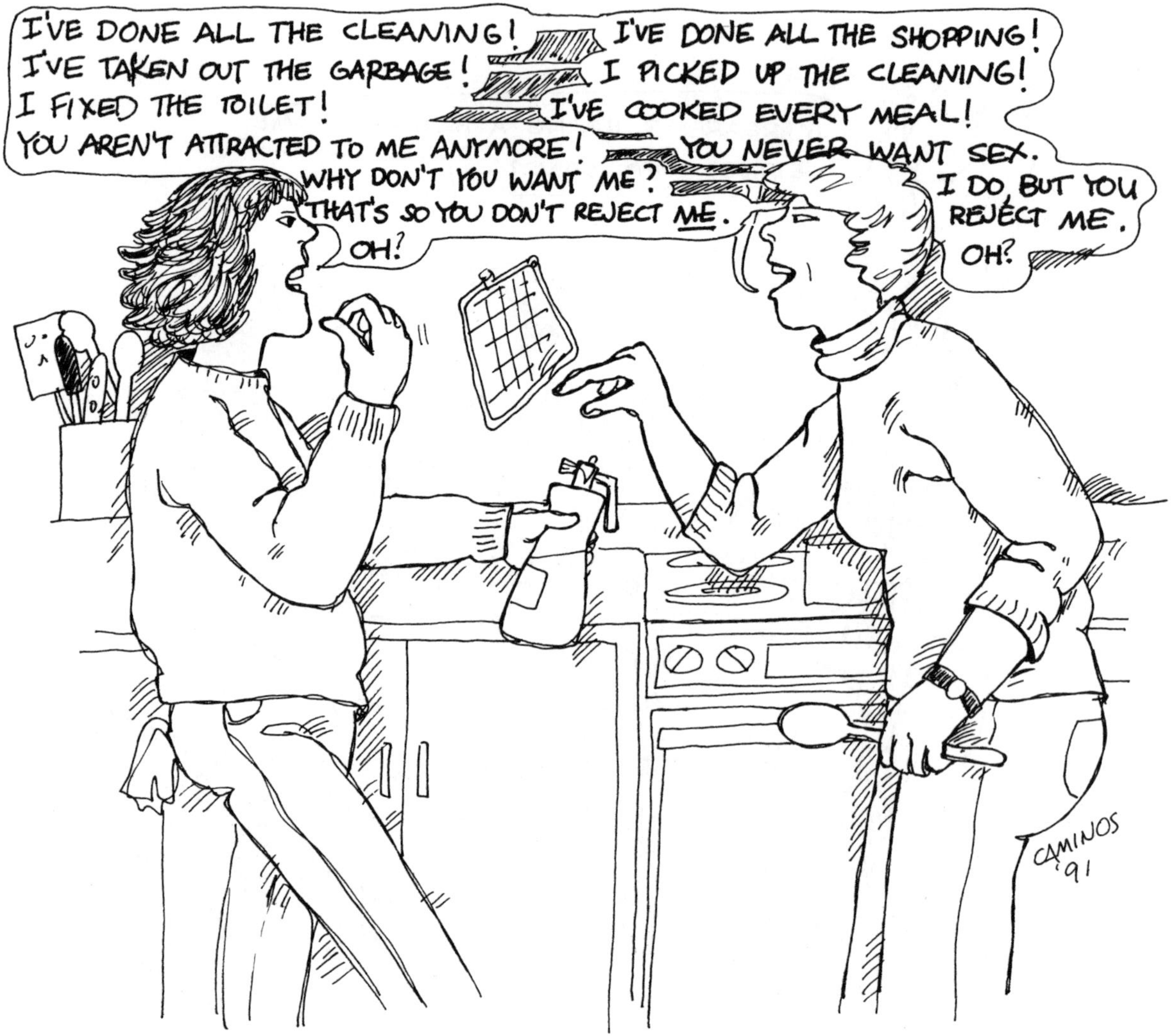
I'VE DONE ALL THE CLEANING!
I'VE DONE ALL THE SHOPPING!
I'VE TAKEN OUT THE GARBAGE!
I PICKED UP THE CLEANING!
I FIXED THE TOILET!
I'VE COOKED EVERY MEAL!
YOU AREN'T ATTRACTED TO ME ANYMORE!
YOU NEVER WANT SEX.
WHY DON'T YOU WANT ME?
I DO, BUT YOU REJECT ME.
THAT'S SO YOU DON'T REJECT ME.
OH?
OH?
CAMINOS '91

I'M LEAVING YOU. WE GET ALONG TOO WELL. THERE'S NO DRAMA IN OUR RELATIONSHIP.
CAMINOS '92

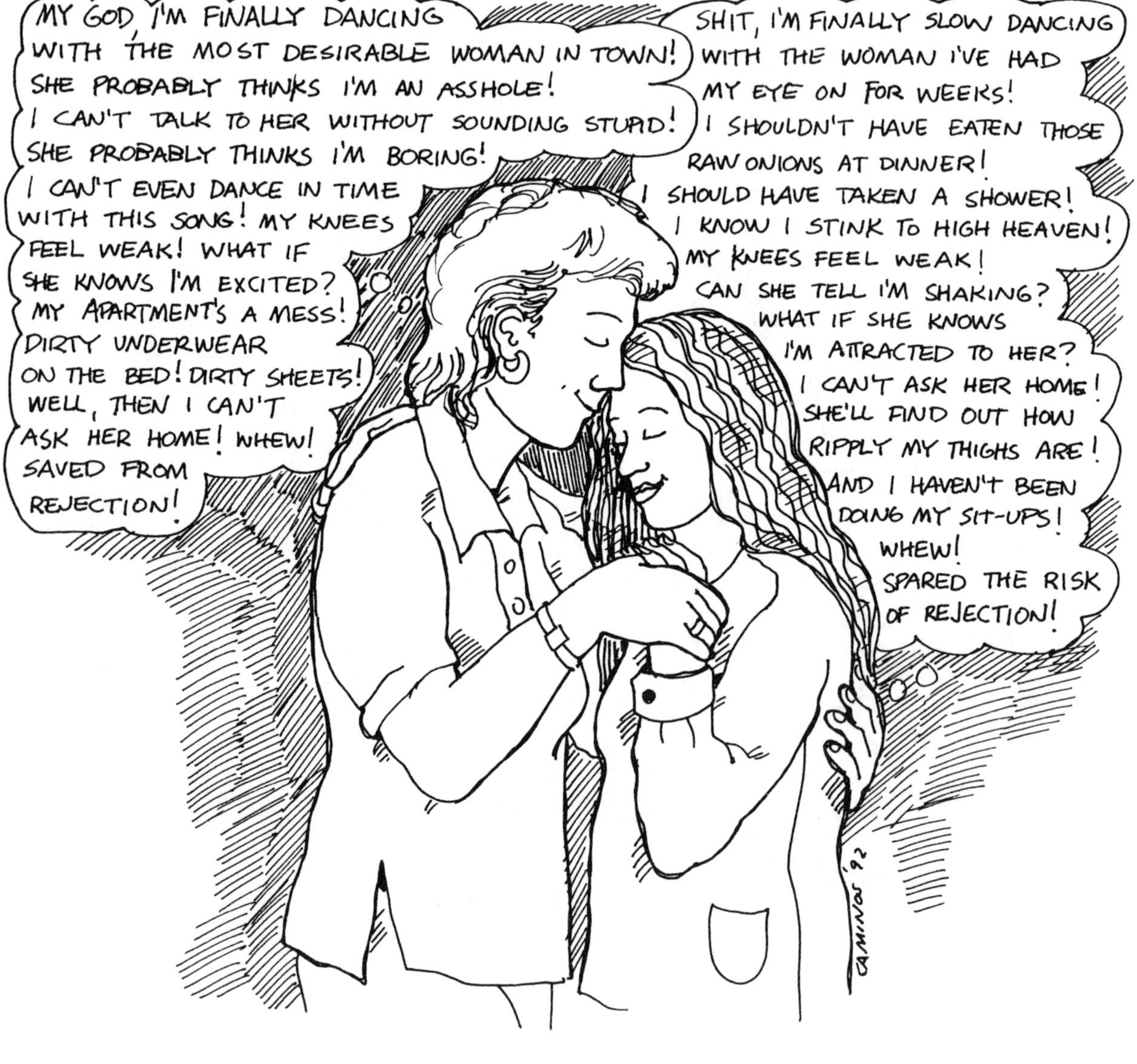
MY GOD, I'M FINALLY DANCING WITH THE MOST DESIRABLE WOMAN IN TOWN! SHE PROBABLY THINKS I'M AN ASSHOLE! I CAN'T TALK TO HER WITHOUT SOUNDING STUPID! SHE PROBABLY THINKS I'M BORING! I CAN'T EVEN DANCE IN TIME WITH THIS SONG! MY KNEES FEEL WEAK! WHAT IF SHE KNOWS I'M EXCITED? MY APARTMENT'S A MESS! DIRTY UNDERWEAR ON THE BED! DIRTY SHEETS! WELL, THEN I CAN'T ASK HER HOME! WHEW! SAVED FROM REJECTION!
SHIT, I'M FINALLY SLOW DANCING WITH THE WOMAN I'VE HAD MY EYE ON FOR WEEKS! I SHOULDN'T HAVE EATEN THOSE RAW ONIONS AT DINNER! I SHOULD HAVE TAKEN A SHOWER! I KNOW I STINK TO HIGH HEAVEN! MY KNEES FEEL WEAK! CAN SHE TELL I'M SHAKING? WHAT IF SHE KNOWS I'M ATTRACTED TO HER? I CAN'T ASK HER HOME! SHE'LL FIND OUT HOW RIPPLY MY THIGHS ARE! AND I HAVEN'T BEEN DOING MY SIT-UPS! WHEW! SPARED THE RISK OF REJECTION!
CAMINOS '92

WELL, AS OF THIS CONCERT, JOANNE IS STILL WITH MARY BETH, LINDA HAS A PERM THAT DIDN'T TAKE, NANCY'S GAINED AT LEAST 20 LBS., MARSHA SEEMS TO BE CHEATING WITH SUE'S LOVER, EILEEN, JEAN'S GOT A BIG HICKEY ON HER NECK, DIANE'S HAVING A FIGHT WITH ANN, AND HA HA, OLD SEXY HAS A PIMPLE ON THE END OF HER NOSE.
CAMINOS '92

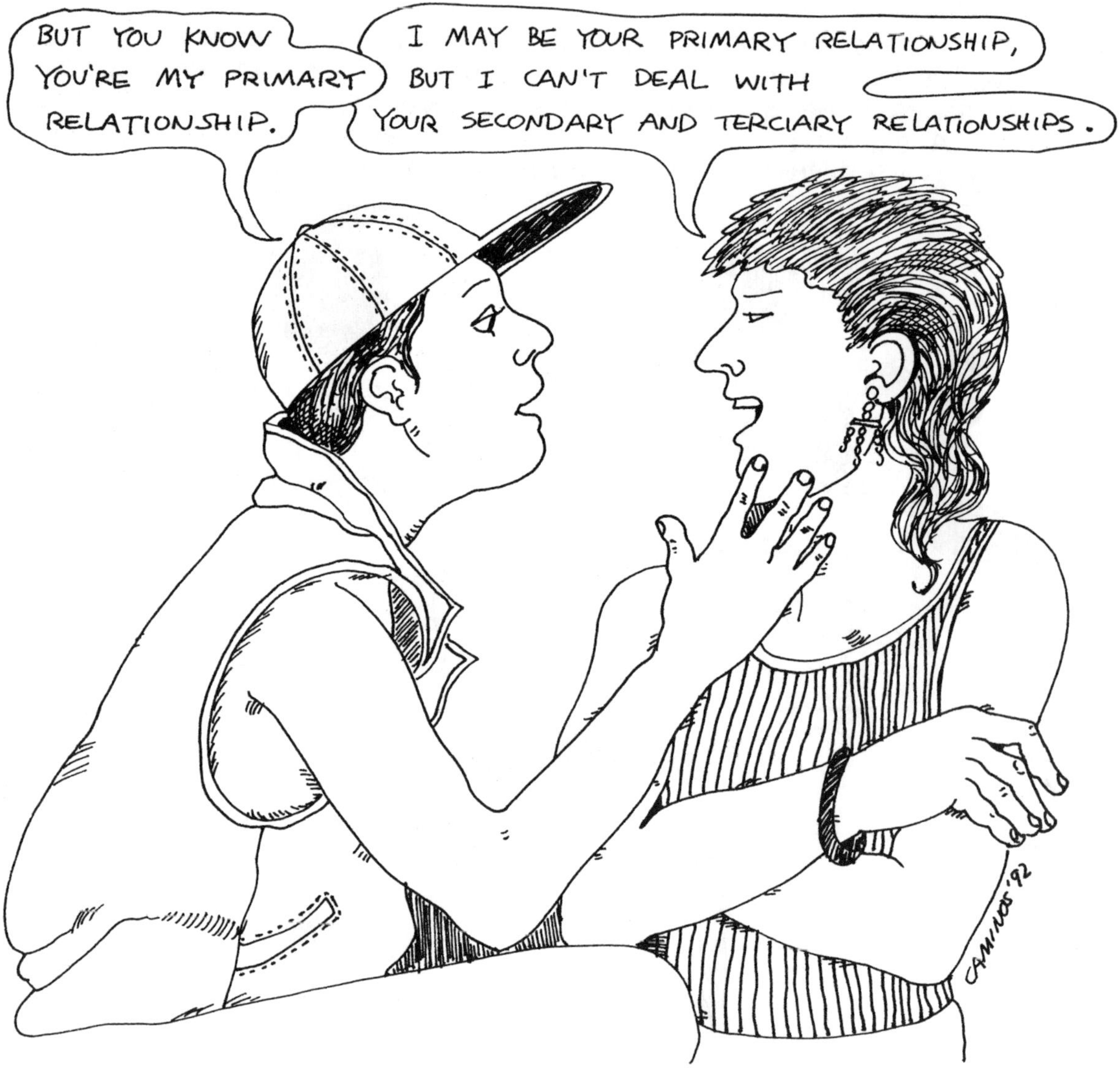
BUT YOU KNOW YOU'RE MY PRIMARY RELATIONSHIP.
I MAY BE YOUR PRIMARY RELATIONSHIP, BUT I CAN'T DEAL WITH YOUR SECONDARY AND TERCIARY RELATIONSHIPS.
CAMINOS '92

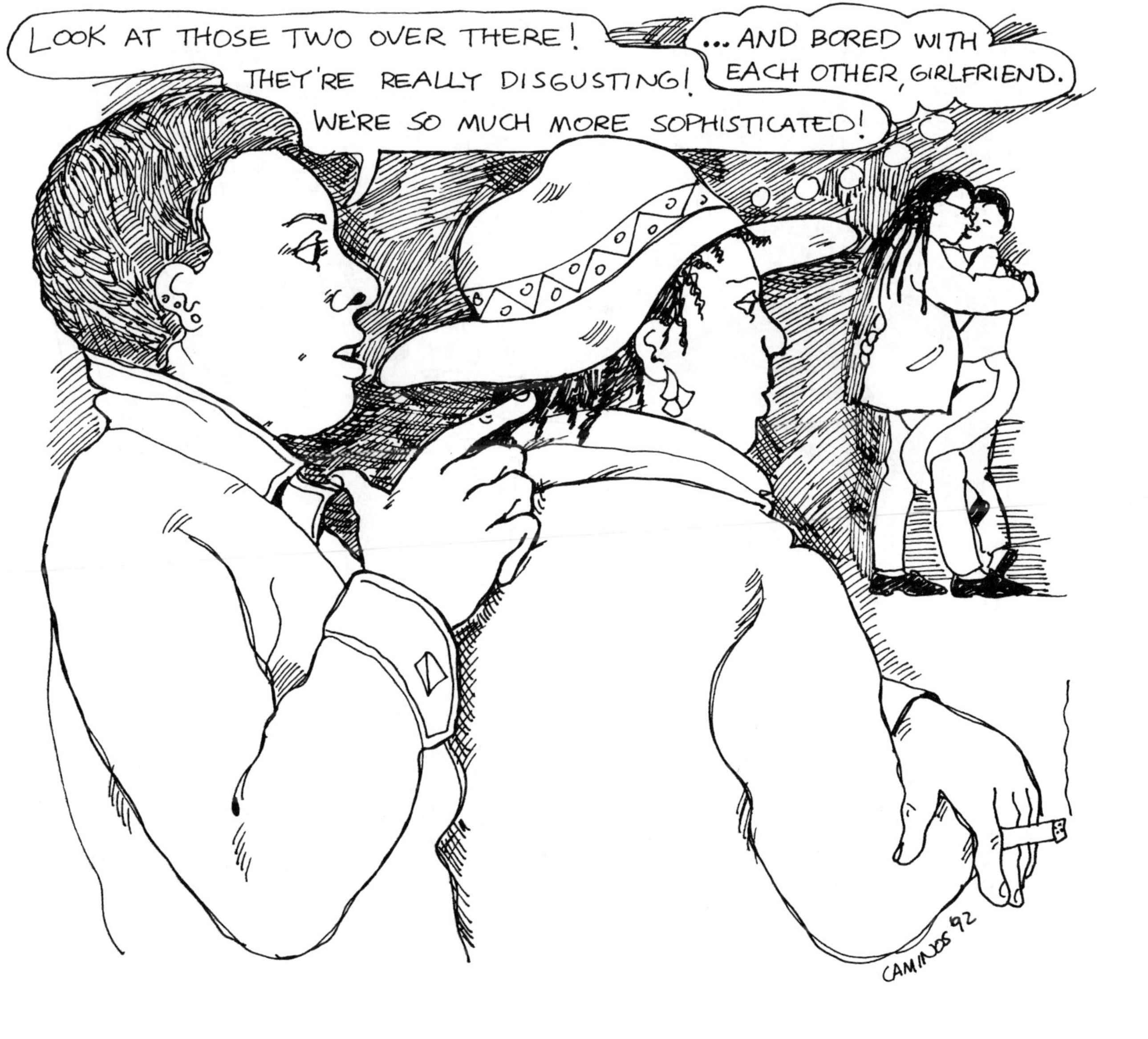
LOOK AT THOSE TWO OVER THERE! THEY'RE REALLY DISGUSTING! WE'RE SO MUCH MORE SOPHISTICATED!
...AND BORED WITH EACH OTHER, GIRLFRIEND.
CAMINOS '92

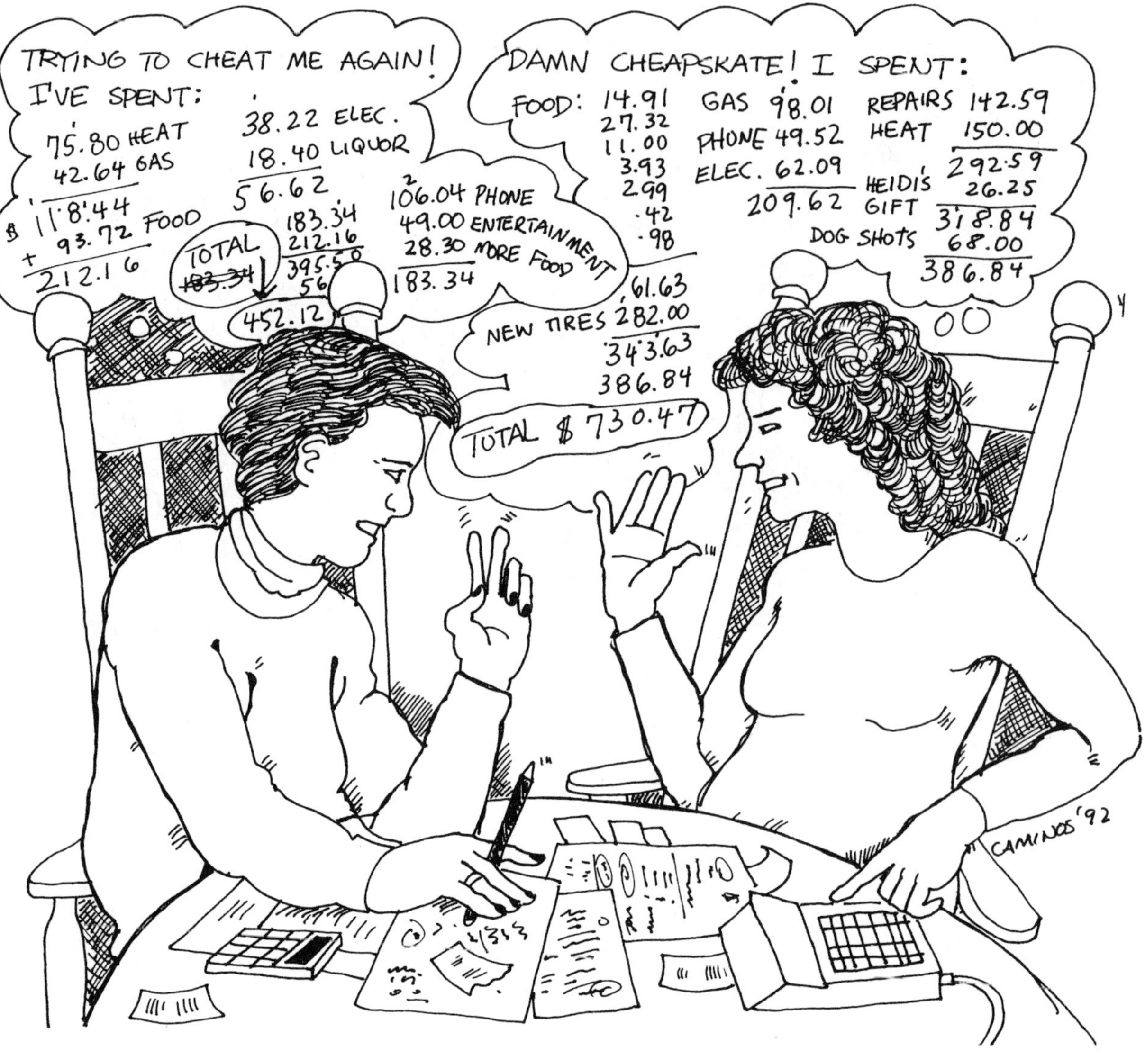
TRYING TO CHEAT ME AGAIN! I'VE SPENT:
75.80 HEAT
42.64 GAS
118.44
+ 93.72 FOOD
212.16
38.22 ELEC.
18.40 LIQUOR
56.62
TOTAL
183.34
452.12
183.34
212.16
106.04 PHONE
49.00 ENTERTAINMENT
28.30 MORE FOOD
183.34
DAMN CHEAPSKATE! I SPENT:
FOOD: 14.91
27.32
11.00
3.93
2.99
.42
.98
61.63
NEW TIRES 282.00
343.63
386.84
TOTAL $730.47
GAS 98.01
PHONE 49.52
ELEC. 62.09
209.62
REPAIRS 142.59
HEAT 150.00
292.59
HEIDI'S GIFT 26.25
318.84
DOG SHOTS 68.00
386.84
CAMINOS '92

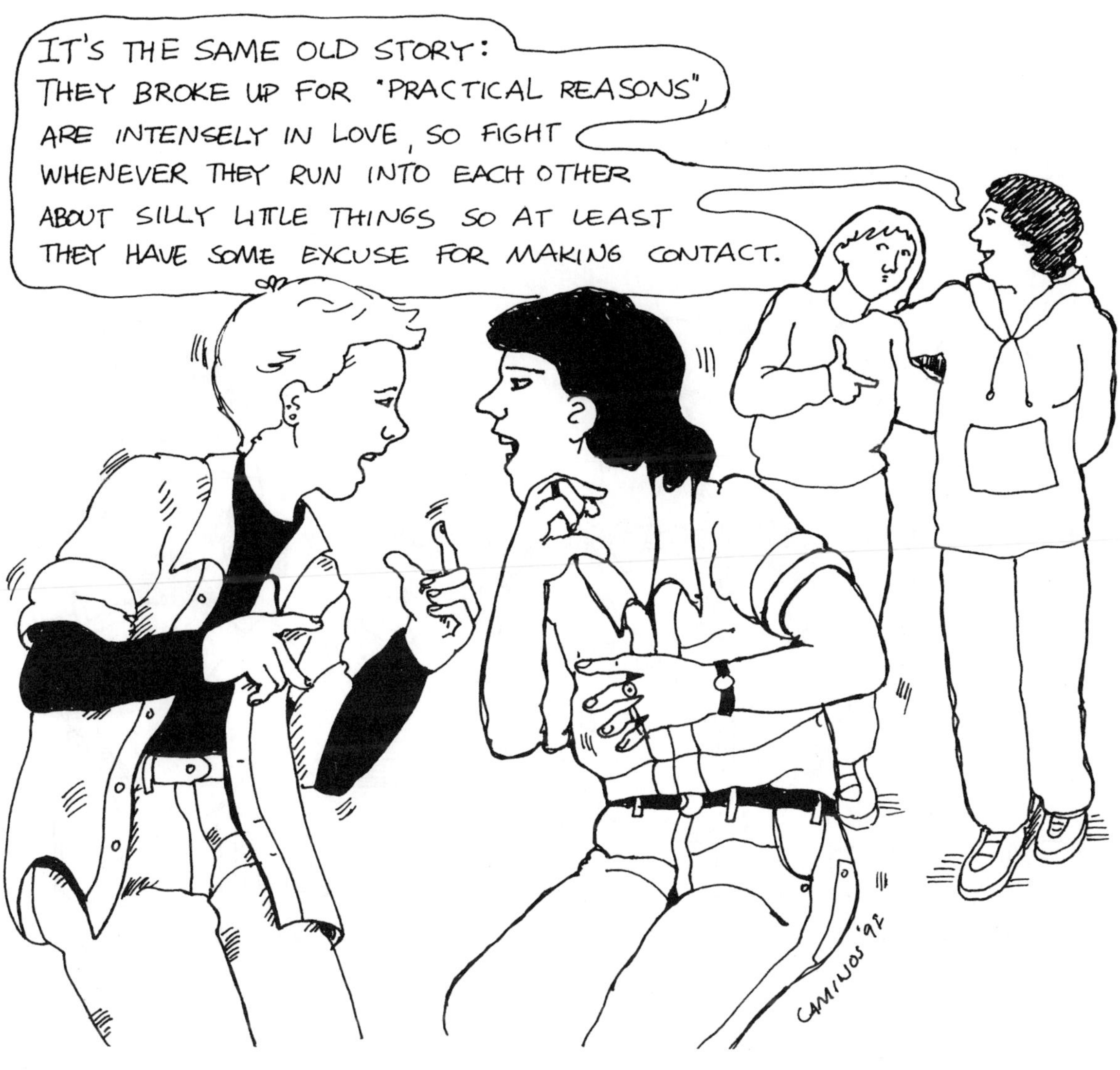
IT'S THE SAME OLD STORY: THEY BROKE UP FOR "PRACTICAL REASONS", ARE INTENSELY IN LOVE, SO FIGHT WHENEVER THEY RUN INTO EACH OTHER ABOUT SILLY LITTLE THINGS SO AT LEAST THEY HAVE SOME EXCUSE FOR MAKING CONTACT.
CAMINOS '92

OH HELL NO, I'M NOT WORRIED. THEY'LL NEVER SLEEP TOGETHER; IT WOULD RUIN THE FUN OF THEIR LITTLE "INTENSITY".
CAMINOS '92

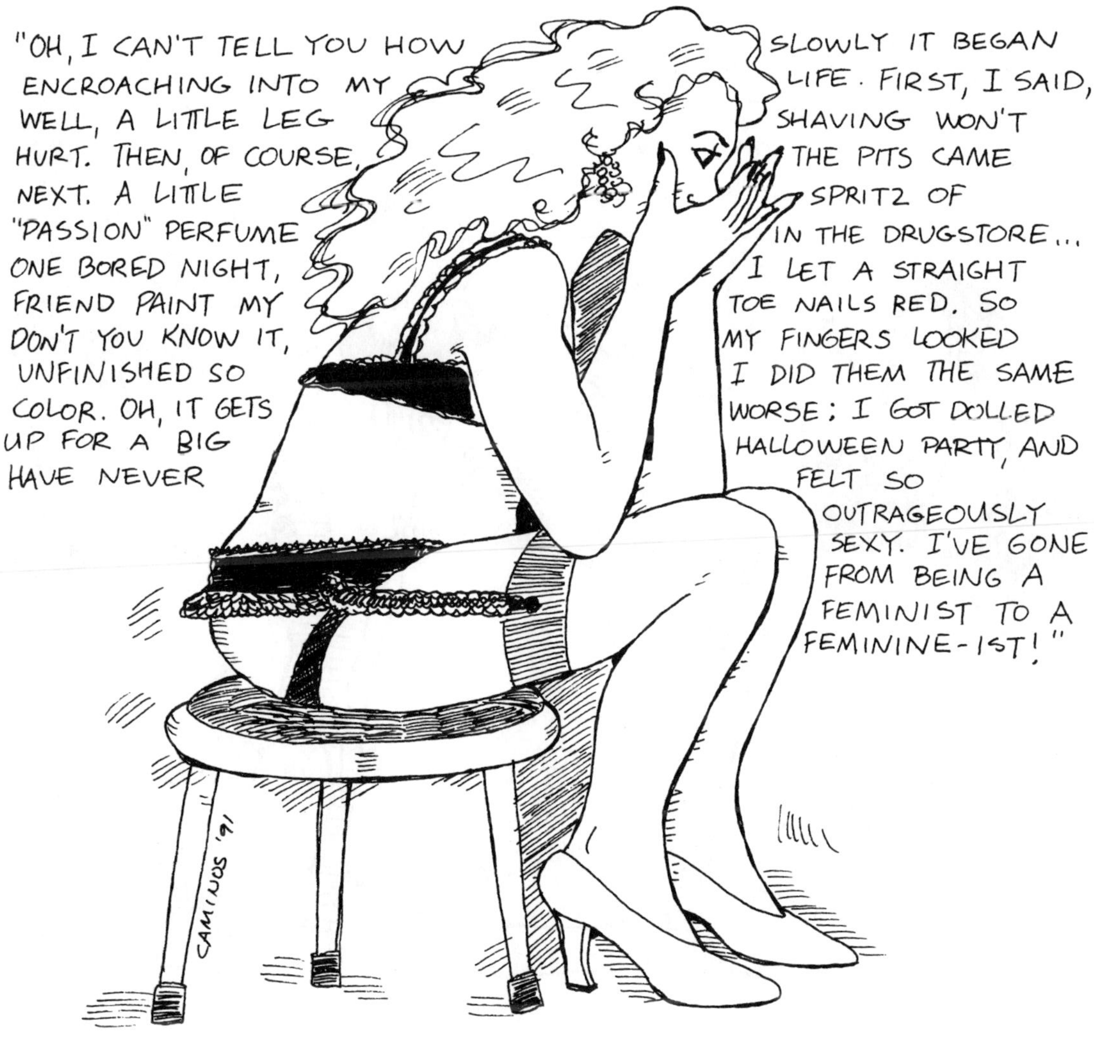
"OH, I CAN'T TELL YOU HOW SLOWLY IT BEGAN
ENCROACHING INTO MY LIFE. FIRST, I SAID,
WELL, A LITTLE LEG SHAVING WON'T
HURT. THEN, OF COURSE, THE PITS CAME
NEXT. A LITTLE SPRITZ OF
"PASSION" PERFUME IN THE DRUGSTORE...
ONE BORED NIGHT, I LET A STRAIGHT
FRIEND PAINT MY TOE NAILS RED. SO
DON'T YOU KNOW IT, MY FINGERS LOOKED
UNFINISHED SO I DID THEM THE SAME
COLOR. OH, IT GETS WORSE; I GOT DOLLED
UP FOR A BIG HALLOWEEN PARTY, AND
HAVE NEVER FELT SO
OUTRAGEOUSLY
SEXY. I'VE GONE
FROM BEING A
FEMINIST TO A
FEMININE-IST!"
CAMINOS '91

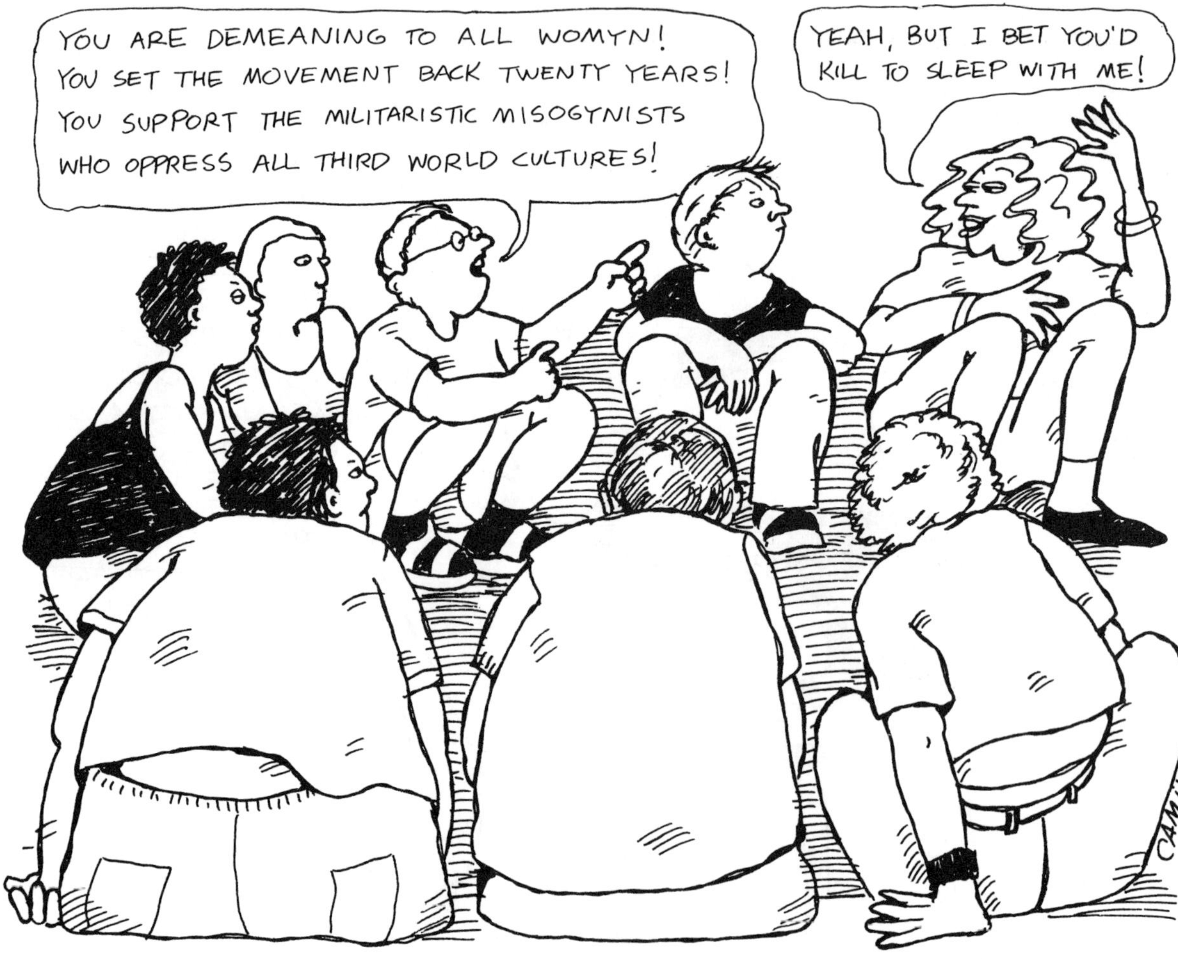
YOU ARE DEMEANING TO ALL WOMYN! YOU SET THE MOVEMENT BACK TWENTY YEARS! YOU SUPPORT THE MILITARISTIC MISOGYNISTS WHO OPPRESS ALL THIRD WORLD CULTURES!
YEAH, BUT I BET YOU'D KILL TO SLEEP WITH ME!
CAMINOS '91

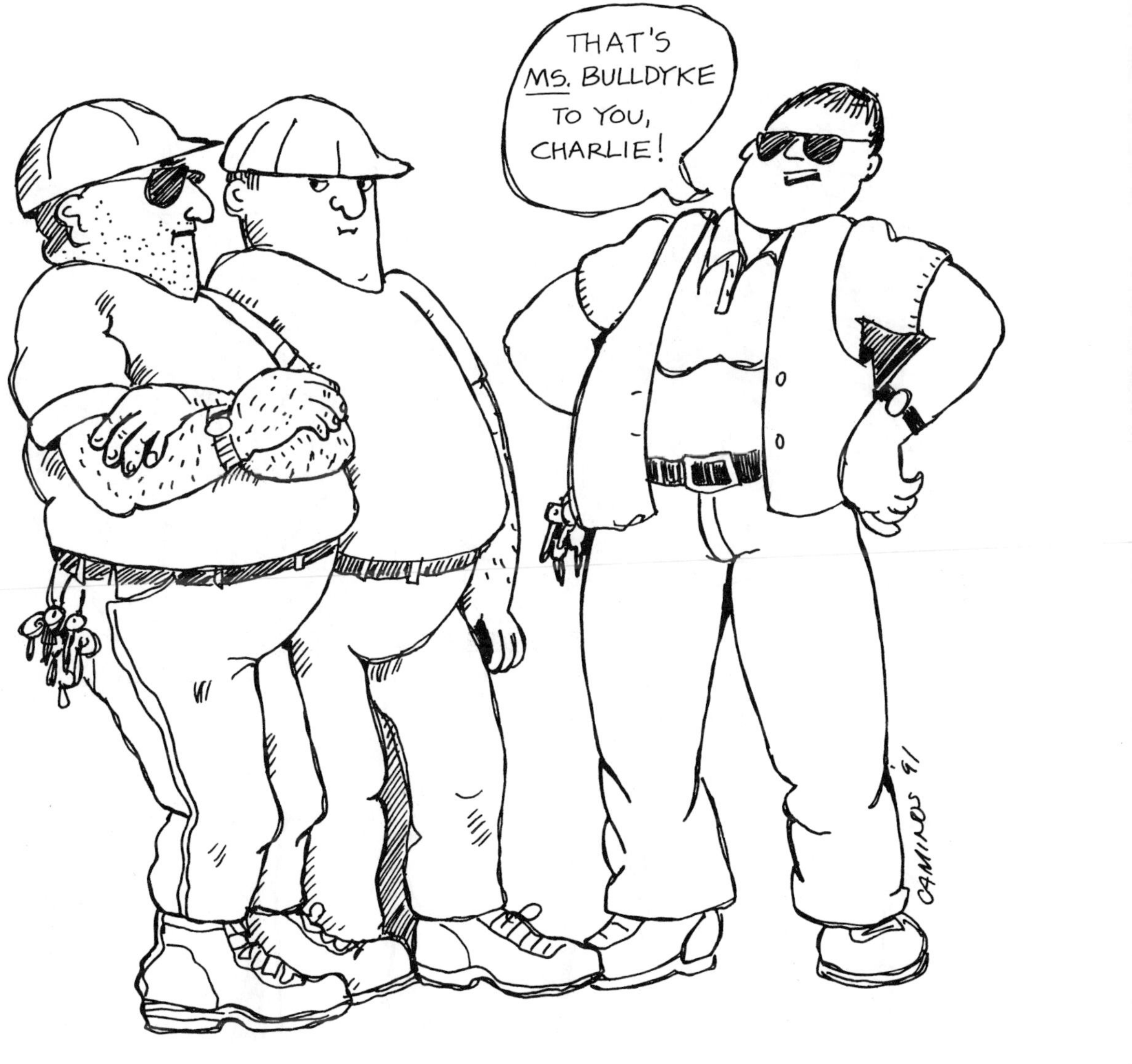
THAT'S MS. BULLDYKE TO YOU, CHARLIE!
CAMINOS '91

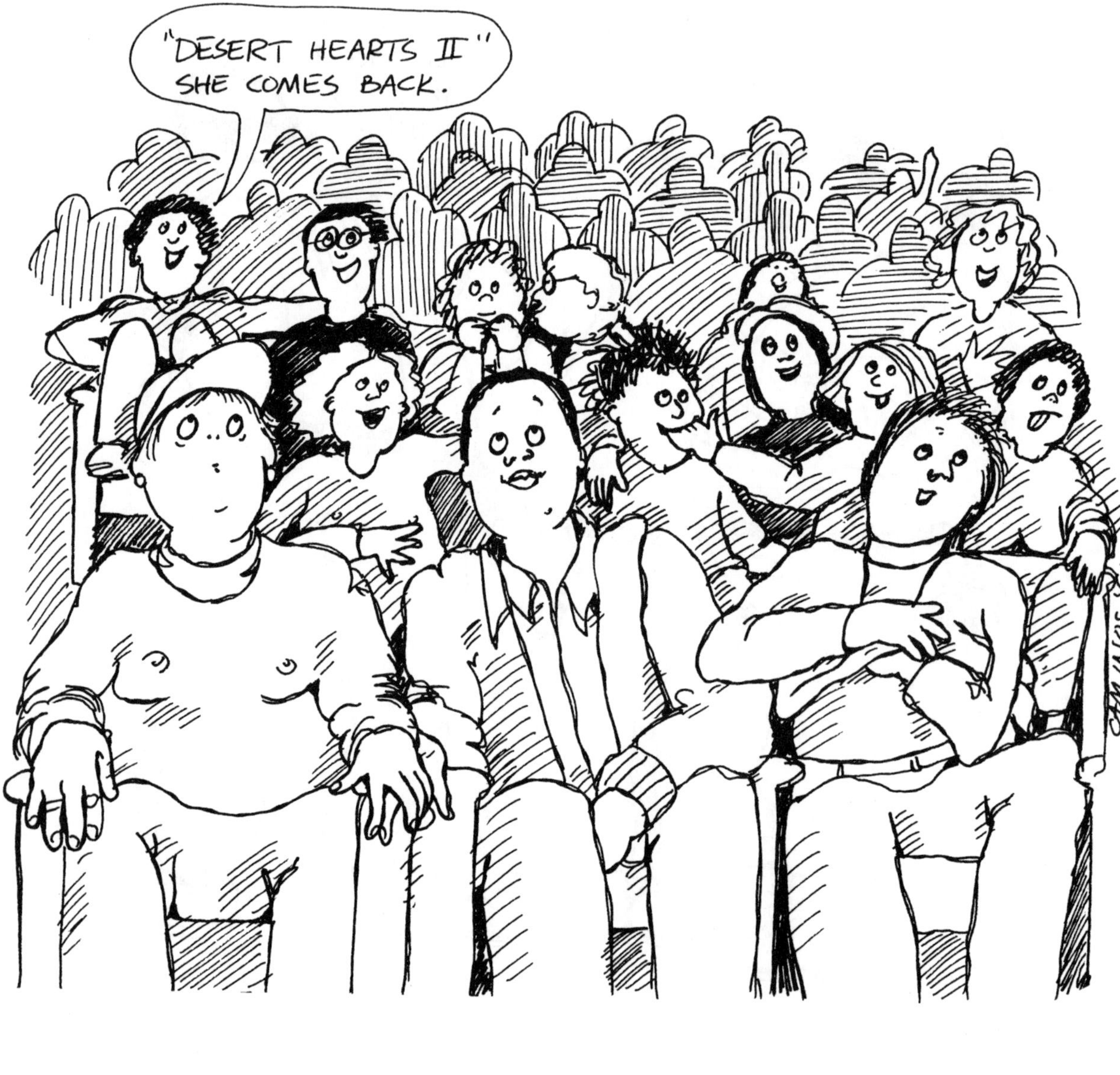
"DESERT HEARTS II"
SHE COMES BACK.
CAMINOS '91

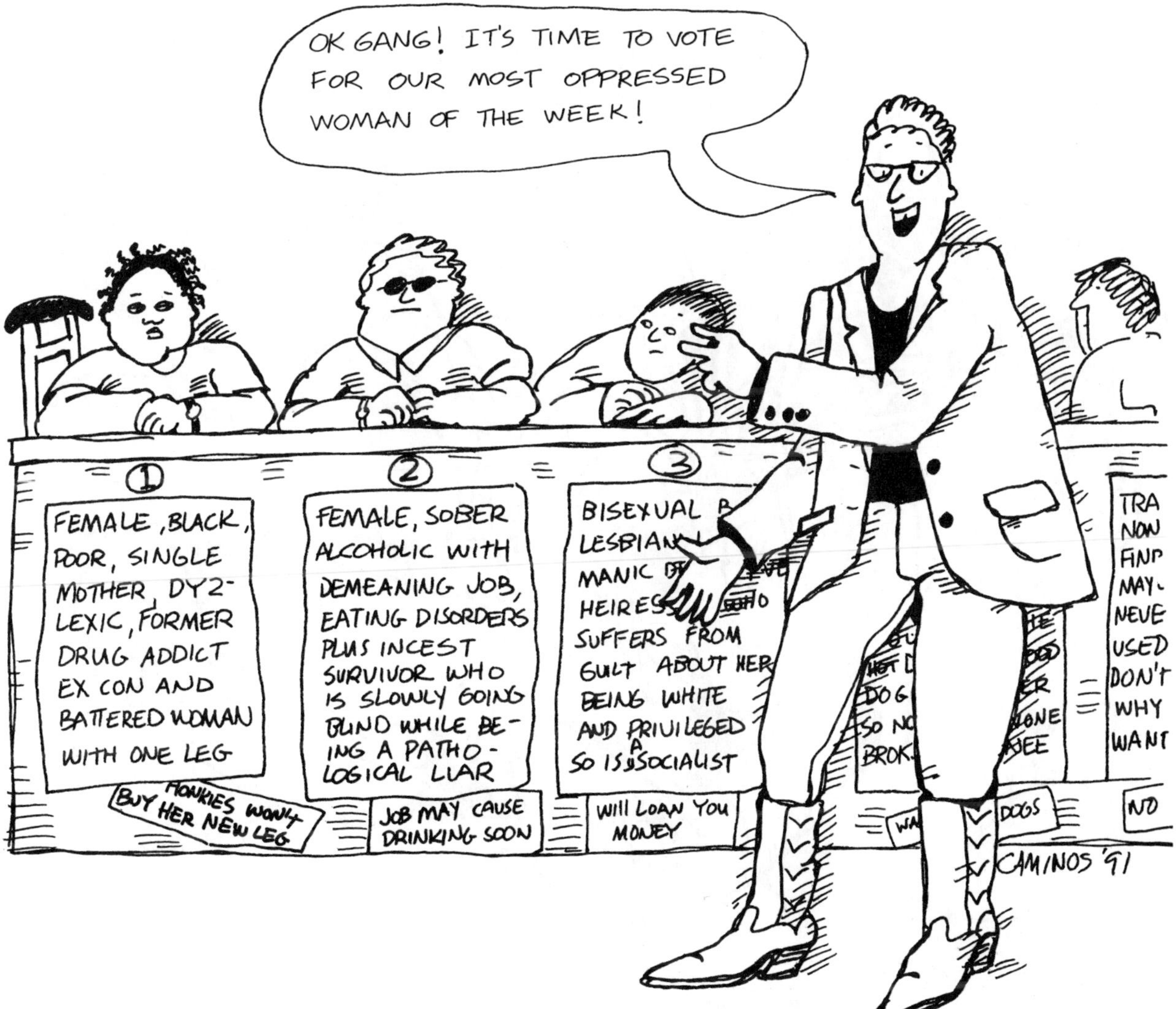

OK GANG! IT'S TIME TO VOTE FOR OUR MOST OPPRESSED WOMAN OF THE WEEK!
1
FEMALE, BLACK, POOR, SINGLE MOTHER, DYZ-LEXIC, FORMER DRUG ADDICT EX CON AND BATTERED WOMAN WITH ONE LEG
HONKIES WON'T BUY HER NEW LEG
2
FEMALE, SOBER ALCOHOLIC WITH DEMEANING JOB, EATING DISORDERS PLUS INCEST SURVIVOR WHO IS SLOWLY GOING BLIND WHILE BE-ING A PATHO-LOGICAL LIAR
JOB MAY CAUSE DRINKING SOON
3
BISEXUAL
LESBIAN
MANIC
SUFFERS FROM GUILT ABOUT HER BEING WHITE AND PRIVILEGED SO IS A SOCIALIST
WILL LOAN YOU MONEY
DOGS
NO
CAMINOS '91

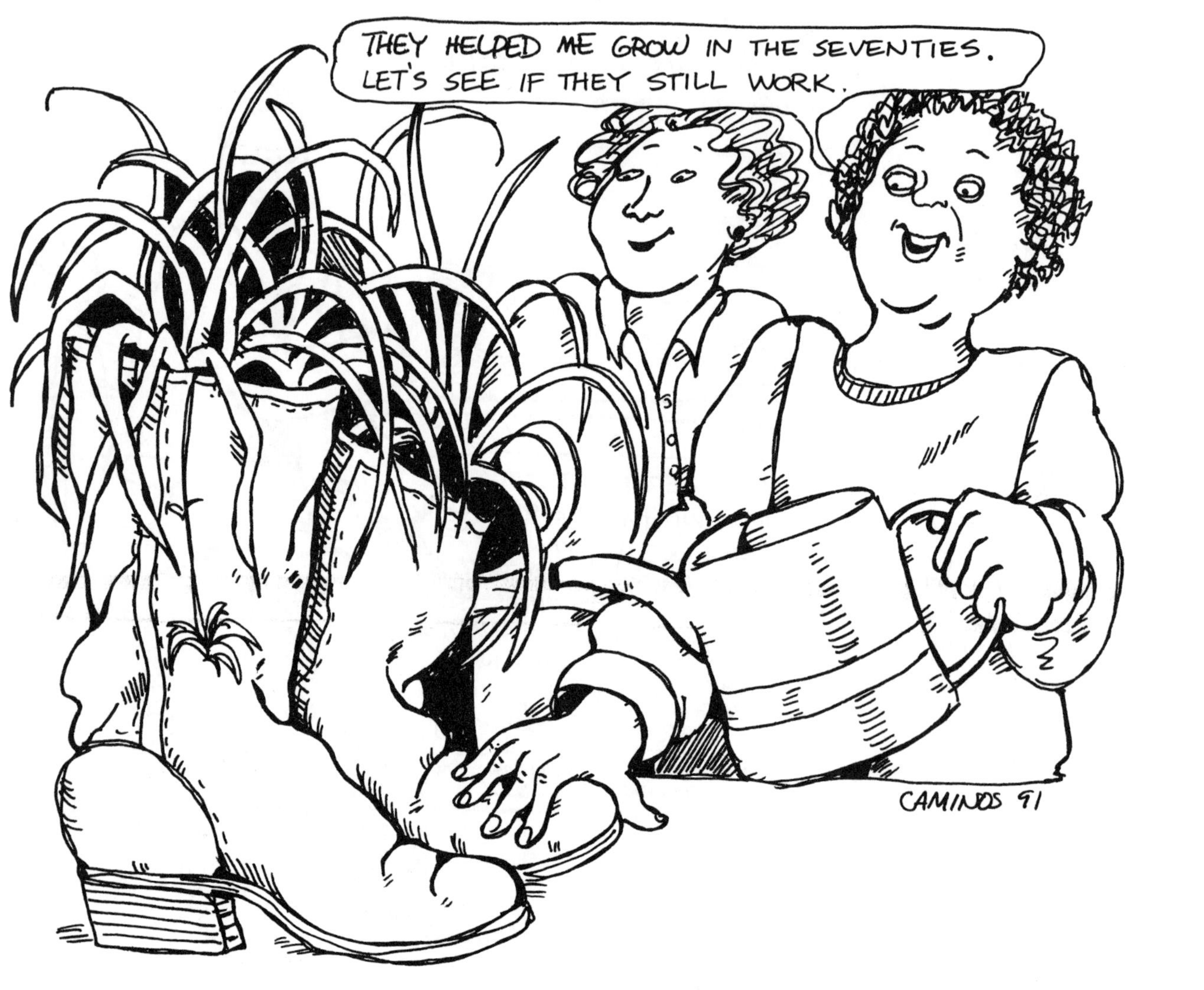
THEY HELPED ME GROW IN THE SEVENTIES. LET'S SEE IF THEY STILL WORK.
CAMINOS 91

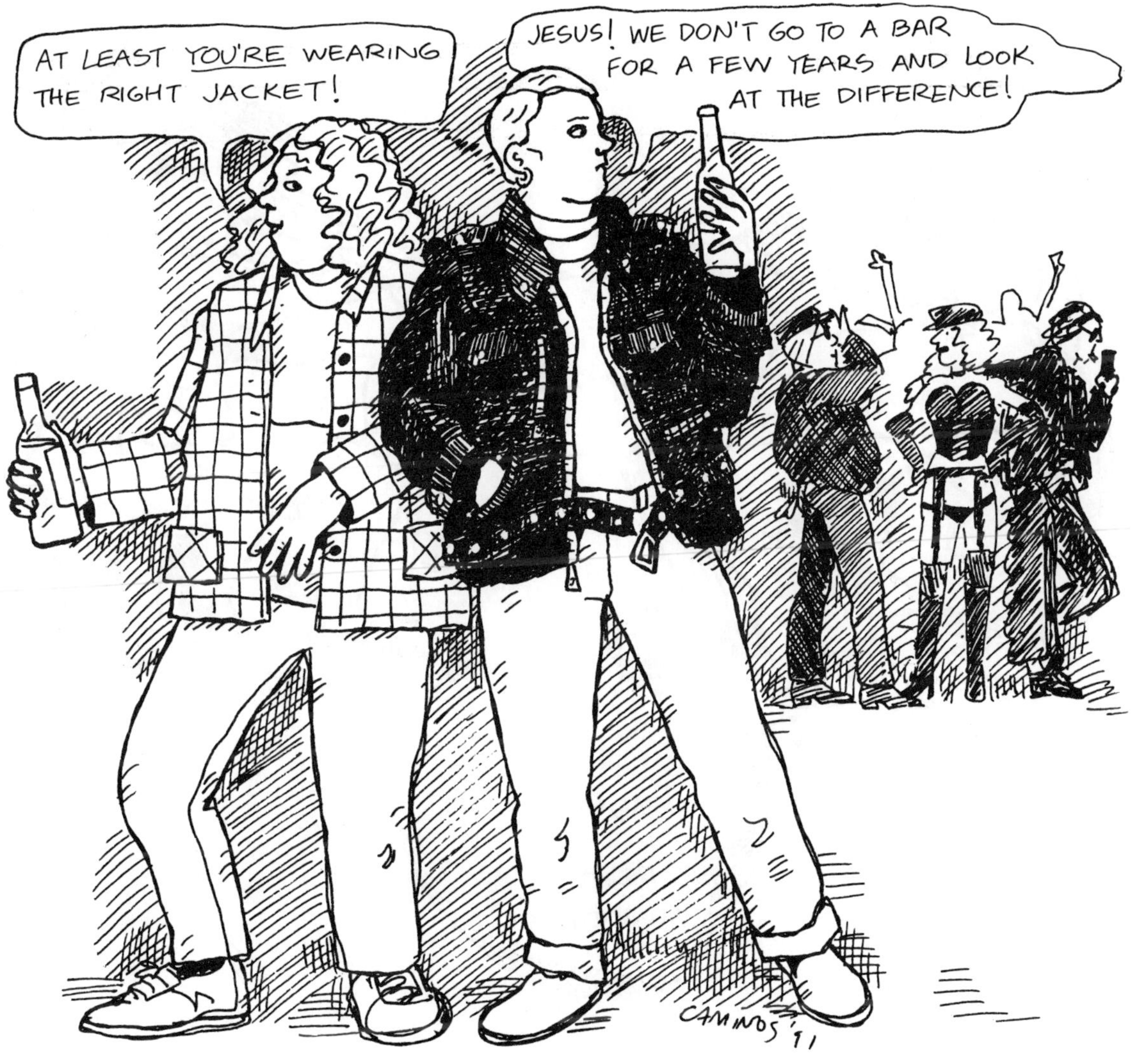
AT LEAST YOU'RE WEARING THE RIGHT JACKET!
JESUS! WE DON'T GO TO A BAR FOR A FEW YEARS AND LOOK AT THE DIFFERENCE!
CAMMOS '91

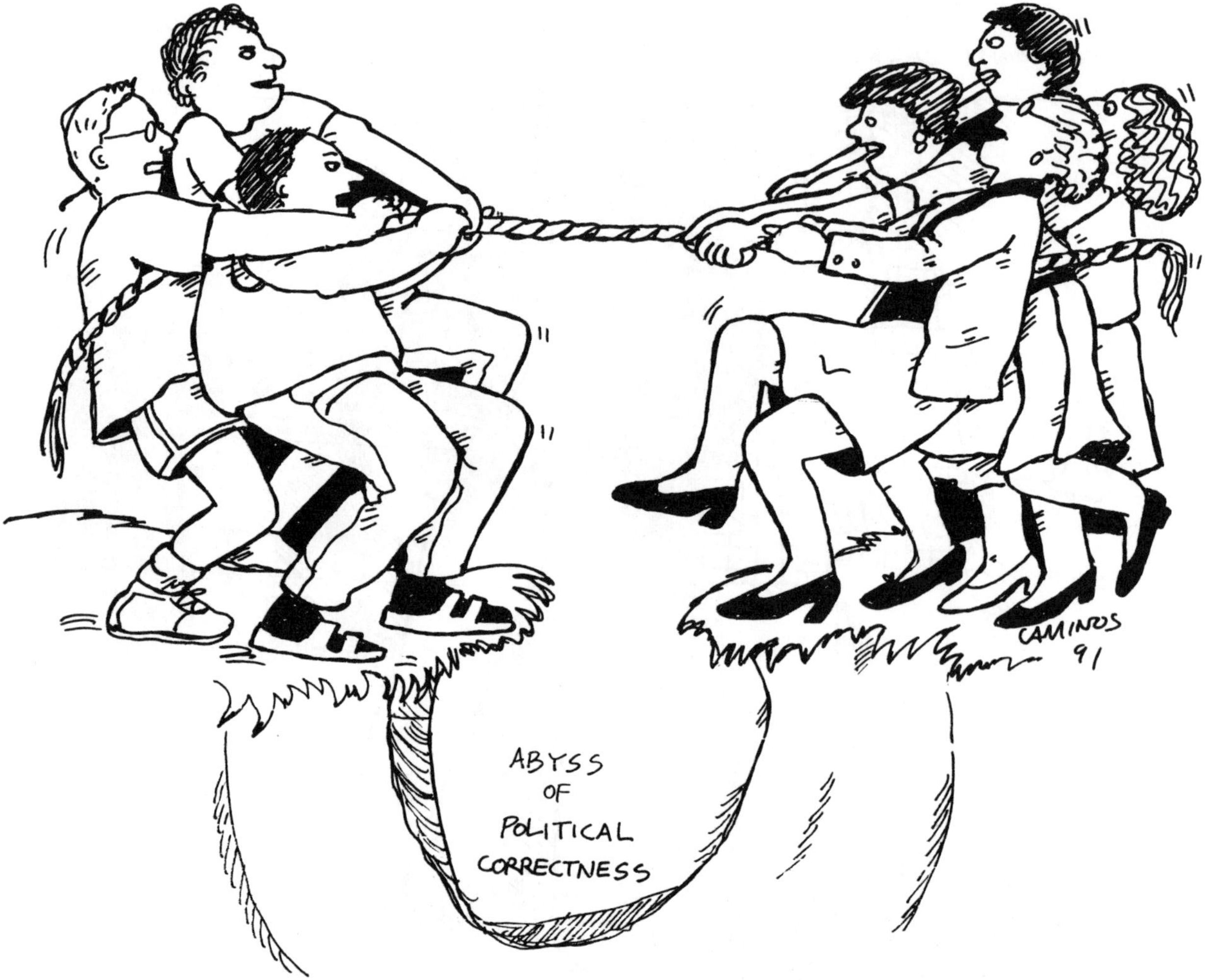
ABYSS
OF
POLITICAL
CORRECTNESS
CAMINOS
91

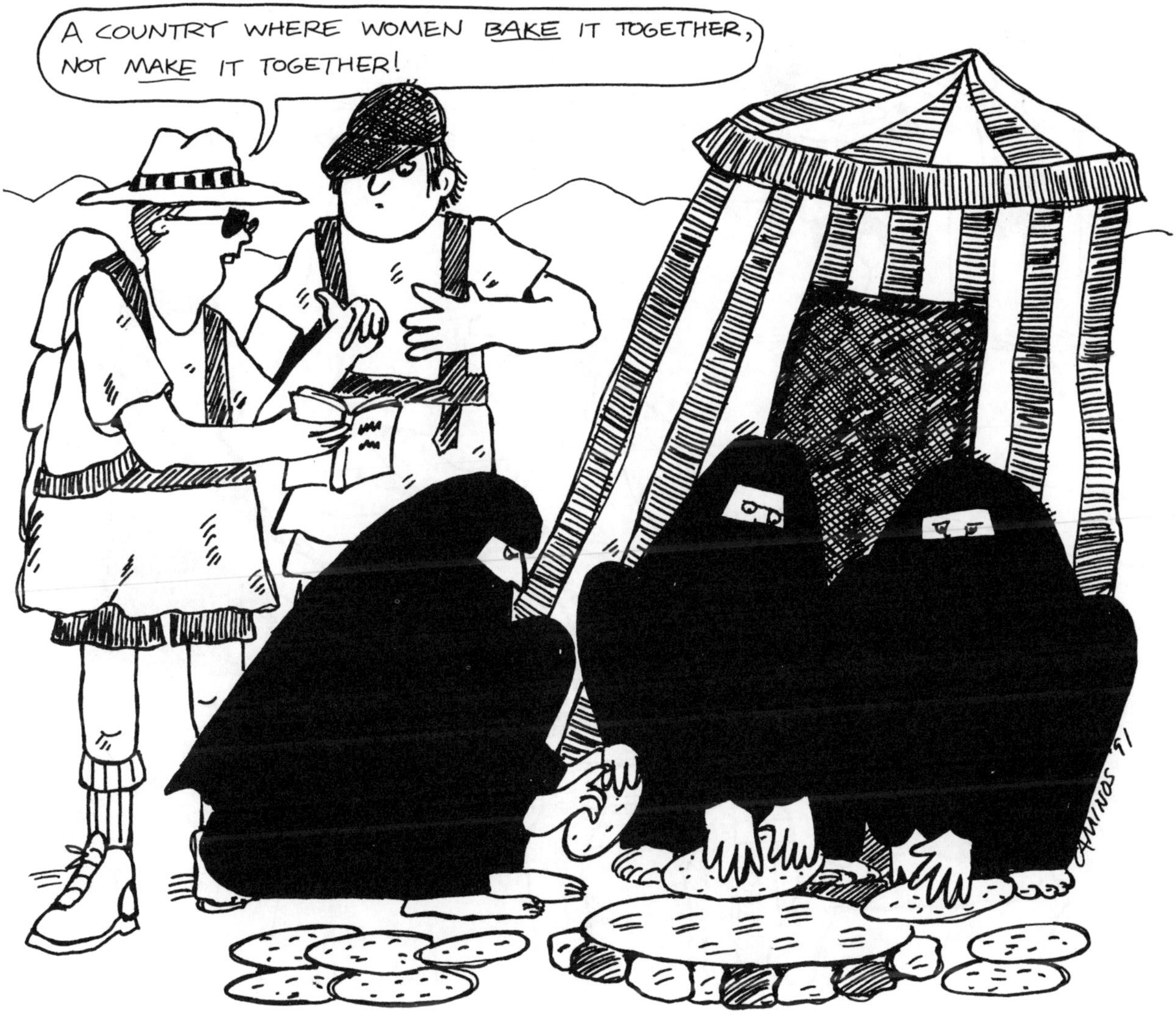
A COUNTRY WHERE WOMEN BAKE IT TOGETHER, NOT MAKE IT TOGETHER!
CAMINOS '91

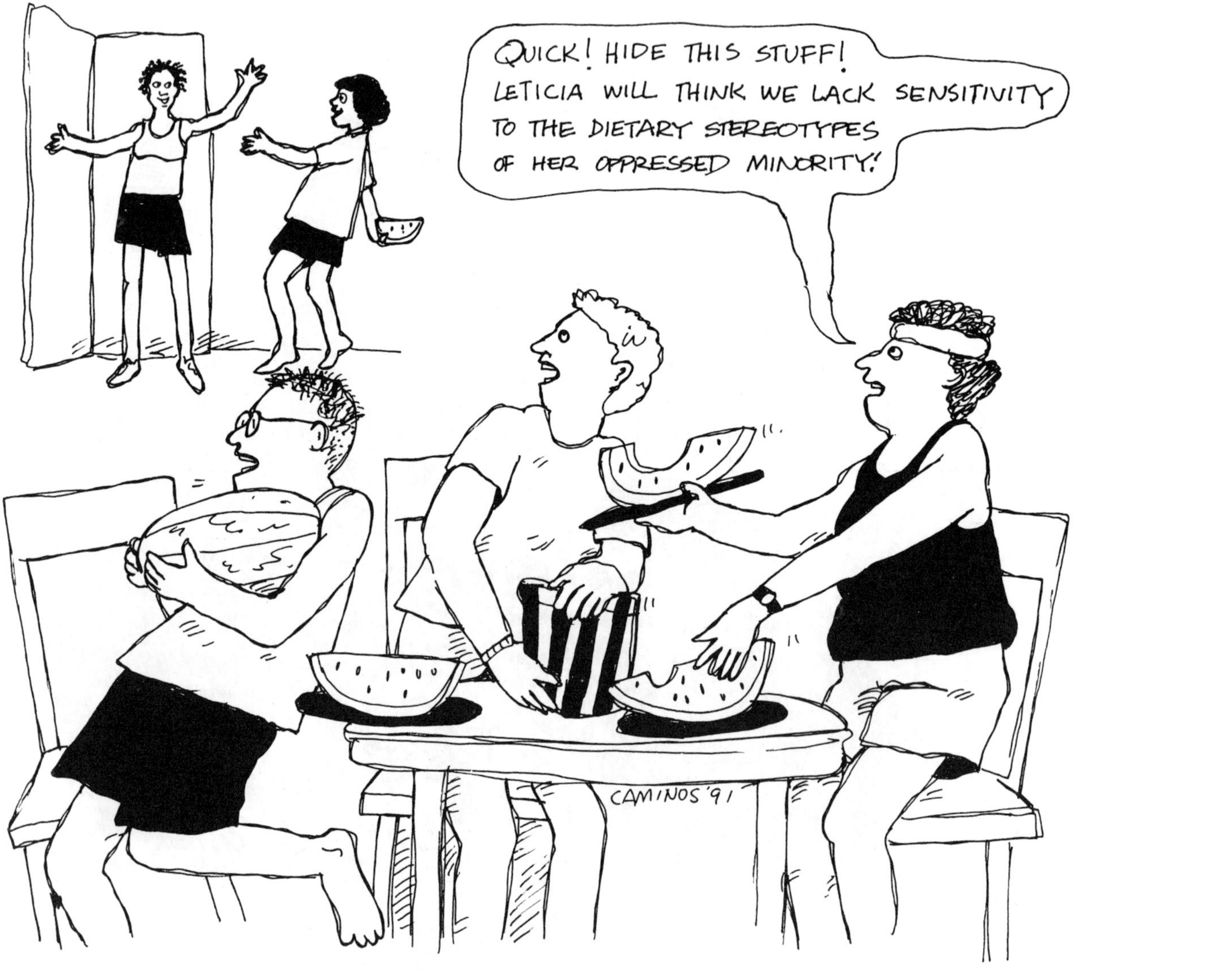
QUICK! HIDE THIS STUFF! LETICIA WILL THINK WE LACK SENSITIVITY TO THE DIETARY STEREOTYPES OF HER OPPRESSED MINORITY!
CAMINOS '91

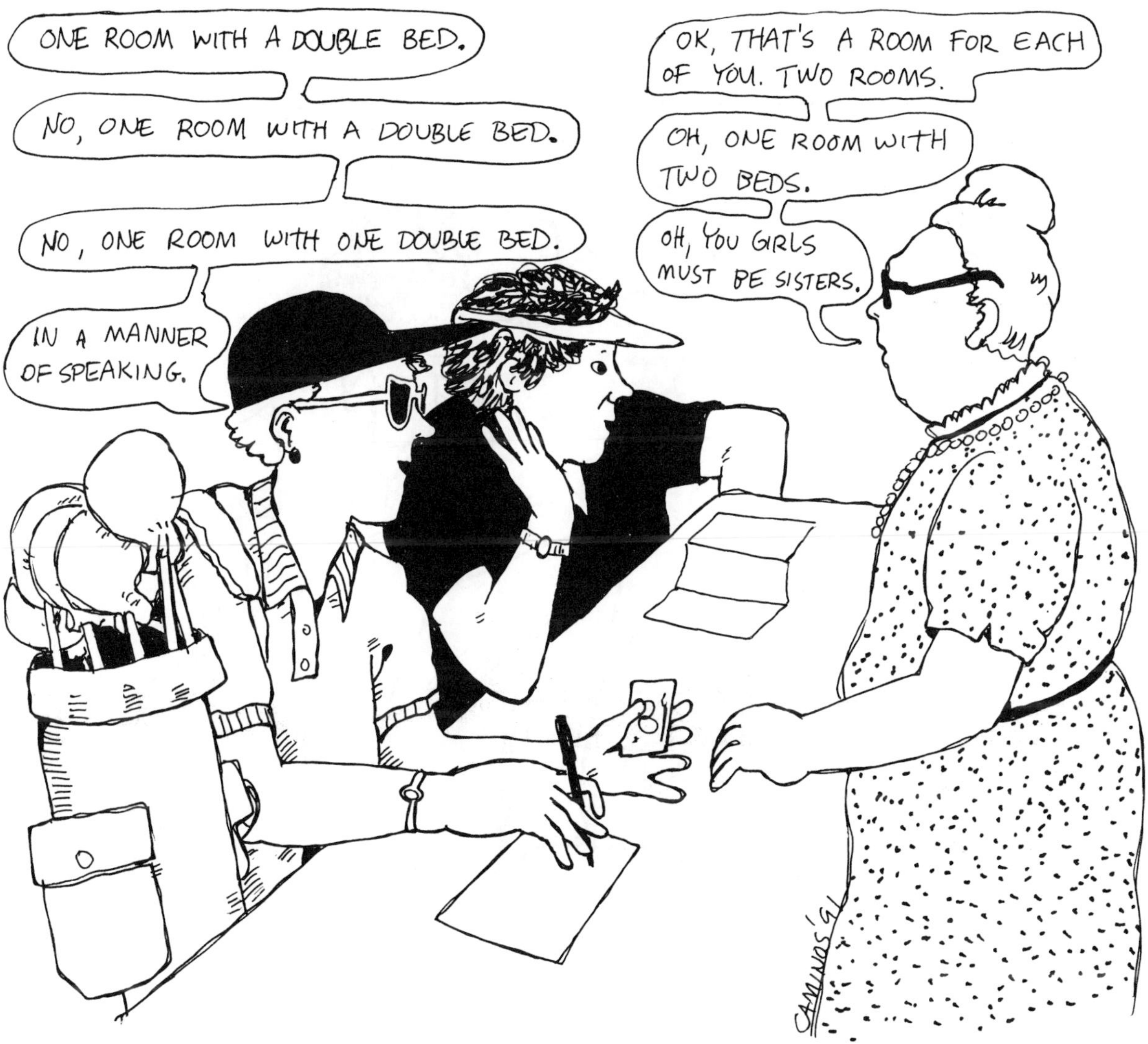
ONE ROOM WITH A DOUBLE BED.
OK, THAT'S A ROOM FOR EACH OF YOU. TWO ROOMS.
NO, ONE ROOM WITH A DOUBLE BED.
OH, ONE ROOM WITH TWO BEDS.
NO, ONE ROOM WITH ONE DOUBLE BED.
OH, YOU GIRLS MUST BE SISTERS.
IN A MANNER OF SPEAKING.
CAMINOS '91

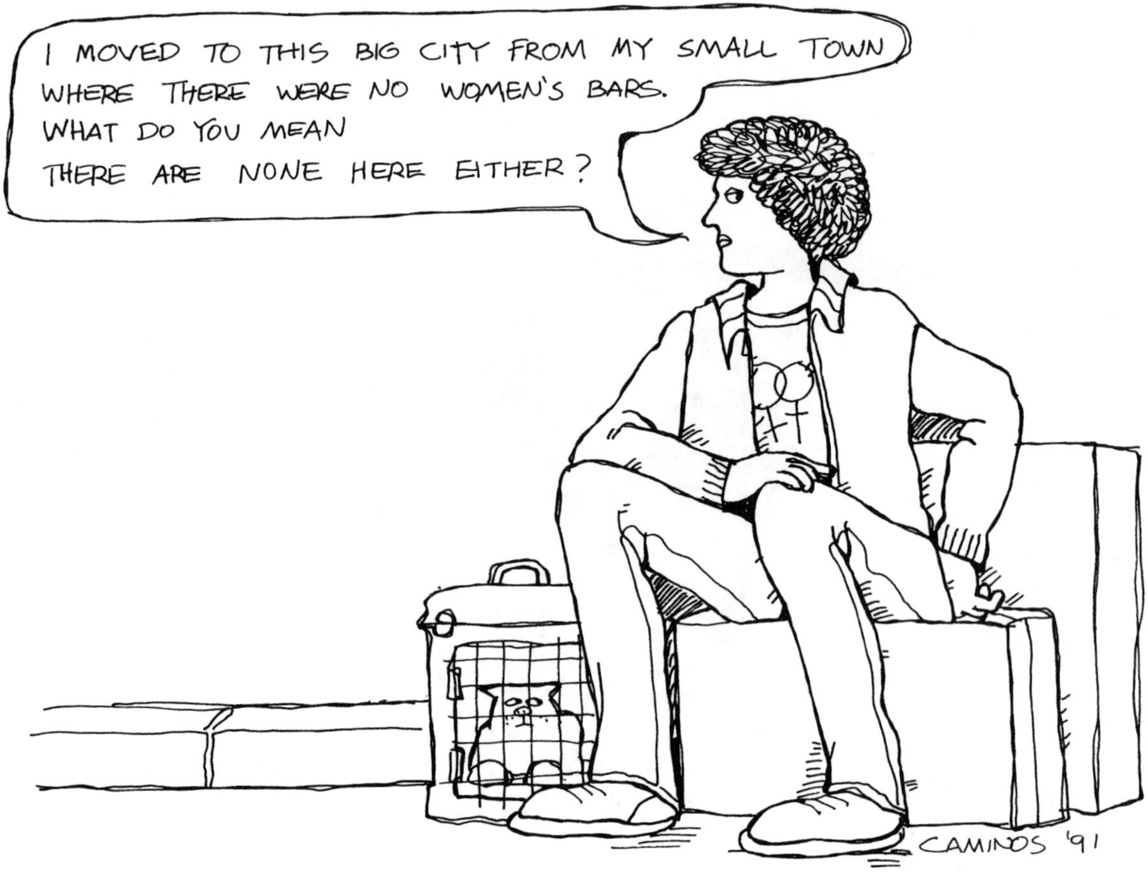
I MOVED TO THIS BIG CITY FROM MY SMALL TOWN
WHERE THERE WERE NO WOMEN'S BARS.
WHAT DO YOU MEAN
THERE ARE NONE HERE EITHER?
CAMINOS '91

FIRST THEY SAID, "CUT OFF YOUR LONG HAIR." SO I DID. THEN THEY SAID, "FORGET THE MAKE-UP." I DID SO. THEN IT WAS, "YOUR CLOTHES ARE INAPPROPRIATE." SO I BOUGHT APPROPRIATE ONES. THEN THEY TOLD ME MY POLITICS WERE AN EMBARRASSMENT TO THE MOVEMENT. I CHANGED THEM. I JOINED A CONSCIOUSNESS RAISING GROUP, AND BECAME ENLIGHTENED. THEY SAID, "EAT, ENJOY YOURSELF! FORGET YOUR PENTHOUSE PET FIGURE." SO NOW I'M A FAT SLOB. I'M ALSO ALONE, BORED, AND DEPRESSED, AND WOULD HAVE BEEN MUCH HAPPIER JUST BEING MYSELF.
CAMINOS '91

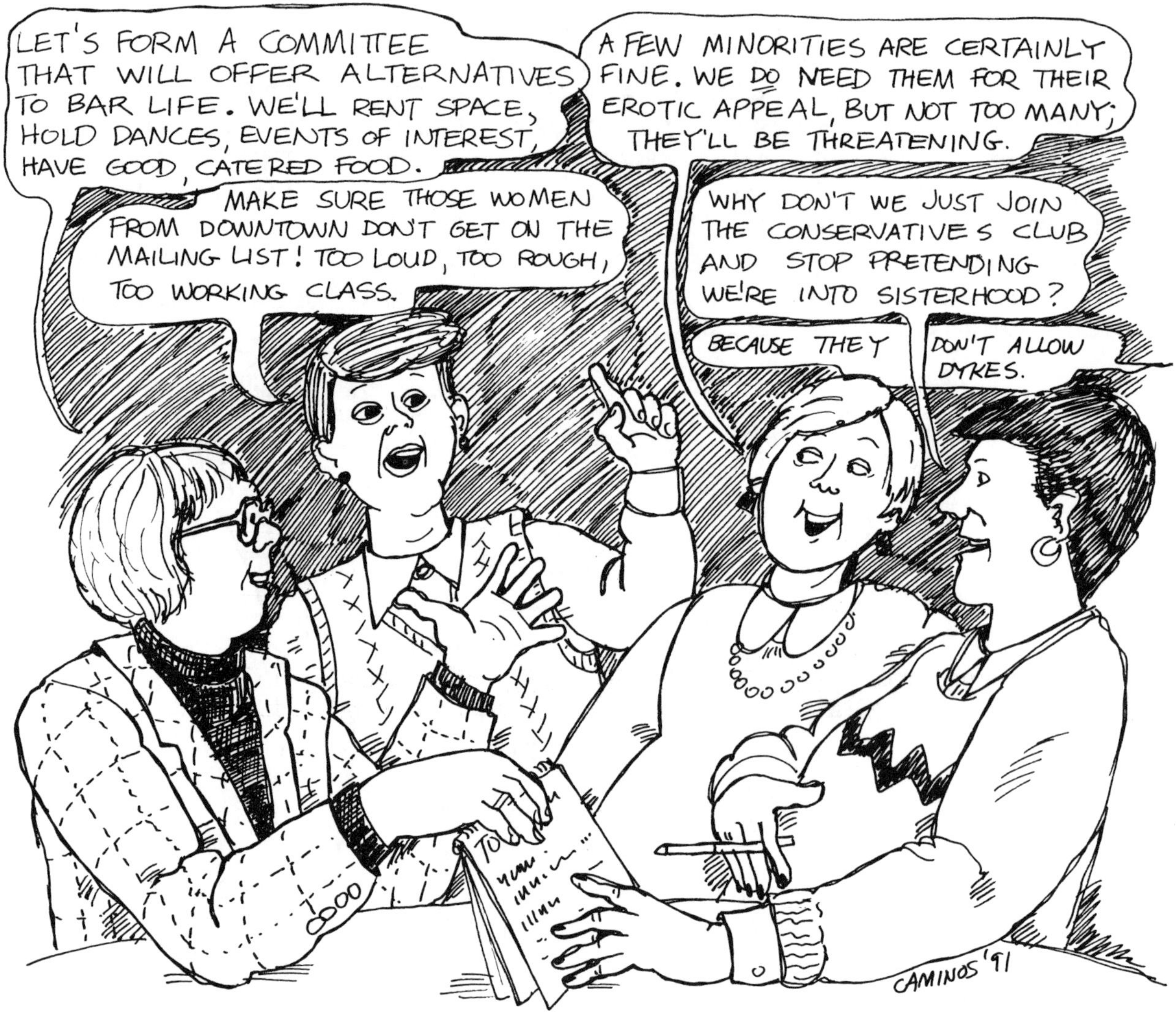
LET'S FORM A COMMITTEE THAT WILL OFFER ALTERNATIVES TO BAR LIFE. WE'LL RENT SPACE, HOLD DANCES, EVENTS OF INTEREST, HAVE GOOD, CATERED FOOD.
MAKE SURE THOSE WOMEN FROM DOWNTOWN DON'T GET ON THE MAILING LIST! TOO LOUD, TOO ROUGH, TOO WORKING CLASS.
A FEW MINORITIES ARE CERTAINLY FINE. WE DO NEED THEM FOR THEIR EROTIC APPEAL, BUT NOT TOO MANY; THEY'LL BE THREATENING.
WHY DON'T WE JUST JOIN THE CONSERVATIVES CLUB AND STOP PRETENDING WE'RE INTO SISTERHOOD?
BECAUSE THEY
DON'T ALLOW DYKES.
CAMINOS '91

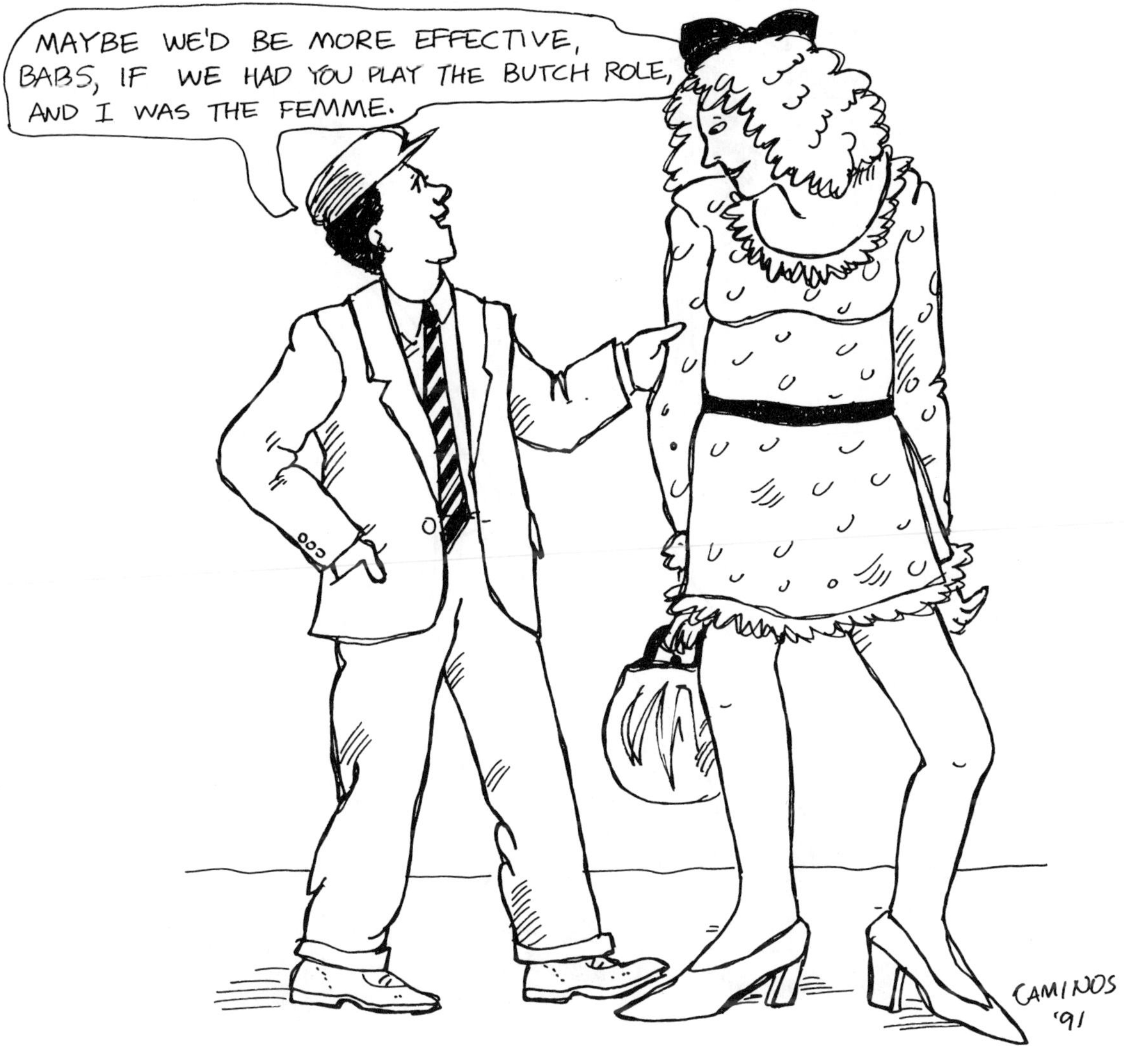
MAYBE WE'D BE MORE EFFECTIVE, BABS, IF WE HAD YOU PLAY THE BUTCH ROLE, AND I WAS THE FEMME.
CAMINOS '91

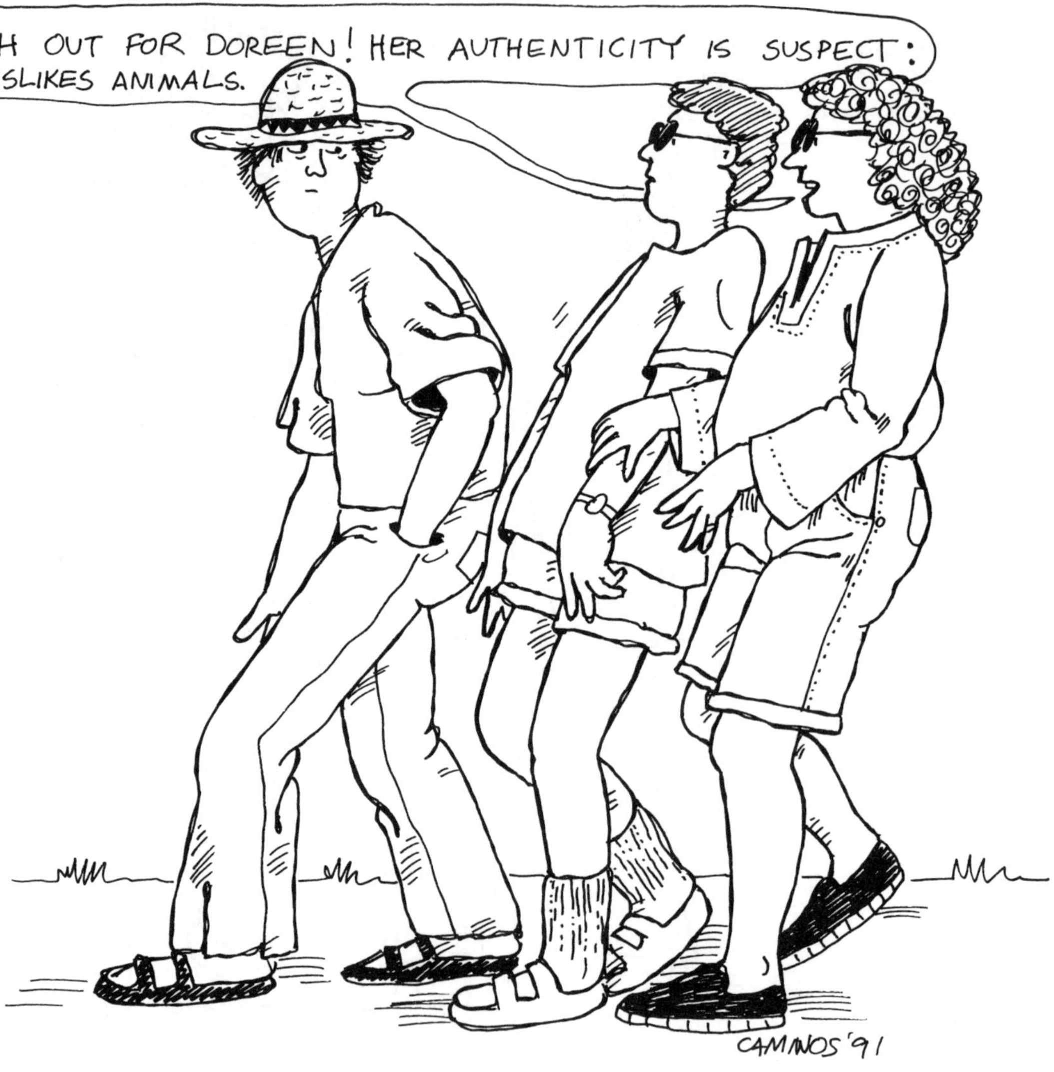
WATCH OUT FOR DOREEN! HER AUTHENTICITY IS SUSPECT: SHE DISLIKES ANIMALS.
CAMINOS '91

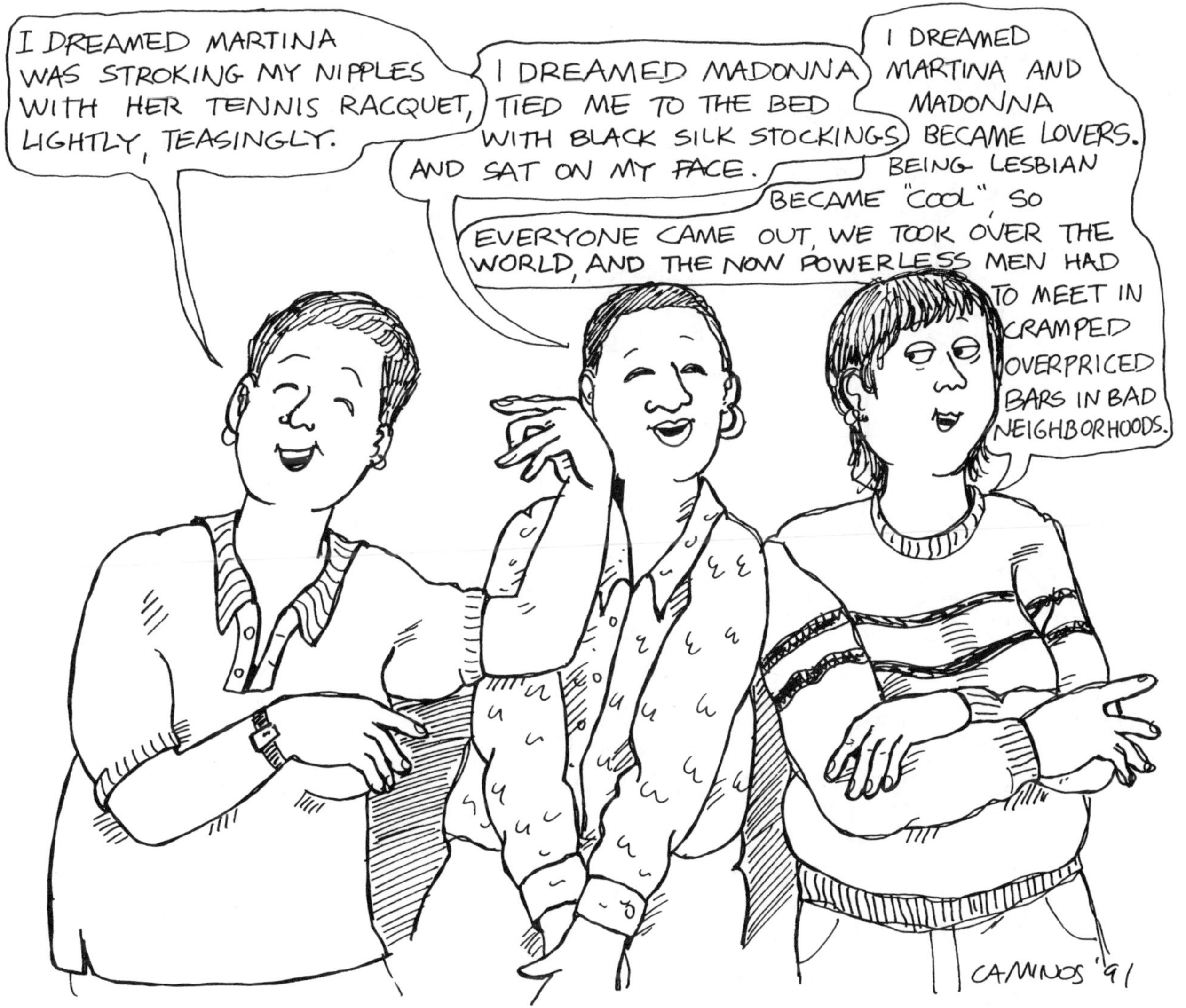
I DREAMED MARTINA WAS STROKING MY NIPPLES WITH HER TENNIS RACQUET, LIGHTLY, TEASINGLY.
I DREAMED MADONNA TIED ME TO THE BED WITH BLACK SILK STOCKINGS AND SAT ON MY FACE.
I DREAMED MARTINA AND MADONNA BECAME LOVERS. BEING LESBIAN BECAME "COOL", SO EVERYONE CAME OUT, WE TOOK OVER THE WORLD, AND THE NOW POWERLESS MEN HAD TO MEET IN CRAMPED OVERPRICED BARS IN BAD NEIGHBORHOODS.
CAMINOS '91

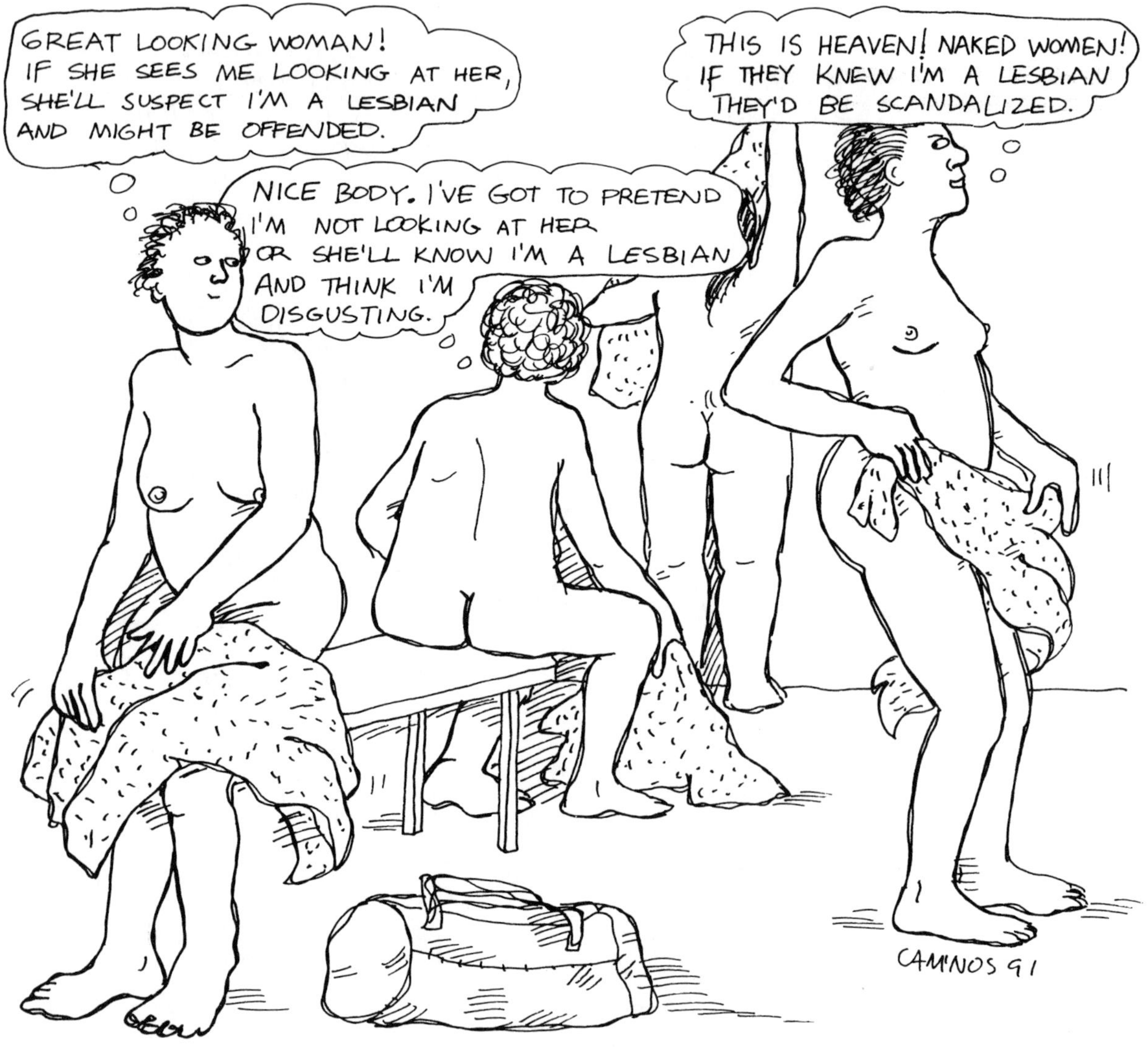
GREAT LOOKING WOMAN! IF SHE SEES ME LOOKING AT HER, SHE'LL SUSPECT I'M A LESBIAN AND MIGHT BE OFFENDED.
THIS IS HEAVEN! NAKED WOMEN! IF THEY KNEW I'M A LESBIAN THEY'D BE SCANDALIZED.
NICE BODY. I'VE GOT TO PRETEND I'M NOT LOOKING AT HER OR SHE'LL KNOW I'M A LESBIAN AND THINK I'M DISGUSTING.
CAMINOS 91

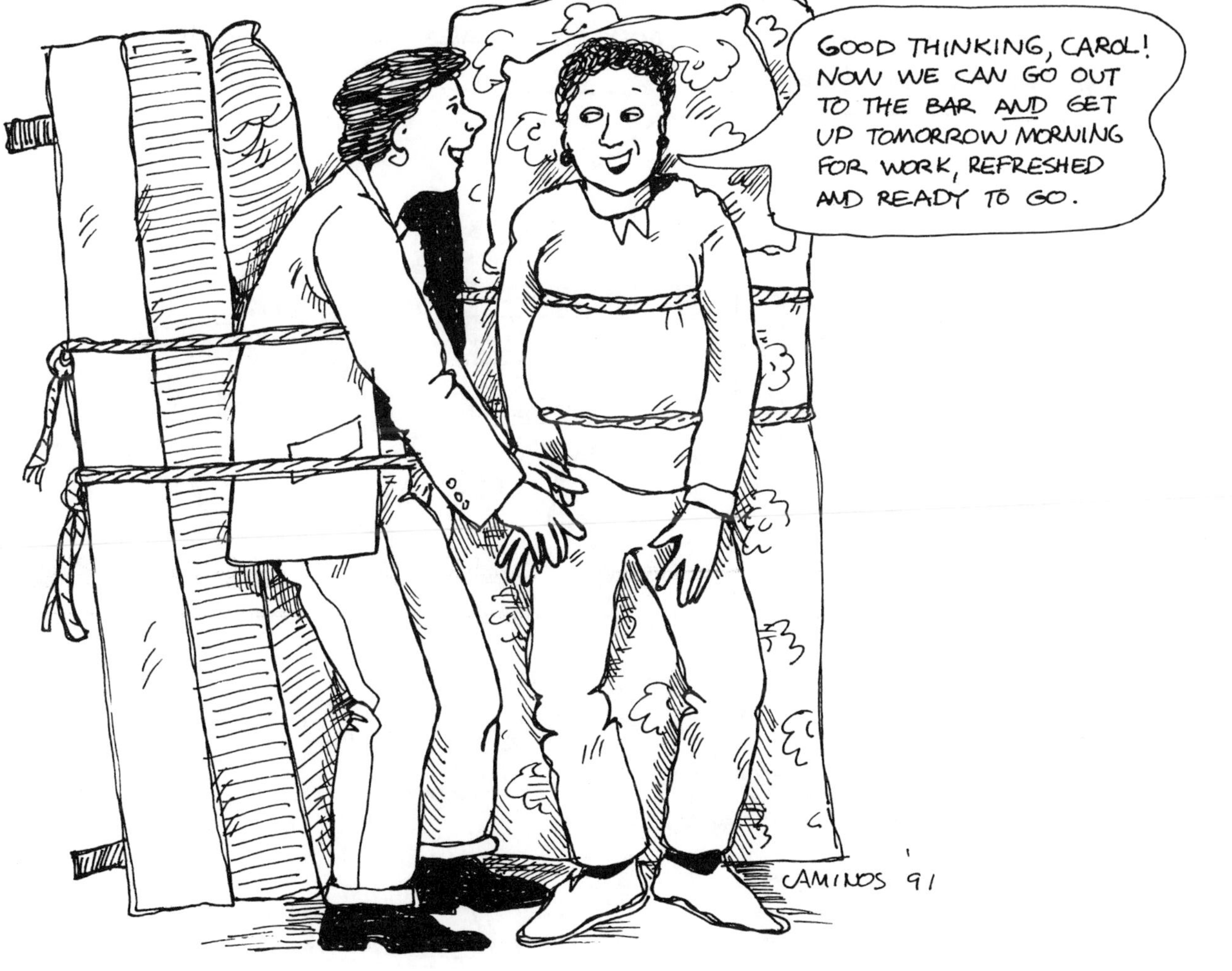
GOOD THINKING, CAROL! NOW WE CAN GO OUT TO THE BAR AND GET UP TOMORROW MORNING FOR WORK, REFRESHED AND READY TO GO.
CAMINOS '91

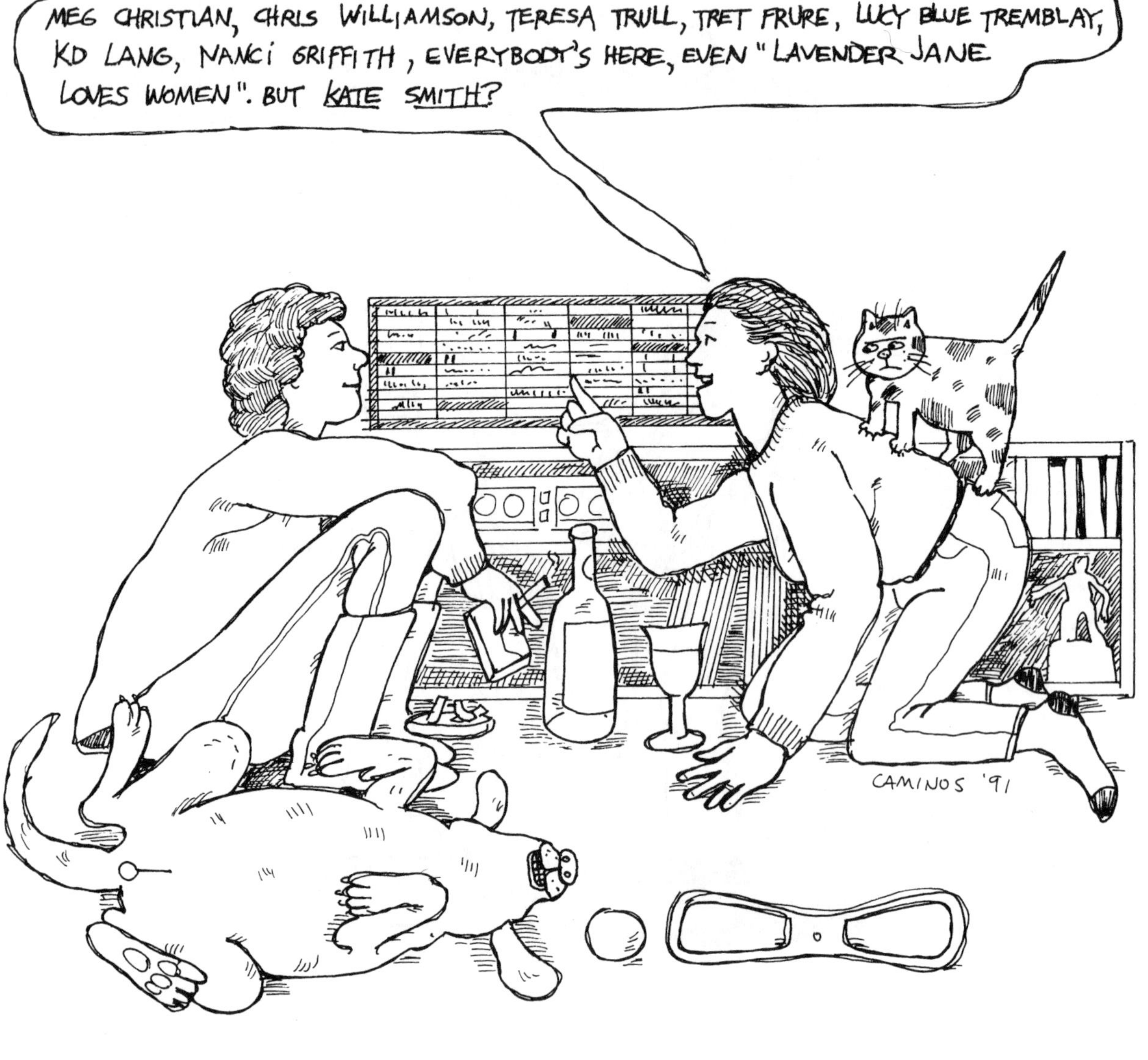
MEG CHRISTIAN, CHRIS WILLIAMSON, TERESA TRULL, TRET FRURE, LUCY BLUE TREMBLAY, KD LANG, NANCI GRIFFITH, EVERYBODY'S HERE, EVEN "LAVENDER JANE LOVES WOMEN". BUT KATE SMITH?
CAMINOS '91

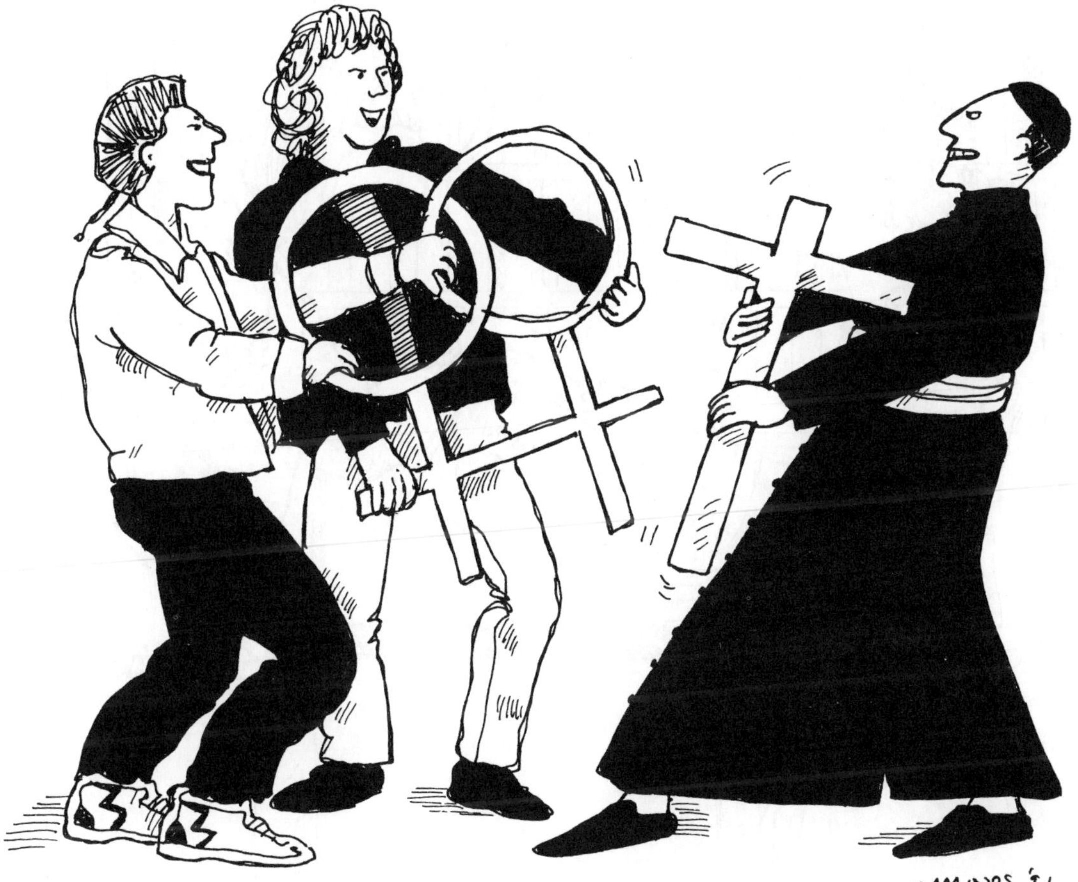
CAMINOS '91

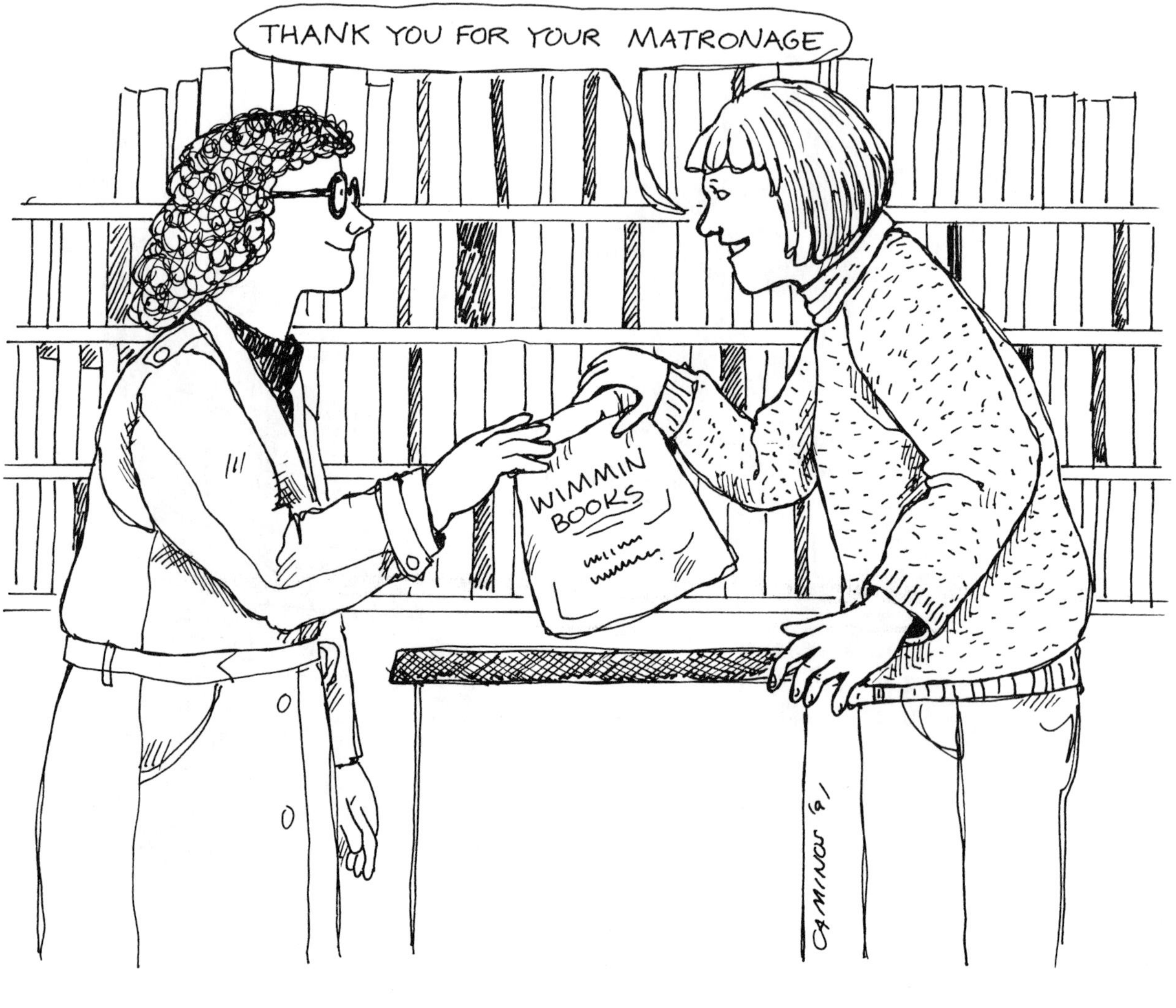
THANK YOU FOR YOUR MATRONAGE
WIMMIN BOOKS

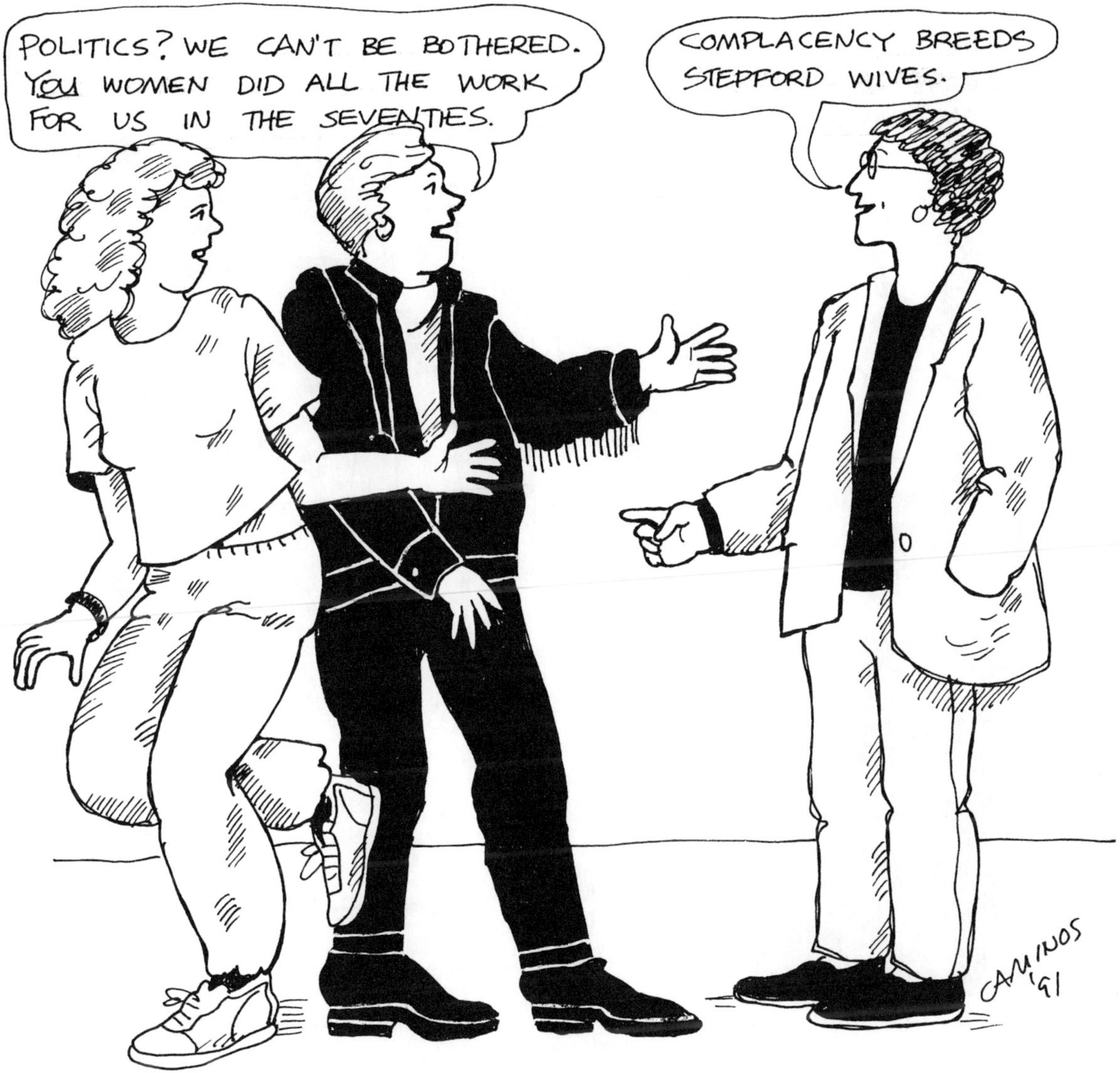
POLITICS? WE CAN'T BE BOTHERED. YOU WOMEN DID ALL THE WORK FOR US IN THE SEVENTIES.
COMPLACENCY BREEDS STEPFORD WIVES.
CAMINOS '91

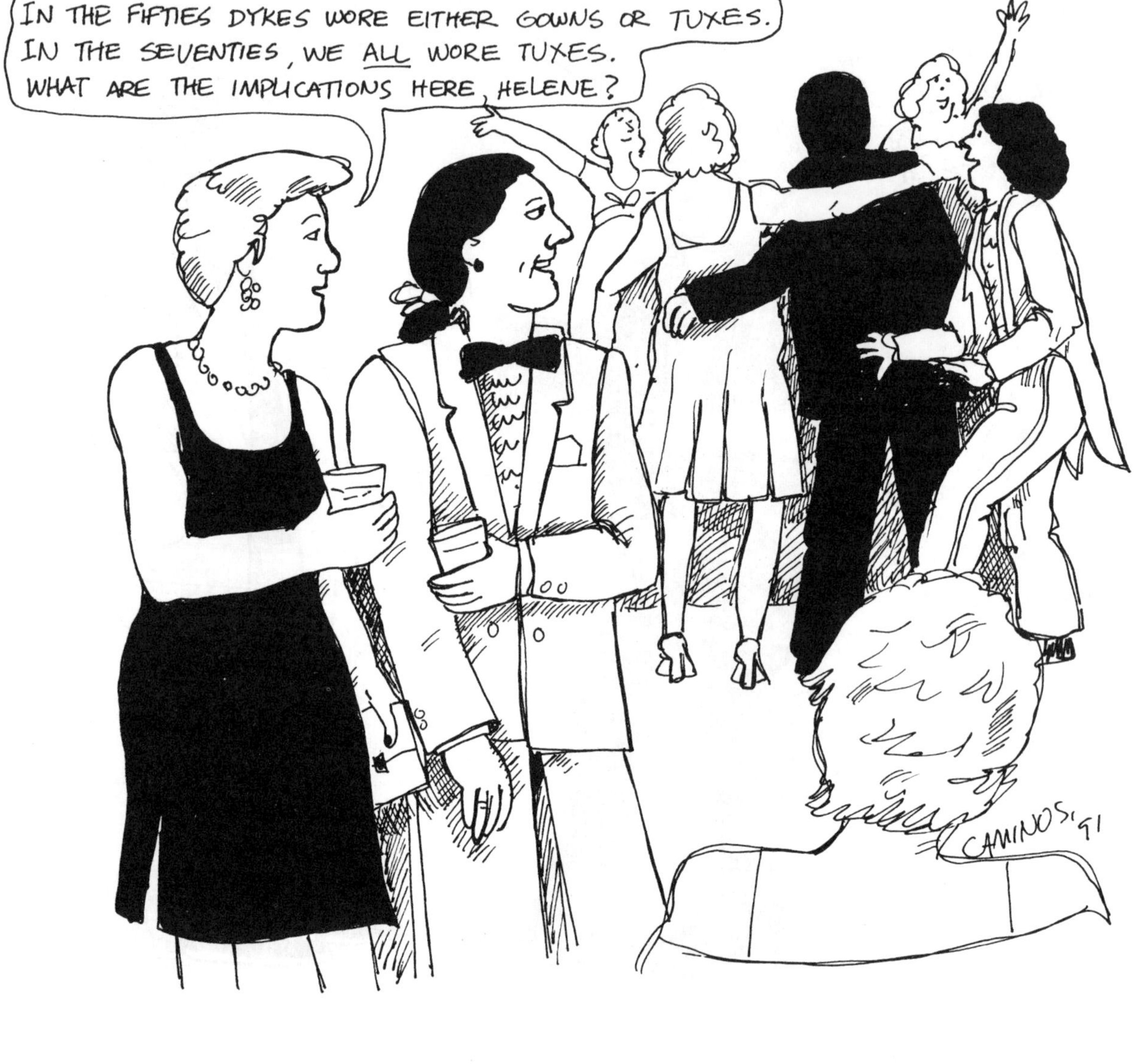
IN THE FIFTIES DYKES WORE EITHER GOWNS OR TUXES. IN THE SEVENTIES, WE ALL WORE TUXES. WHAT ARE THE IMPLICATIONS HERE, HELENE?
CAMINOS '91

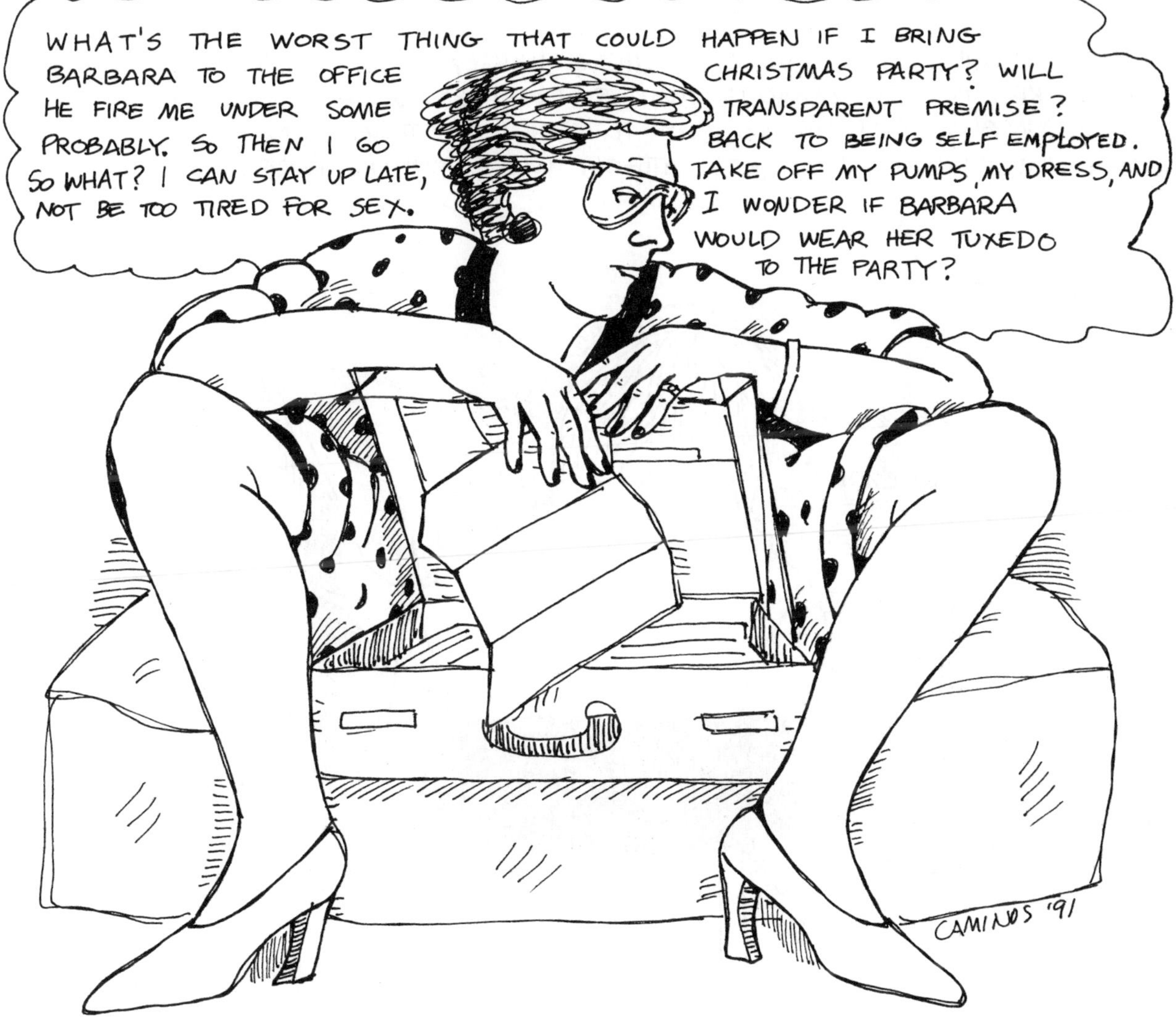
WHAT'S THE WORST THING THAT COULD HAPPEN IF I BRING BARBARA TO THE OFFICE CHRISTMAS PARTY? WILL HE FIRE ME UNDER SOME TRANSPARENT PREMISE? PROBABLY. SO THEN I GO BACK TO BEING SELF EMPLOYED. SO WHAT? I CAN STAY UP LATE, TAKE OFF MY PUMPS, MY DRESS, AND NOT BE TOO TIRED FOR SEX. I WONDER IF BARBARA WOULD WEAR HER TUXEDO TO THE PARTY?
CAMINOS '91

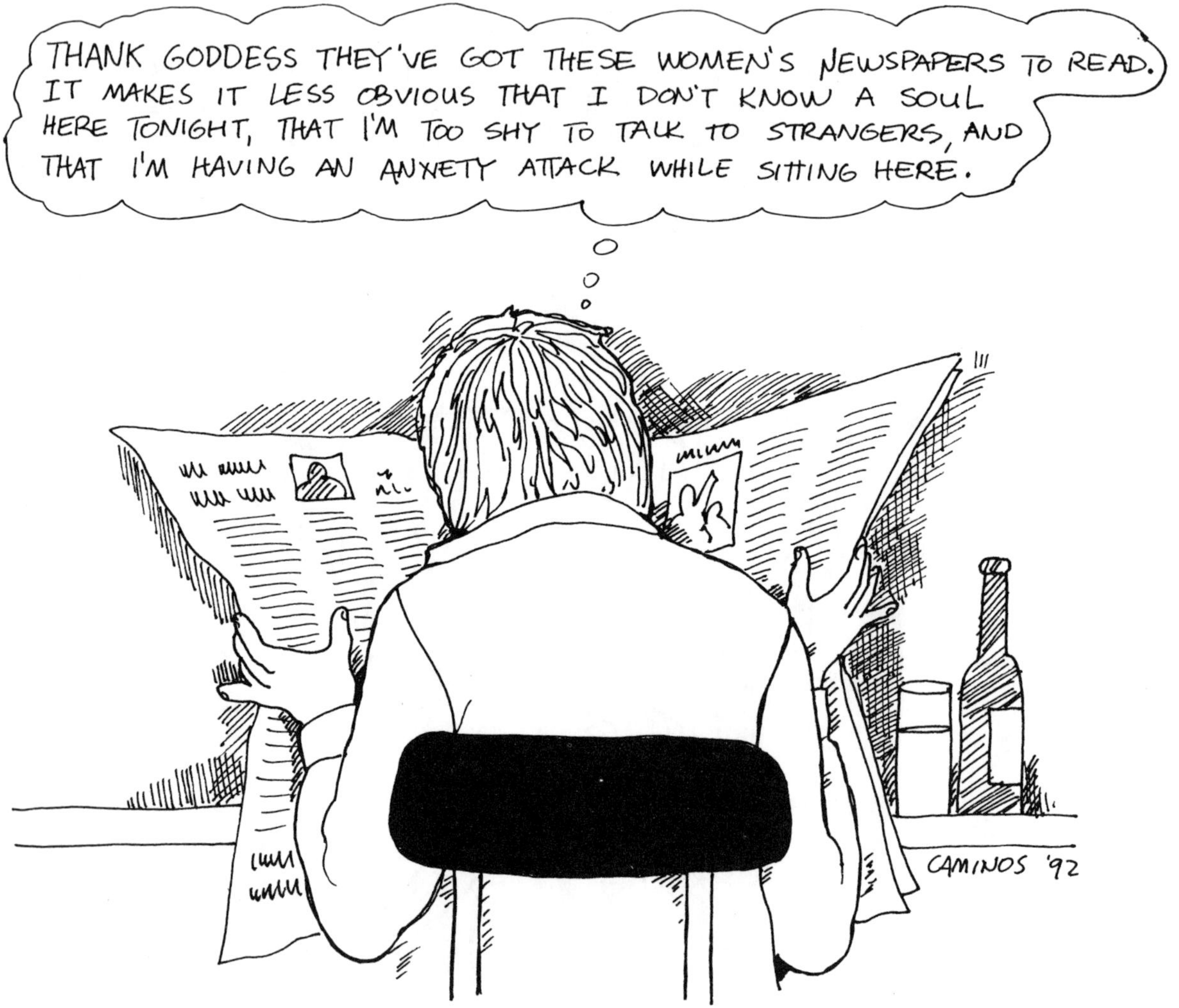
THANK GODDESS THEY'VE GOT THESE WOMEN'S NEWSPAPERS TO READ. IT MAKES IT LESS OBVIOUS THAT I DON'T KNOW A SOUL HERE TONIGHT, THAT I'M TOO SHY TO TALK TO STRANGERS, AND THAT I'M HAVING AN ANXIETY ATTACK WHILE SITTING HERE.
CAMINOS '92

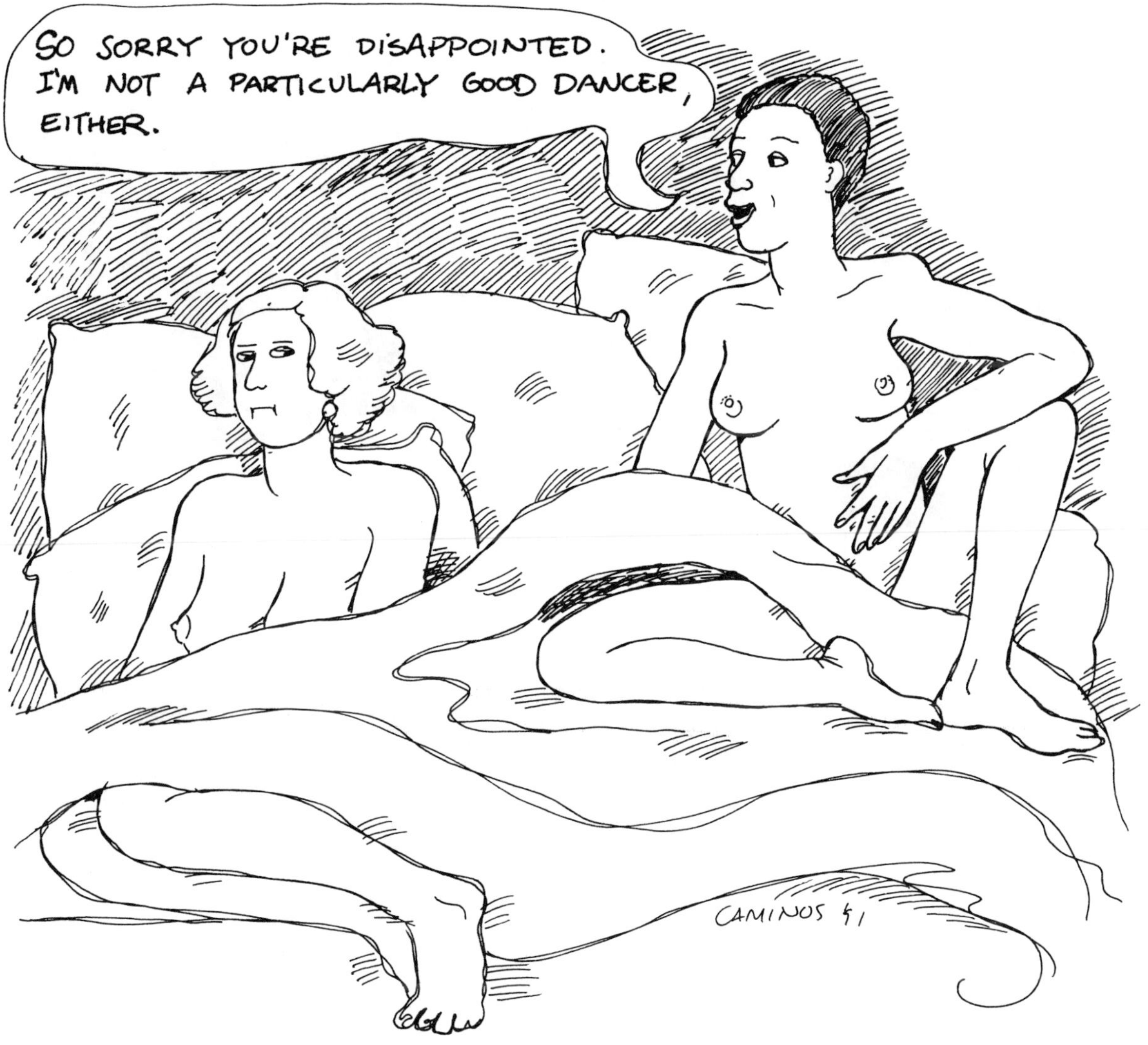
SO SORRY YOU'RE DISAPPOINTED. I'M NOT A PARTICULARLY GOOD DANCER, EITHER.
CAMINOS 91

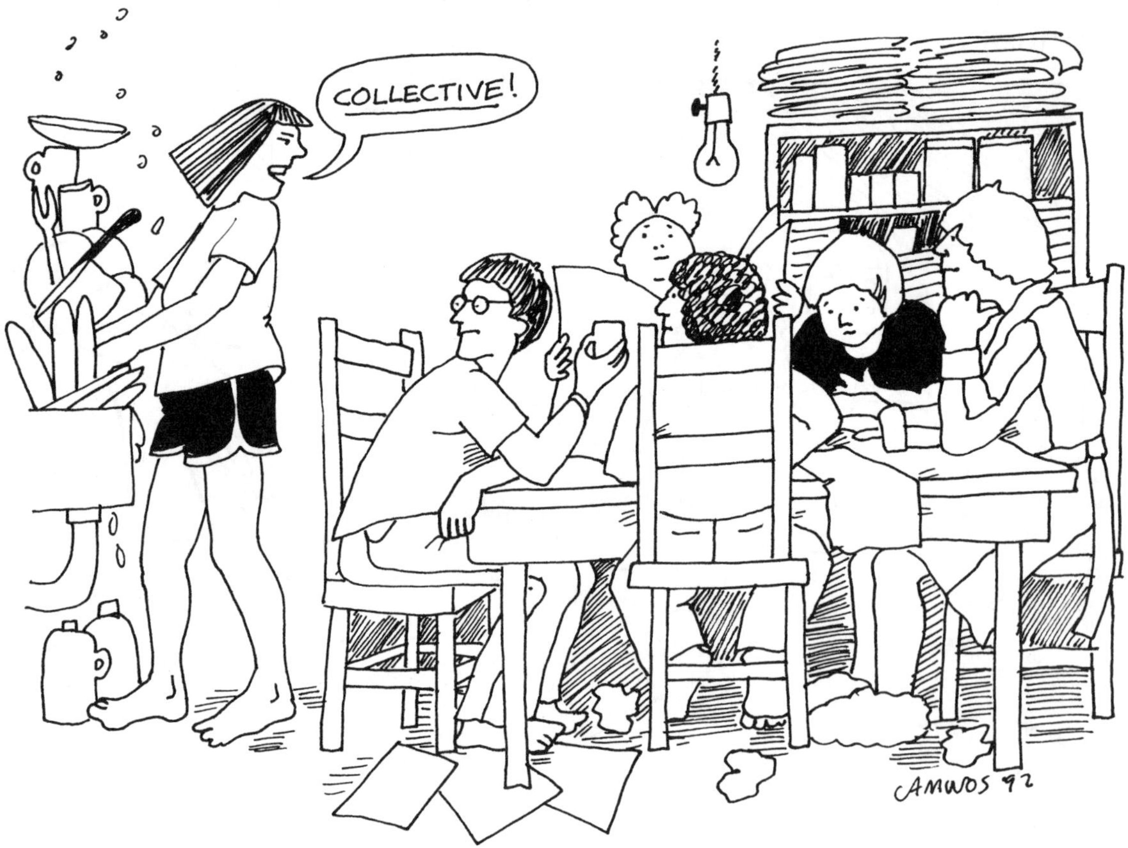
COLLECTIVE!
CAMWOS '92

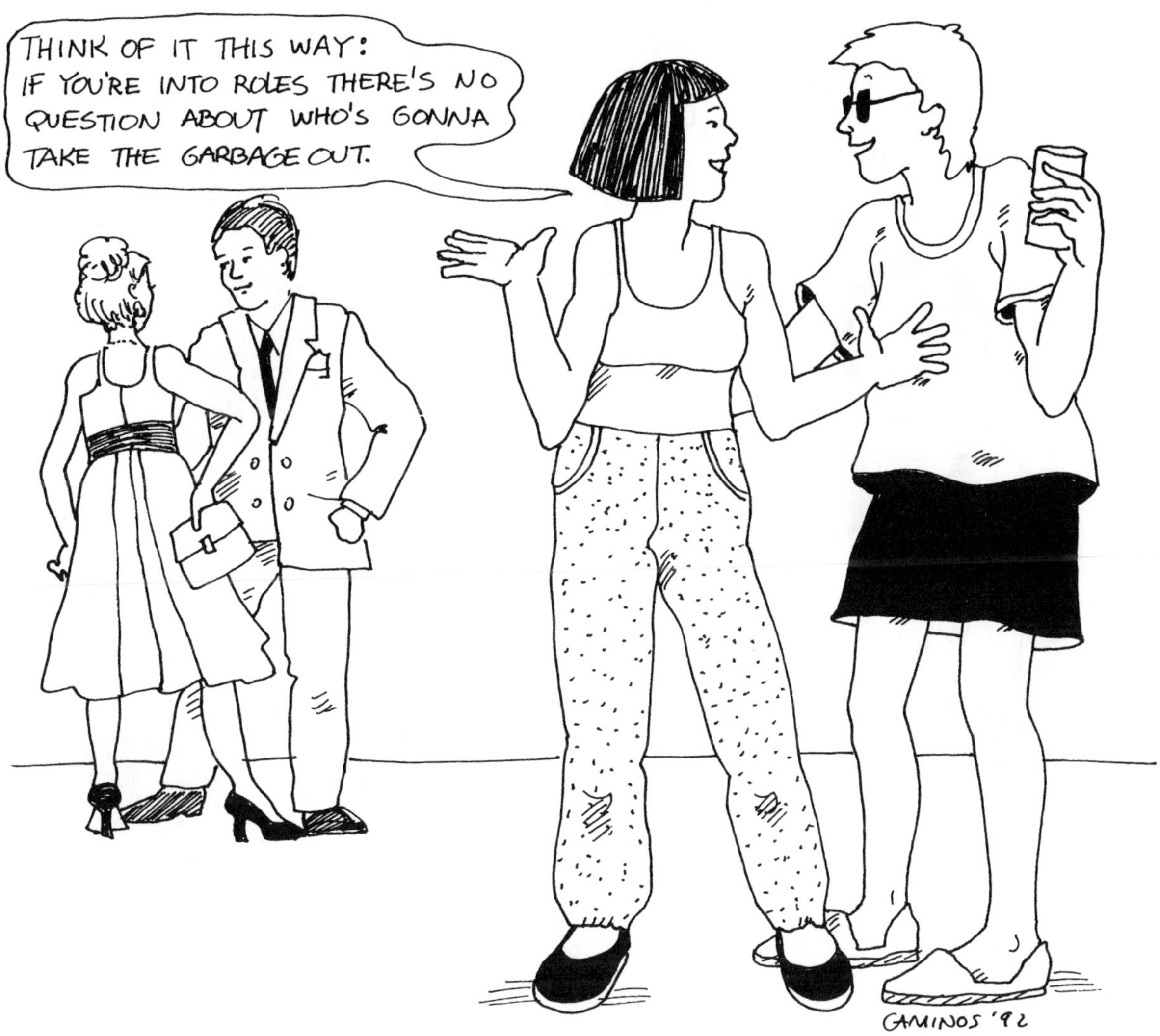
THINK OF IT THIS WAY: IF YOU'RE INTO ROLES THERE'S NO QUESTION ABOUT WHO'S GONNA TAKE THE GARBAGE OUT.
CAMINOS '92

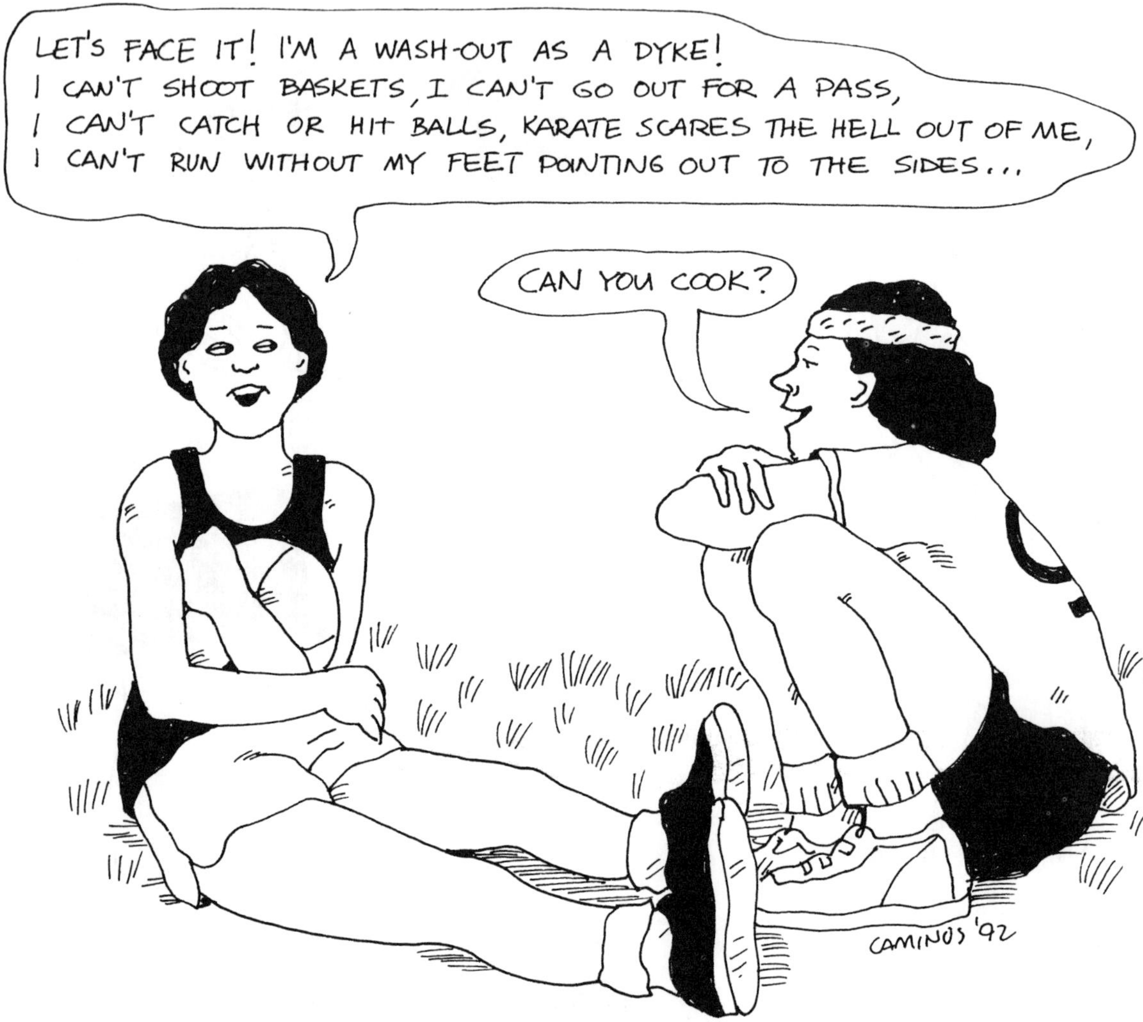
LET'S FACE IT! I'M A WASH-OUT AS A DYKE!
I CAN'T SHOOT BASKETS, I CAN'T GO OUT FOR A PASS,
I CAN'T CATCH OR HIT BALLS, KARATE SCARES THE HELL OUT OF ME,
I CAN'T RUN WITHOUT MY FEET POINTING OUT TO THE SIDES...
CAN YOU COOK?
CAMINOS '92

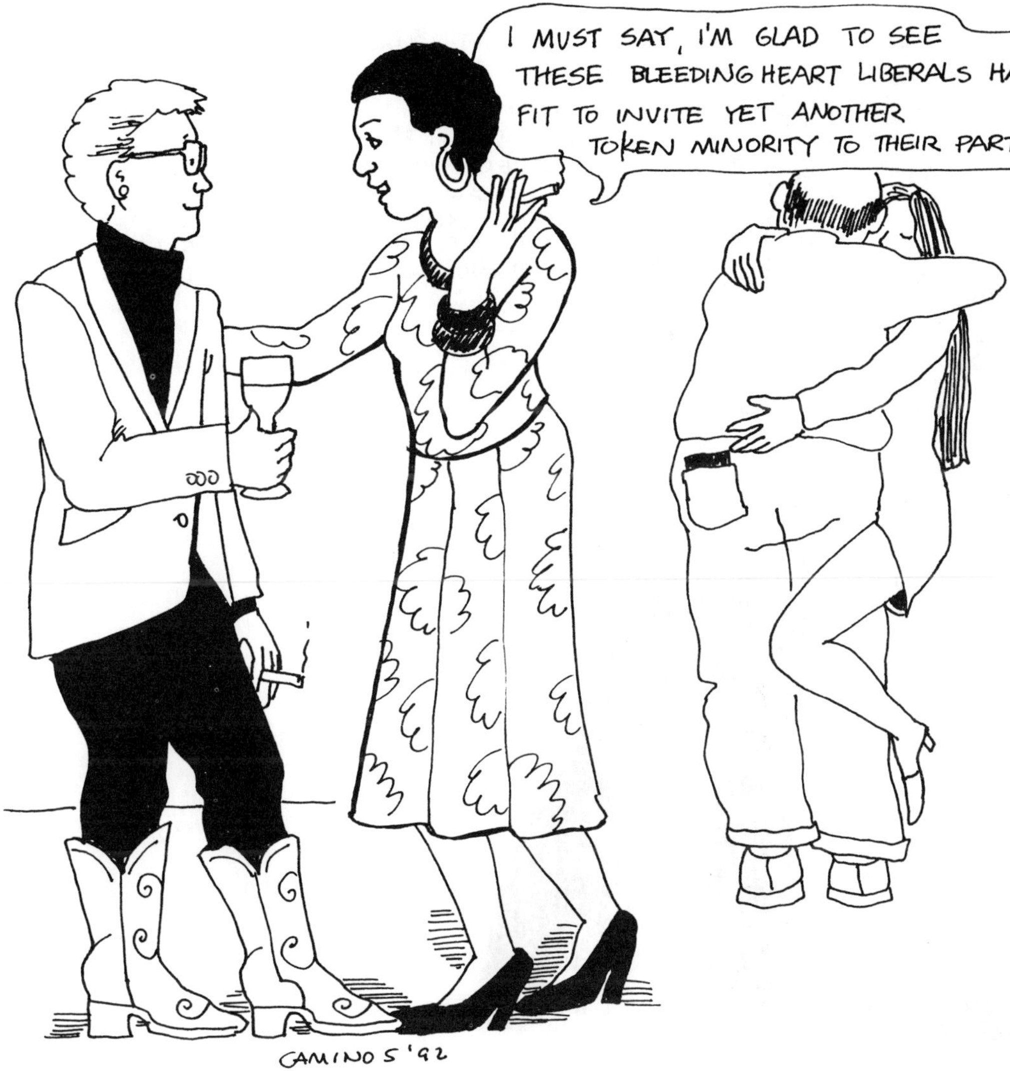
I MUST SAY, I'M GLAD TO SEE THESE BLEEDING HEART LIBERALS HAVE SEEN FIT TO INVITE YET ANOTHER TOKEN MINORITY TO THEIR PARTY.
CAMINOS '92

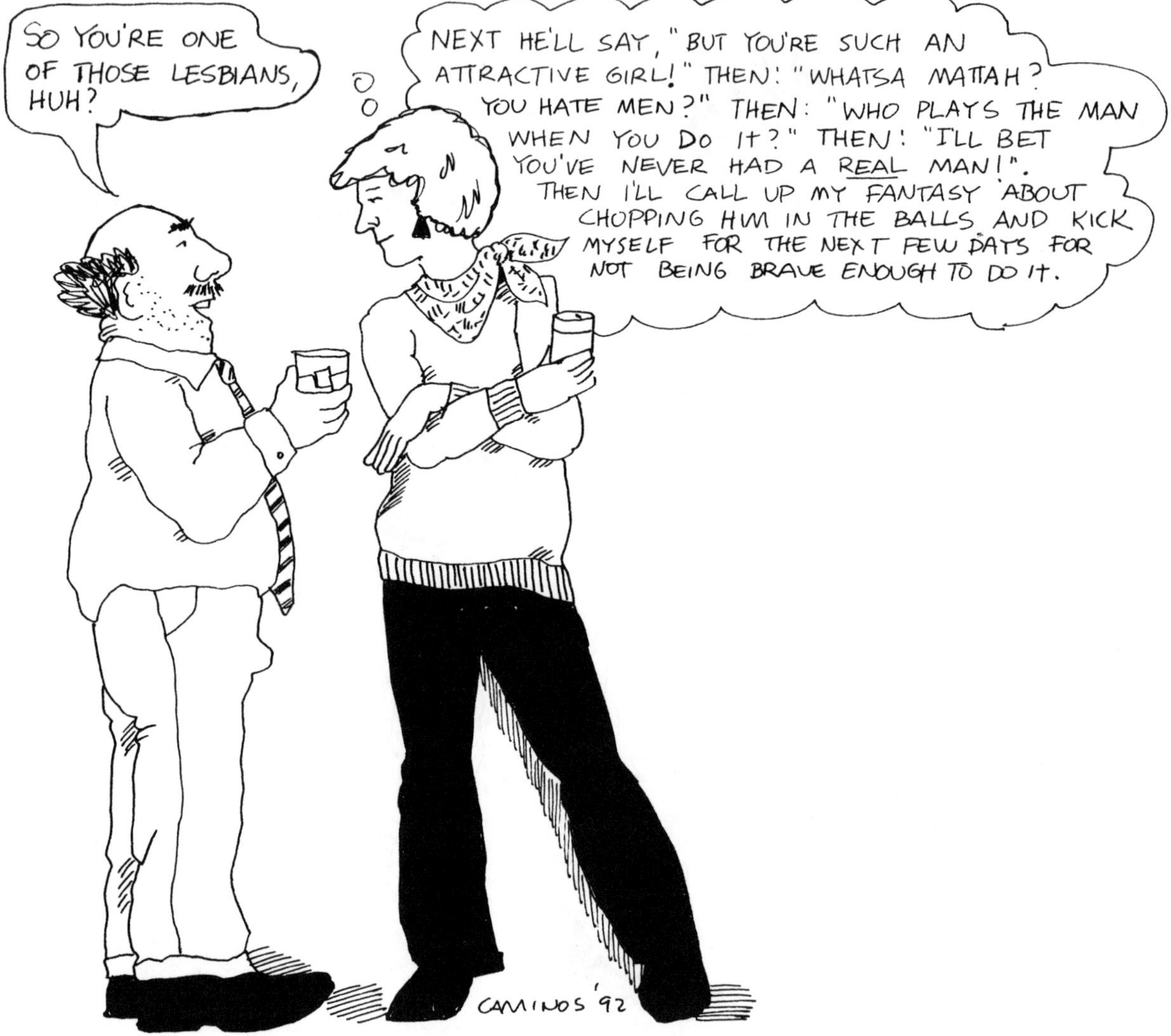
SO YOU'RE ONE OF THOSE LESBIANS, HUH?
NEXT HE'LL SAY, "BUT YOU'RE SUCH AN ATTRACTIVE GIRL!" THEN: "WHATSA MATTAH? YOU HATE MEN?" THEN: "WHO PLAYS THE MAN WHEN YOU DO IT?" THEN: "I'LL BET YOU'VE NEVER HAD A REAL MAN!". THEN I'LL CALL UP MY FANTASY ABOUT CHOPPING HIM IN THE BALLS AND KICK MYSELF FOR THE NEXT FEW DAYS FOR NOT BEING BRAVE ENOUGH TO DO IT.
CAMINOS '92

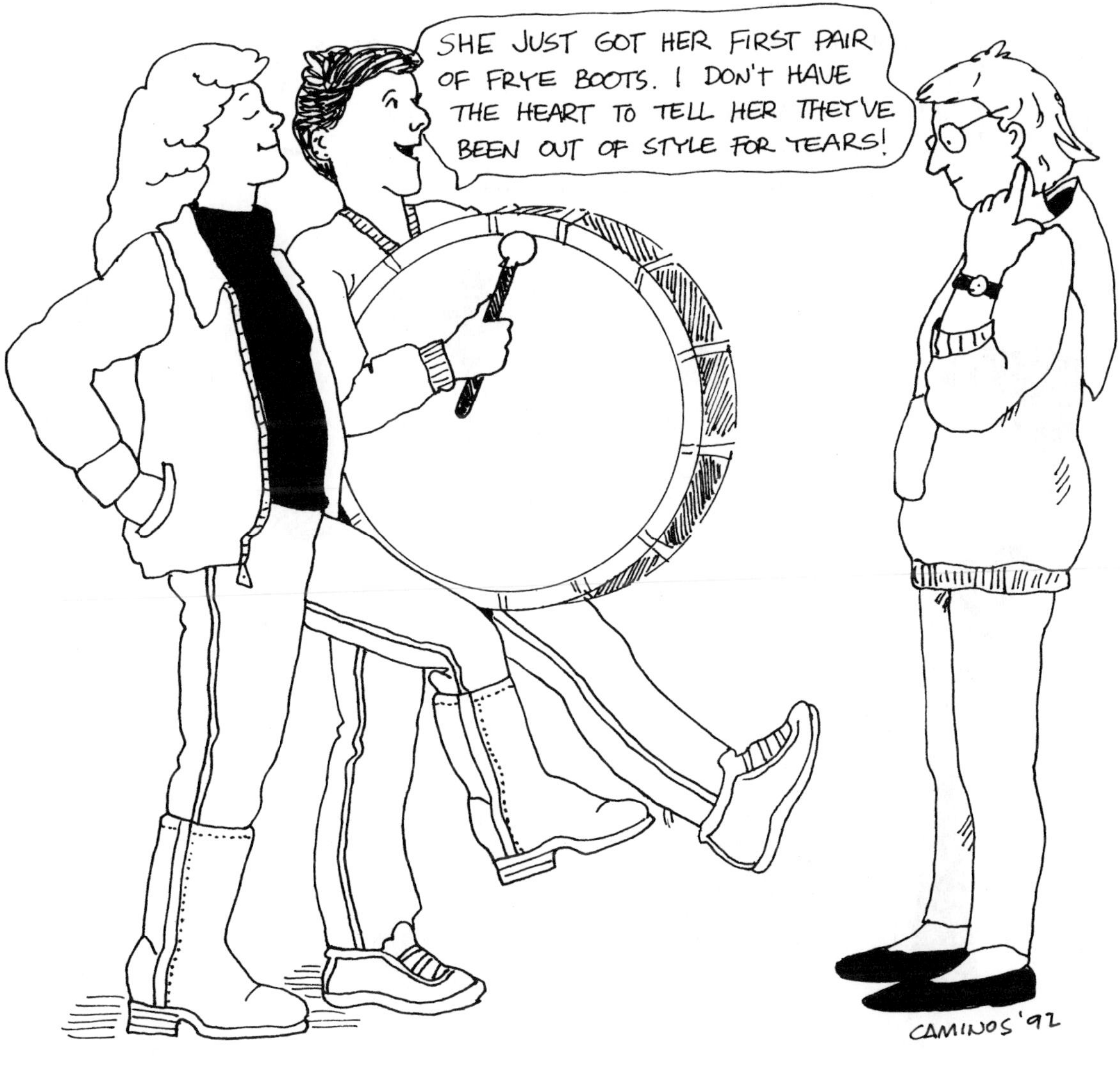
SHE JUST GOT HER FIRST PAIR OF FRYE BOOTS. I DON'T HAVE THE HEART TO TELL HER THEY'VE BEEN OUT OF STYLE FOR YEARS!
CAMINOS '92

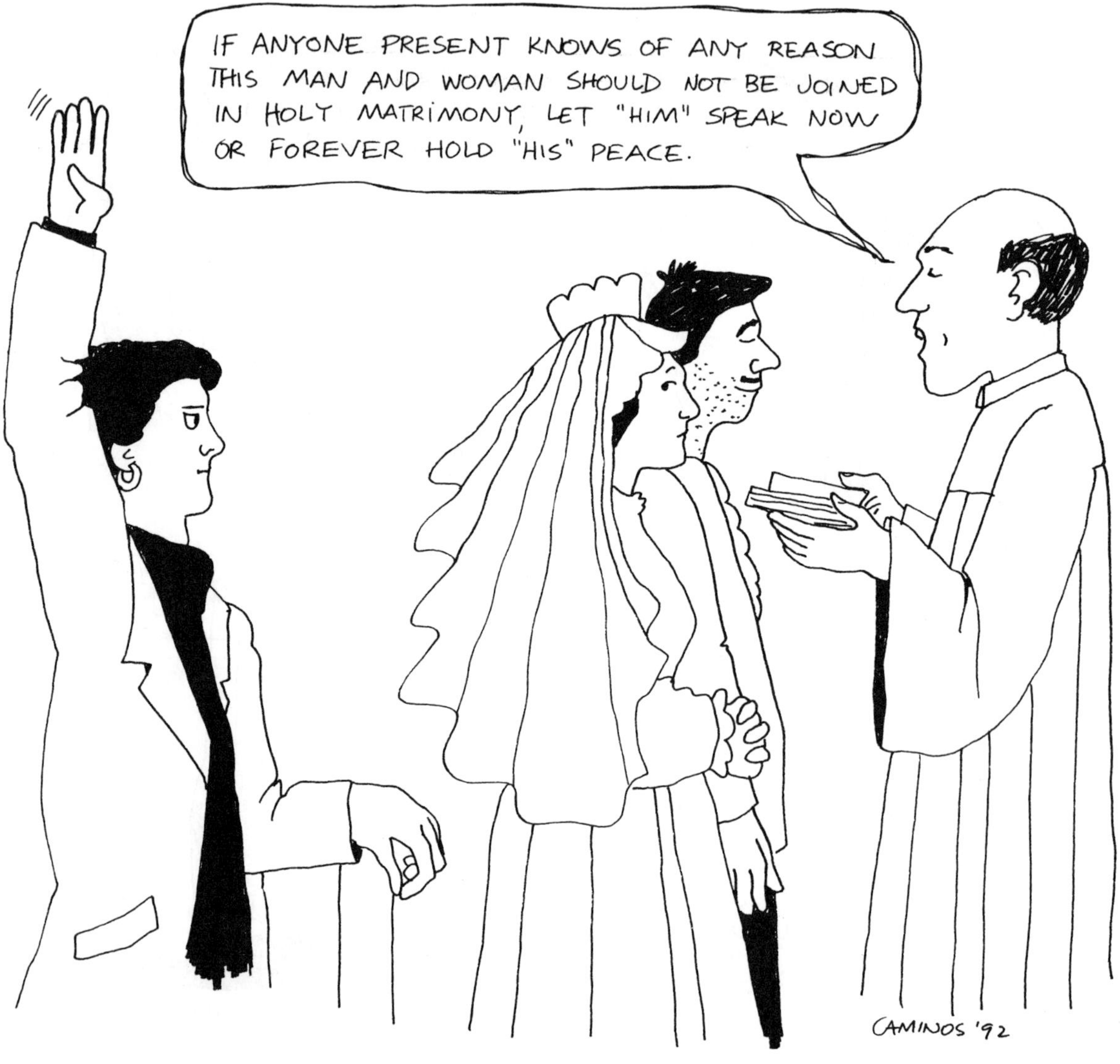
IF ANYONE PRESENT KNOWS OF ANY REASON THIS MAN AND WOMAN SHOULD NOT BE JOINED IN HOLY MATRIMONY, LET "HIM" SPEAK NOW OR FOREVER HOLD "HIS" PEACE.
CAMINOS '92

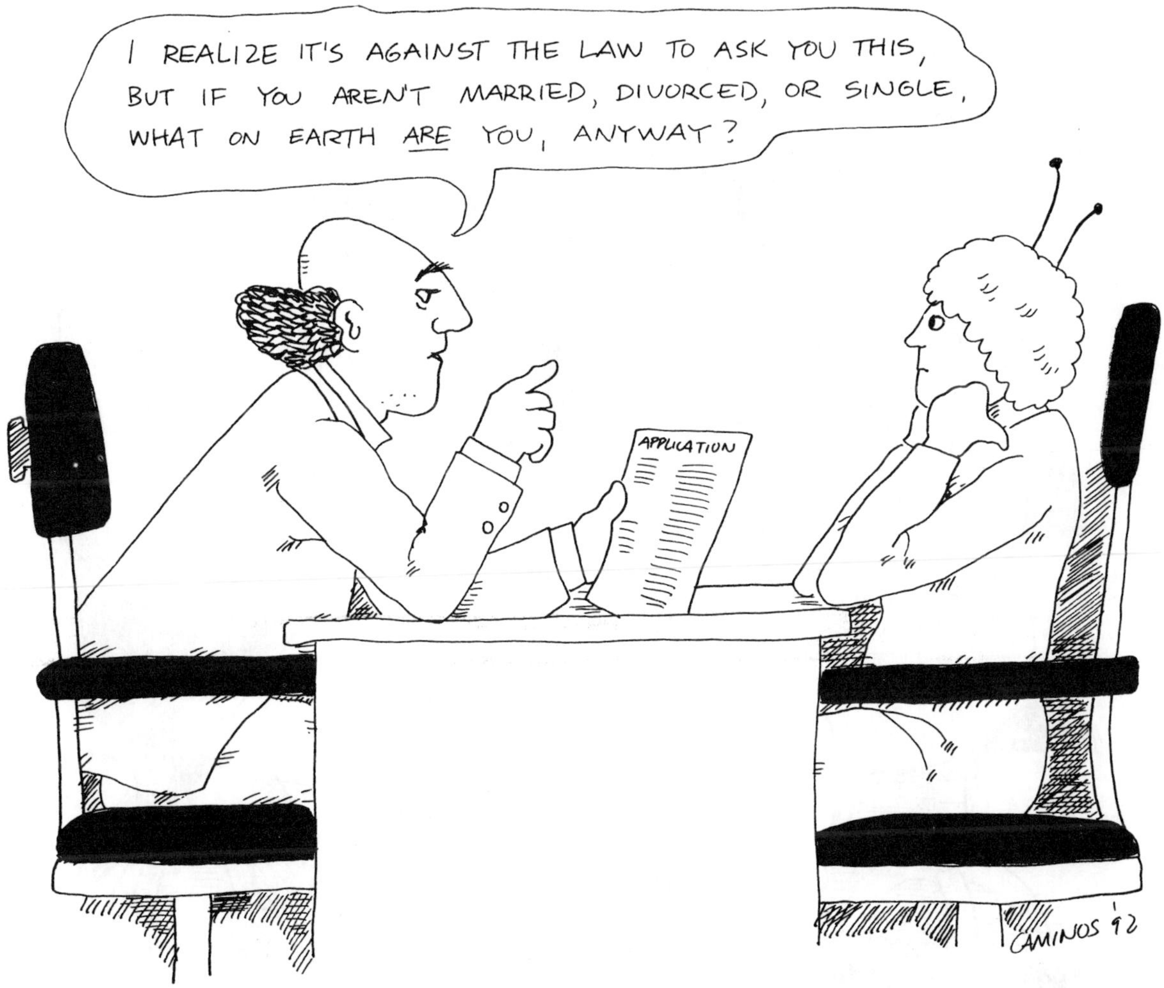
I REALIZE IT'S AGAINST THE LAW TO ASK YOU THIS, BUT IF YOU AREN'T MARRIED, DIVORCED, OR SINGLE, WHAT ON EARTH ARE YOU, ANYWAY?
APPLICATION
CAMINOS '92

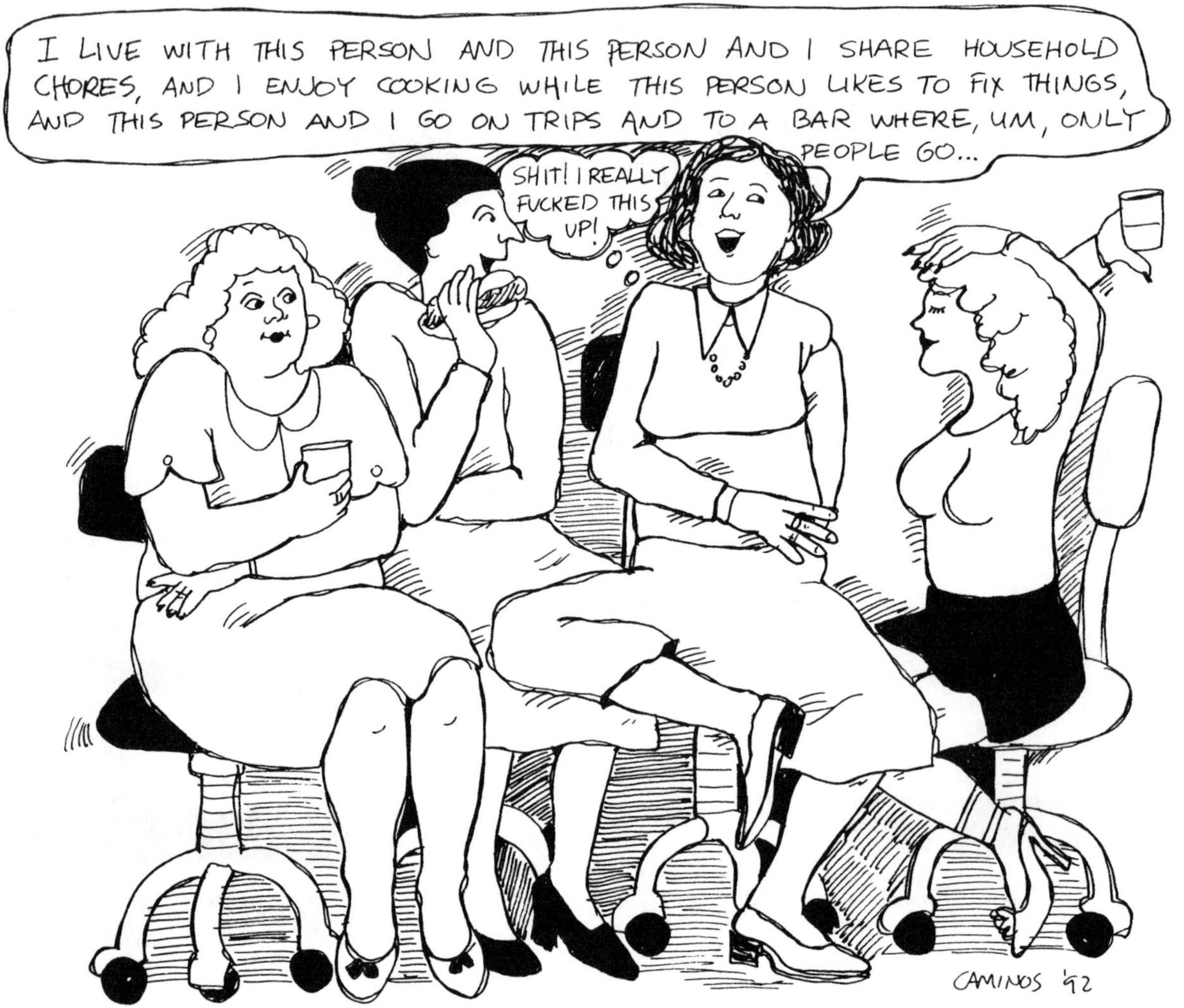
I LIVE WITH THIS PERSON AND THIS PERSON AND I SHARE HOUSEHOLD CHORES, AND I ENJOY COOKING WHILE THIS PERSON LIKES TO FIX THINGS, AND THIS PERSON AND I GO ON TRIPS AND TO A BAR WHERE, UM, ONLY PEOPLE GO...
SHIT! I REALLY FUCKED THIS UP!
CAMINOS '92

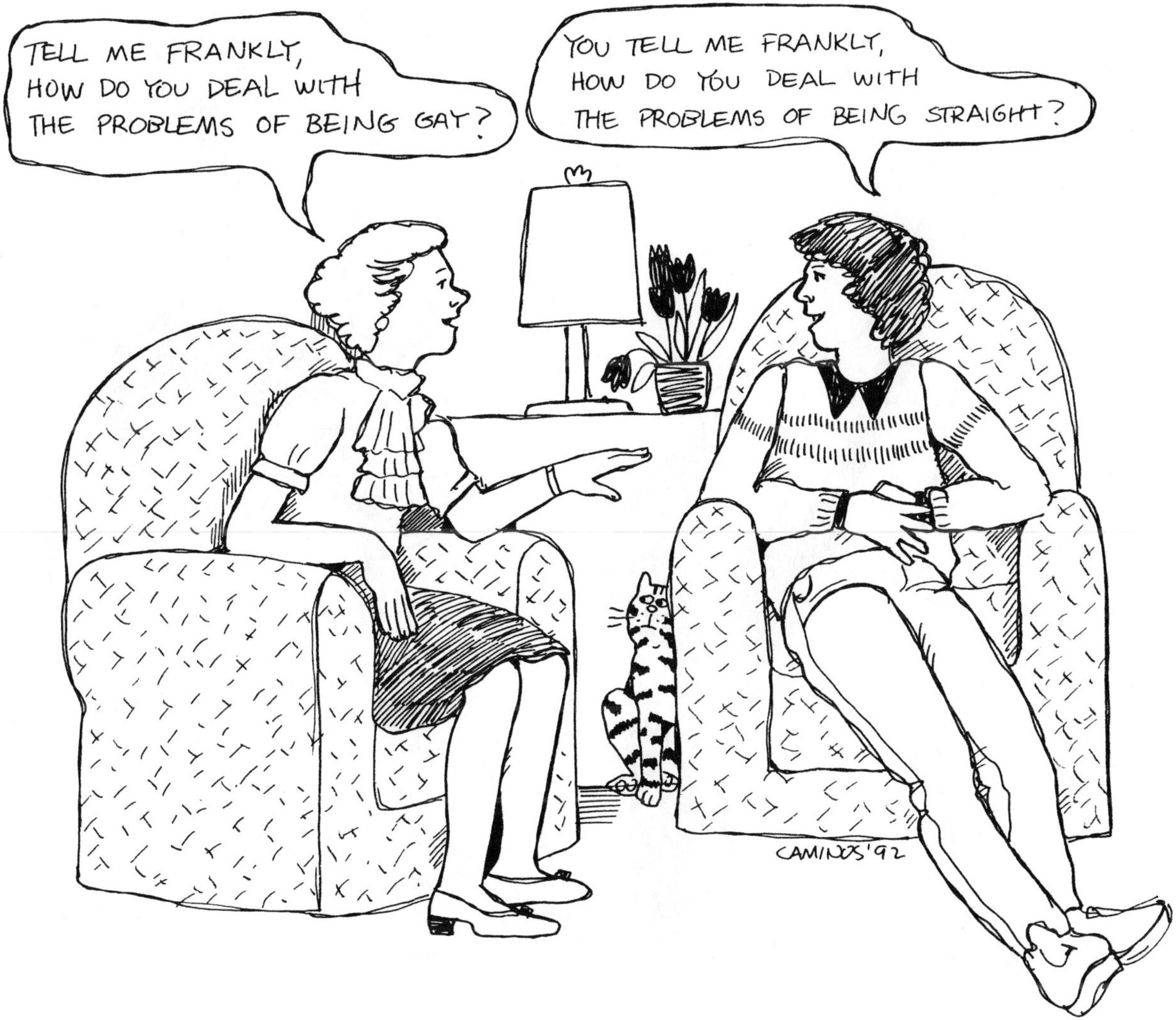
TELL ME FRANKLY, HOW DO YOU DEAL WITH THE PROBLEMS OF BEING GAY?
YOU TELL ME FRANKLY, HOW DO YOU DEAL WITH THE PROBLEMS OF BEING STRAIGHT?
CAMINOS '92

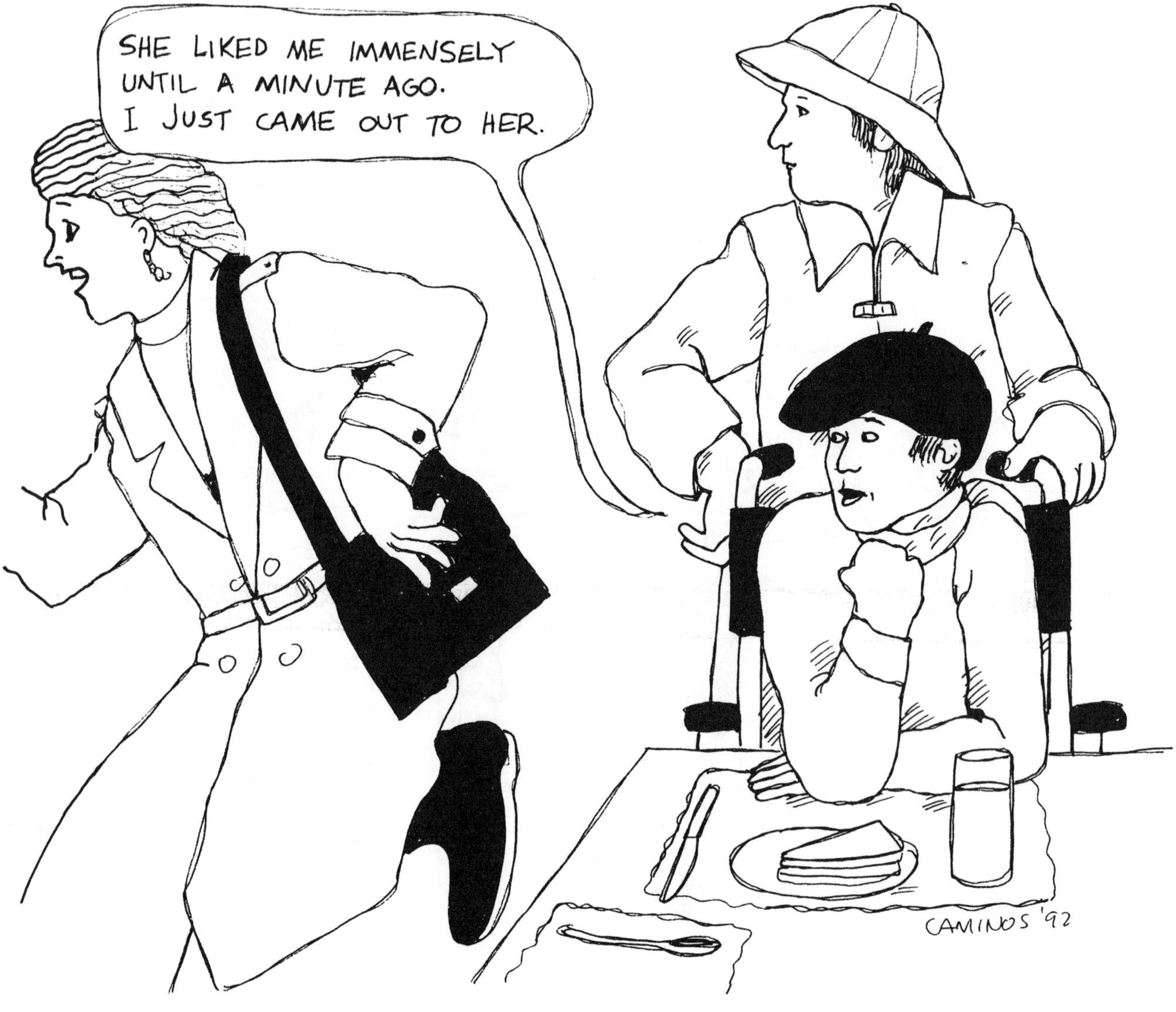
SHE LIKED ME IMMENSELY UNTIL A MINUTE AGO. I JUST CAME OUT TO HER.
CAMINOS '92

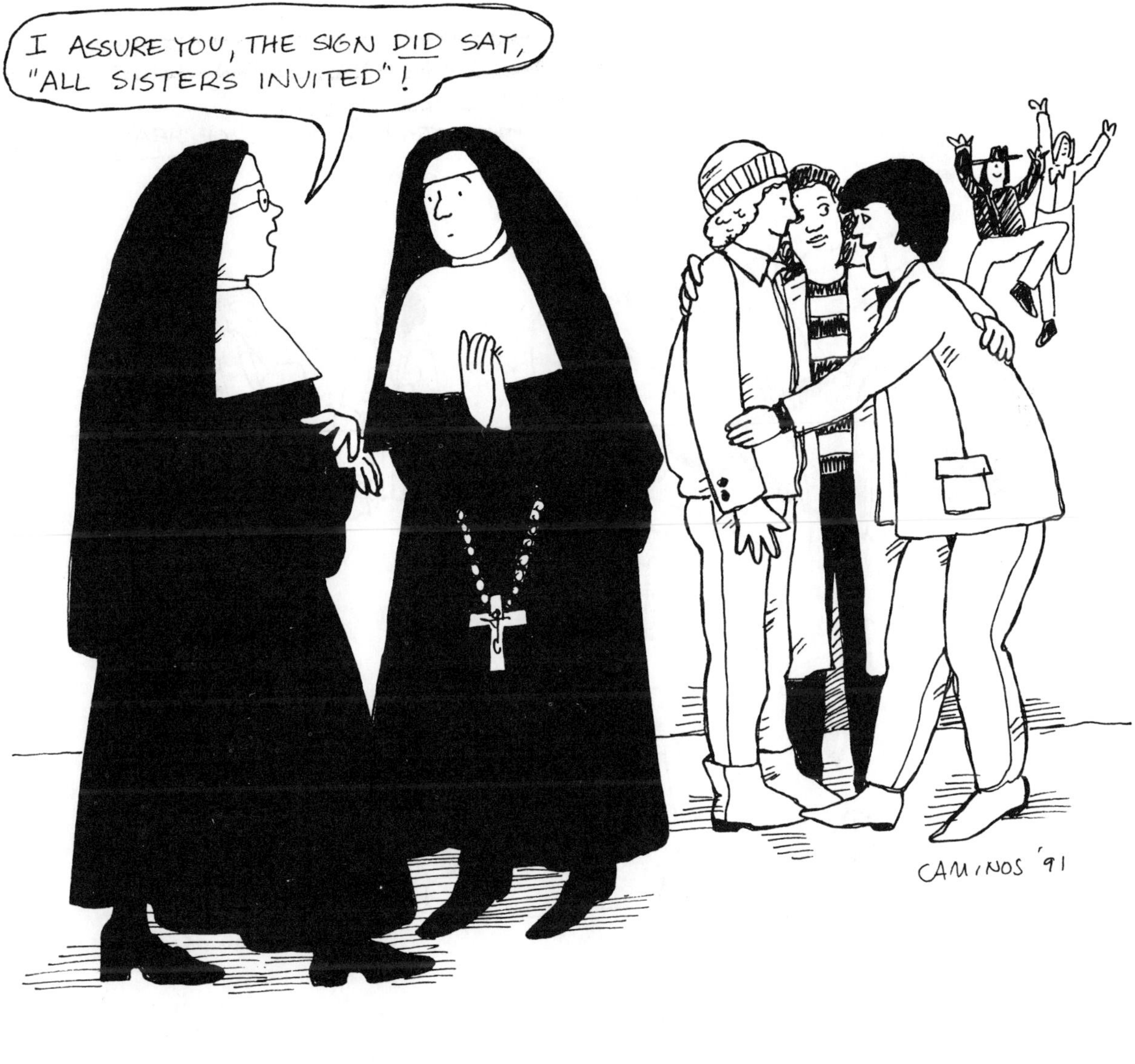
I ASSURE YOU, THE SIGN DID SAT, "ALL SISTERS INVITED"!
CAMINOS '91

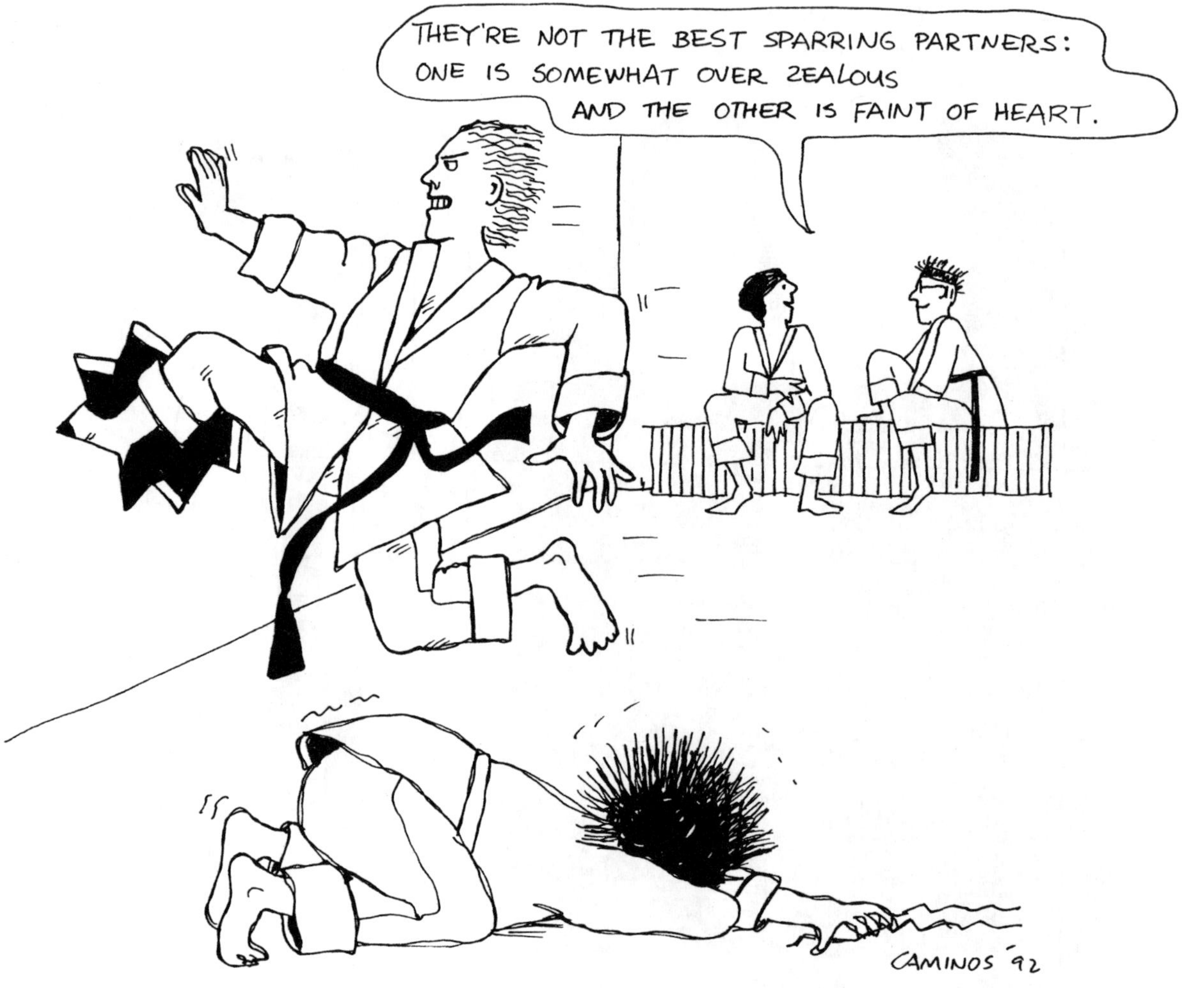
THEY'RE NOT THE BEST SPARRING PARTNERS: ONE IS SOMEWHAT OVER ZEALOUS AND THE OTHER IS FAINT OF HEART.
CAMINOS '92

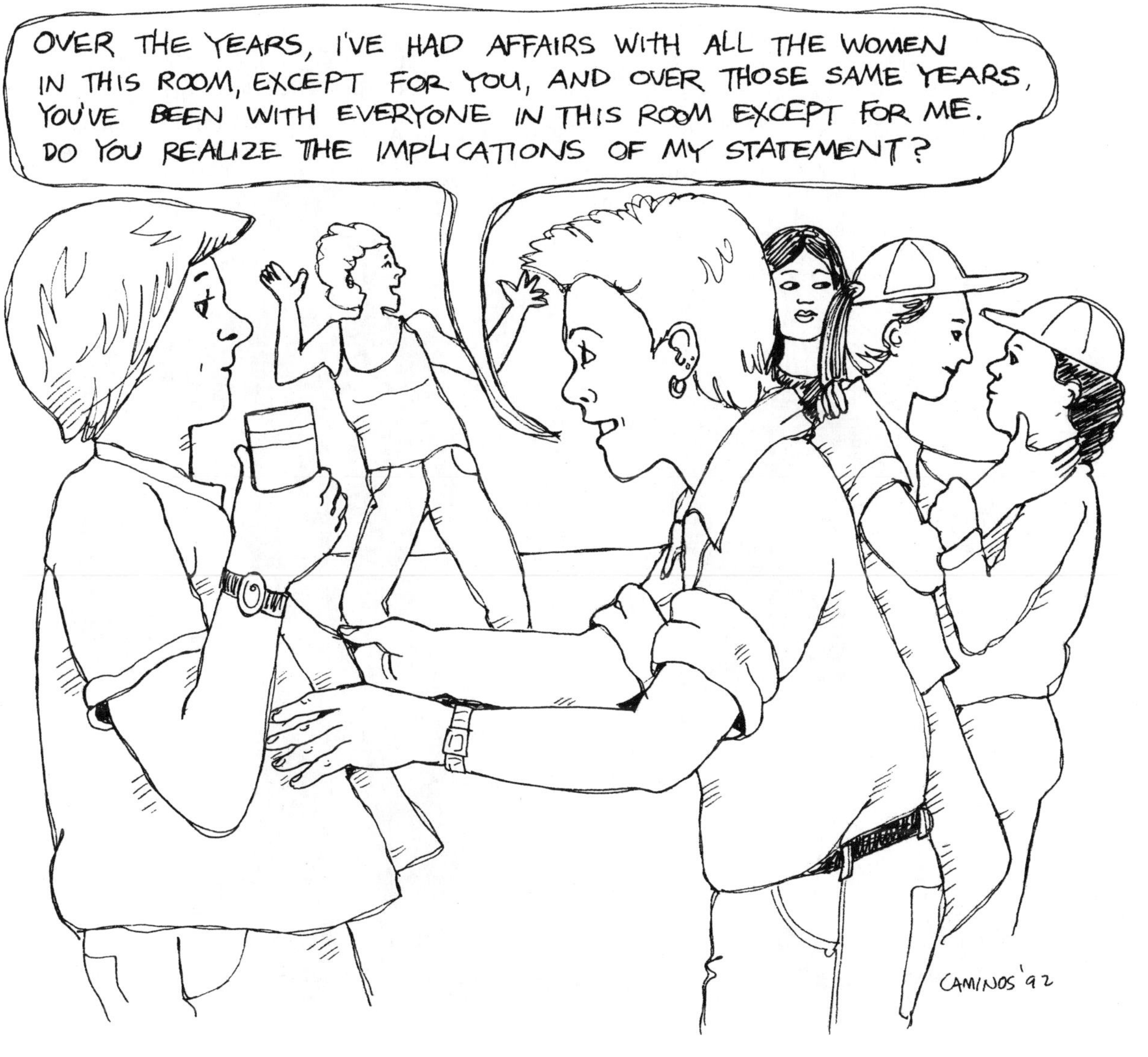
OVER THE YEARS, I'VE HAD AFFAIRS WITH ALL THE WOMEN IN THIS ROOM, EXCEPT FOR YOU, AND OVER THOSE SAME YEARS, YOU'VE BEEN WITH EVERYONE IN THIS ROOM EXCEPT FOR ME. DO YOU REALIZE THE IMPLICATIONS OF MY STATEMENT?
CAMINOS '92

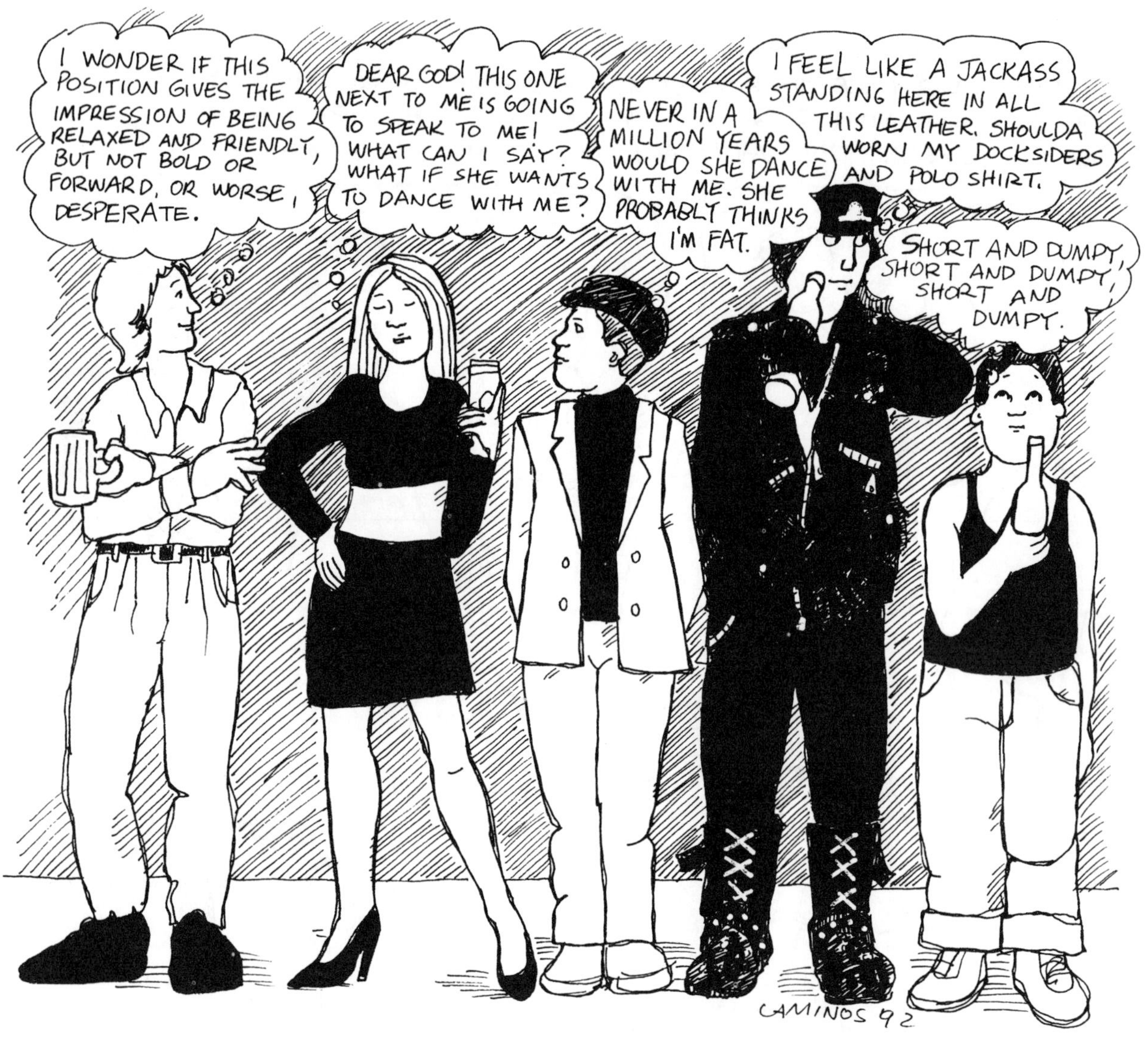
I WONDER IF THIS POSITION GIVES THE IMPRESSION OF BEING RELAXED AND FRIENDLY, BUT NOT BOLD OR FORWARD, OR WORSE, DESPERATE.
DEAR GOD! THIS ONE NEXT TO ME IS GOING TO SPEAK TO ME! WHAT CAN I SAY? WHAT IF SHE WANTS TO DANCE WITH ME?
NEVER IN A MILLION YEARS WOULD SHE DANCE WITH ME. SHE PROBABLY THINKS I'M FAT.
I FEEL LIKE A JACKASS STANDING HERE IN ALL THIS LEATHER. SHOULDA WORN MY DOCKSIDERS AND POLO SHIRT.
SHORT AND DUMPY, SHORT AND DUMPY, SHORT AND DUMPY.
CAMINOS 92

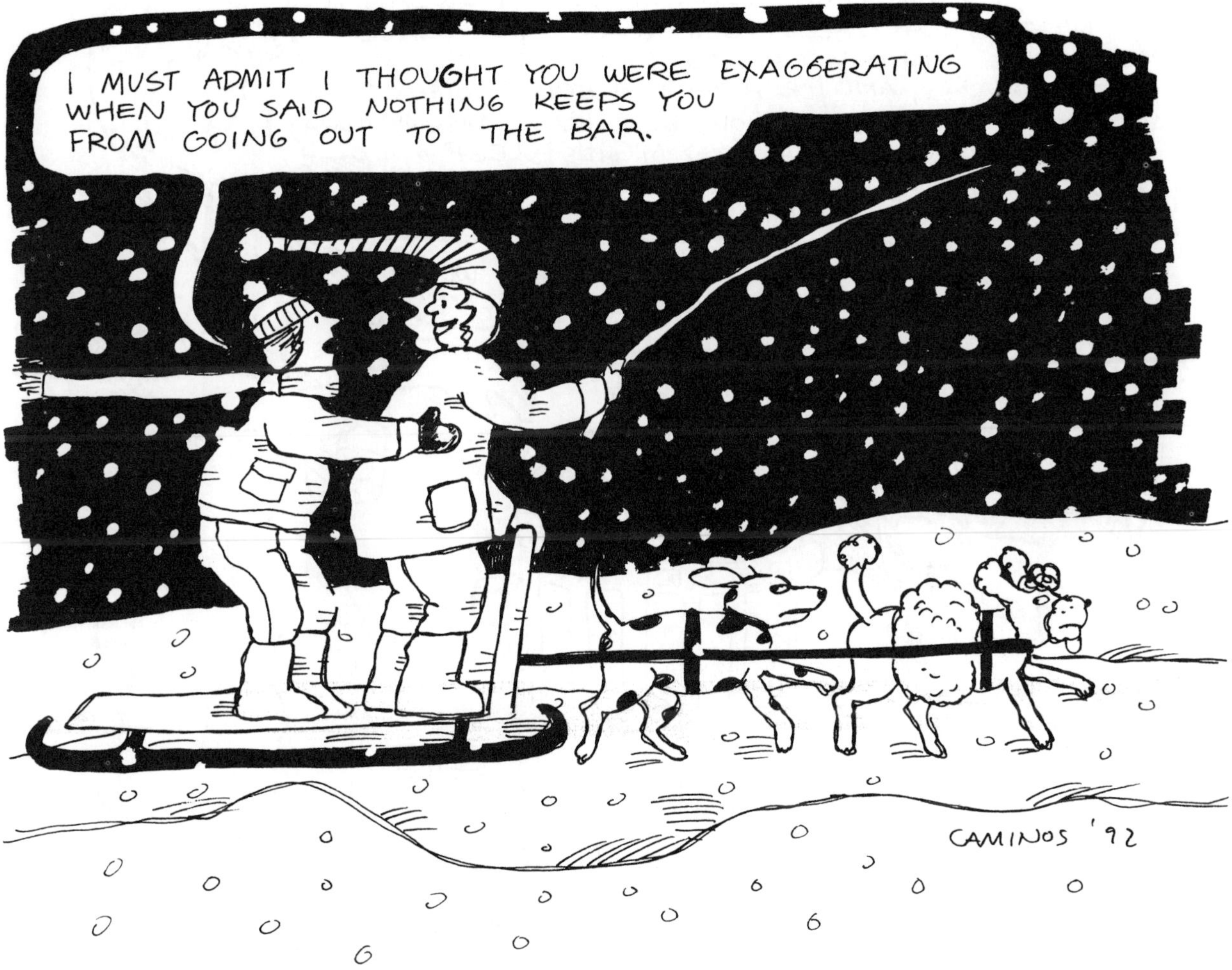
I MUST ADMIT I THOUGHT YOU WERE EXAGGERATING WHEN YOU SAID NOTHING KEEPS YOU FROM GOING OUT TO THE BAR.
CAMINOS '92

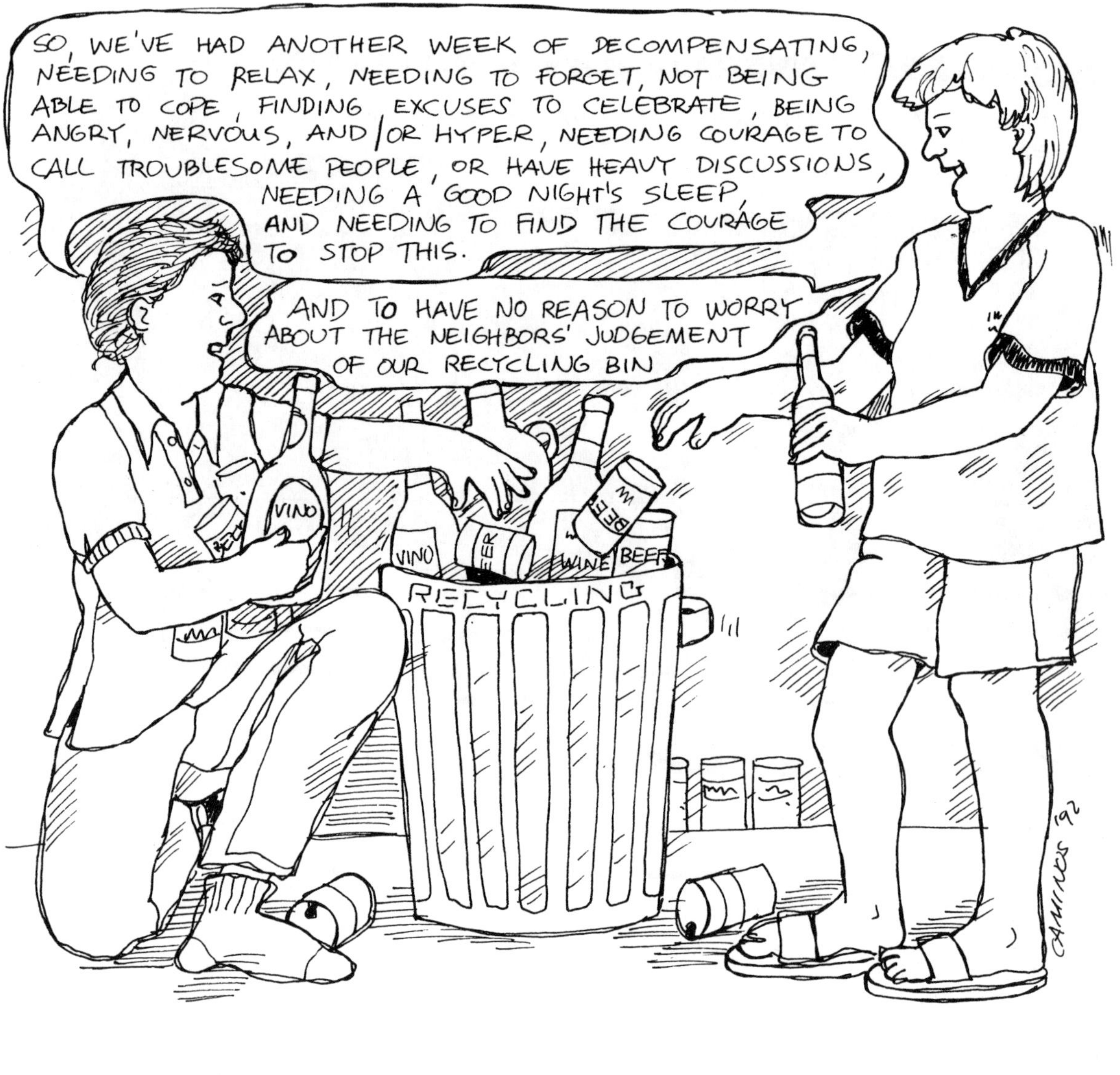
SO, WE'VE HAD ANOTHER WEEK OF DECOMPENSATING, NEEDING TO RELAX, NEEDING TO FORGET, NOT BEING ABLE TO COPE, FINDING EXCUSES TO CELEBRATE, BEING ANGRY, NERVOUS, AND/OR HYPER, NEEDING COURAGE TO CALL TROUBLESOME PEOPLE, OR HAVE HEAVY DISCUSSIONS, NEEDING A GOOD NIGHT'S SLEEP, AND NEEDING TO FIND THE COURAGE TO STOP THIS.
AND TO HAVE NO REASON TO WORRY ABOUT THE NEIGHBORS' JUDGEMENT OF OUR RECYCLING BIN
VINO
VINO
WINE
BEER
RECYCLING
CAMINOS '92

WELL, FIRST I QUIT SMOKING. THEN I QUIT DRINKING. I DEVELOPED AN OBSESSIVE URGE FOR CHOCOLATE. I GAVE THAT UP, ONLY TO FIND THE EATING OF POTATO CHIPS BECAME A PROBLEM. WHEN I GAVE UP THE CHIPS, I BEGAN BUYING LOTTERY TICKETS, JUST A FEW AT FIRST, BUT THEN A FEW MORE AND A FEW MORE, YOU KNOW. LOTTERY TICKETS EXPOSED A GAMBLING ADDICTION WHICH QUICKLY CAUSED ME TO TAKE CASINO TRIPS, THESE PACKAGE TOURS, WHICH CREATED AN ADDICTION TO TRAVELING. I EVEN WENT TO COUNTRIES OPPRESSIVE TO WOMEN. AND JUST WHEN I THOUGHT I'D HIT BOTTOM, I TURNED ON THE TV TO BLOCK OUT THE NEED TO LOOK AT TRAVEL BROCHURES, AND LO AND BEHOLD, THERE WAS THIS SHOPPING BY PHONE SHOW...
CAMINOS '91

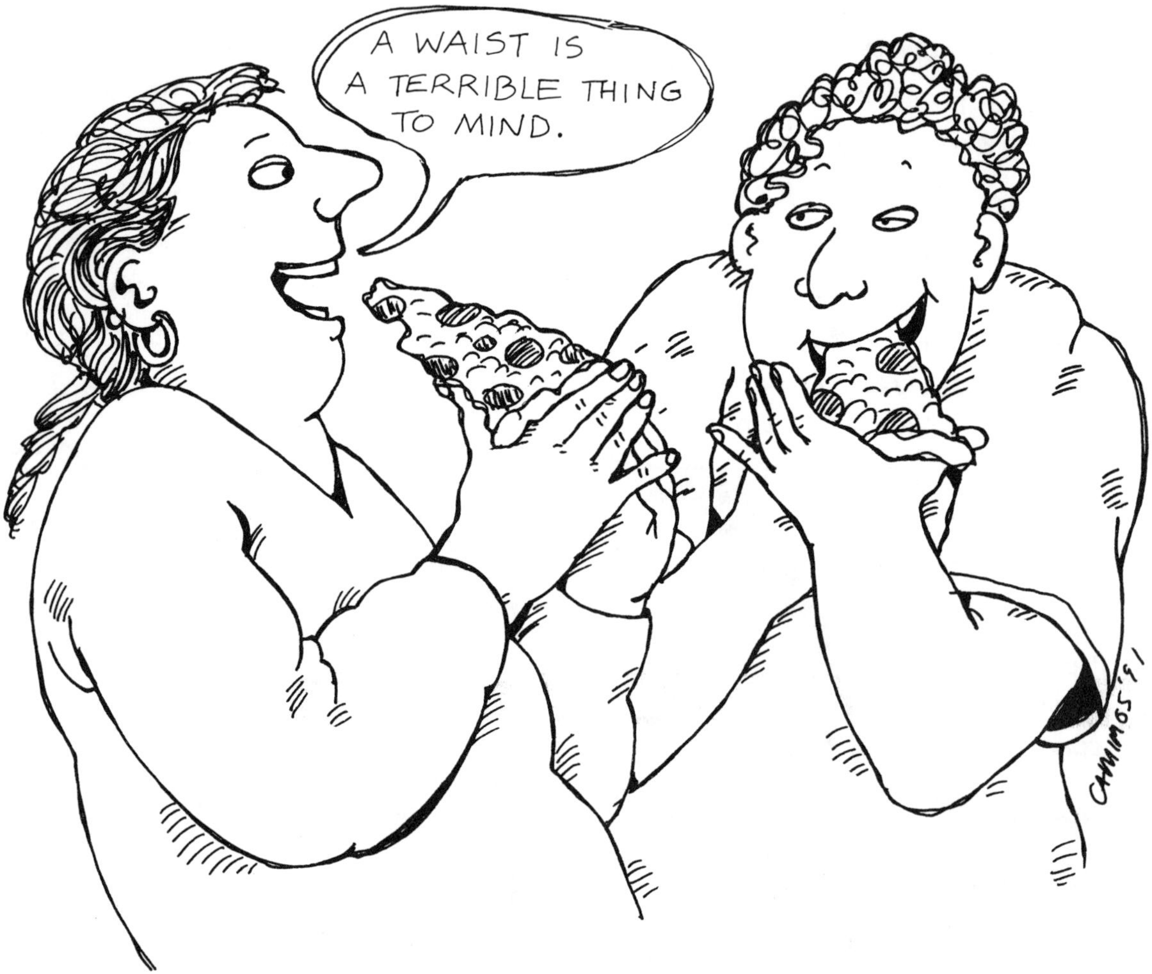
A WAIST IS A TERRIBLE THING TO MIND.

HM, SUPPORT GROUPS: ACOA FOR BISEXUAL ASIANS, AFRICAN ANCESTRAL WIMMIN UNITED FOR SOCIETAL CHANGE, BUTCH/FEMME SOCIETY, EULENSPIEGEL SOCIETY, GIRTH AND MIRTH, LAS BUENAS AMIGAS, LAVENDER BYTES, MOONFIRE SPIRITUALITY CIRCLE, LESBIAN SCUBA DIVING, SEXANON, EROTICIZING SAFE SEX, TRI-STATE GAYLAXIANS. HOW ABOUT WOMEN WHO PUNISHED THEIR CATS EXCESSIVELY BECAUSE THE CATS INSISTED ON LYING ACROSS THE NEWSPAPER?
VENTS
T GROUPS
SUP
CAMINOS 91

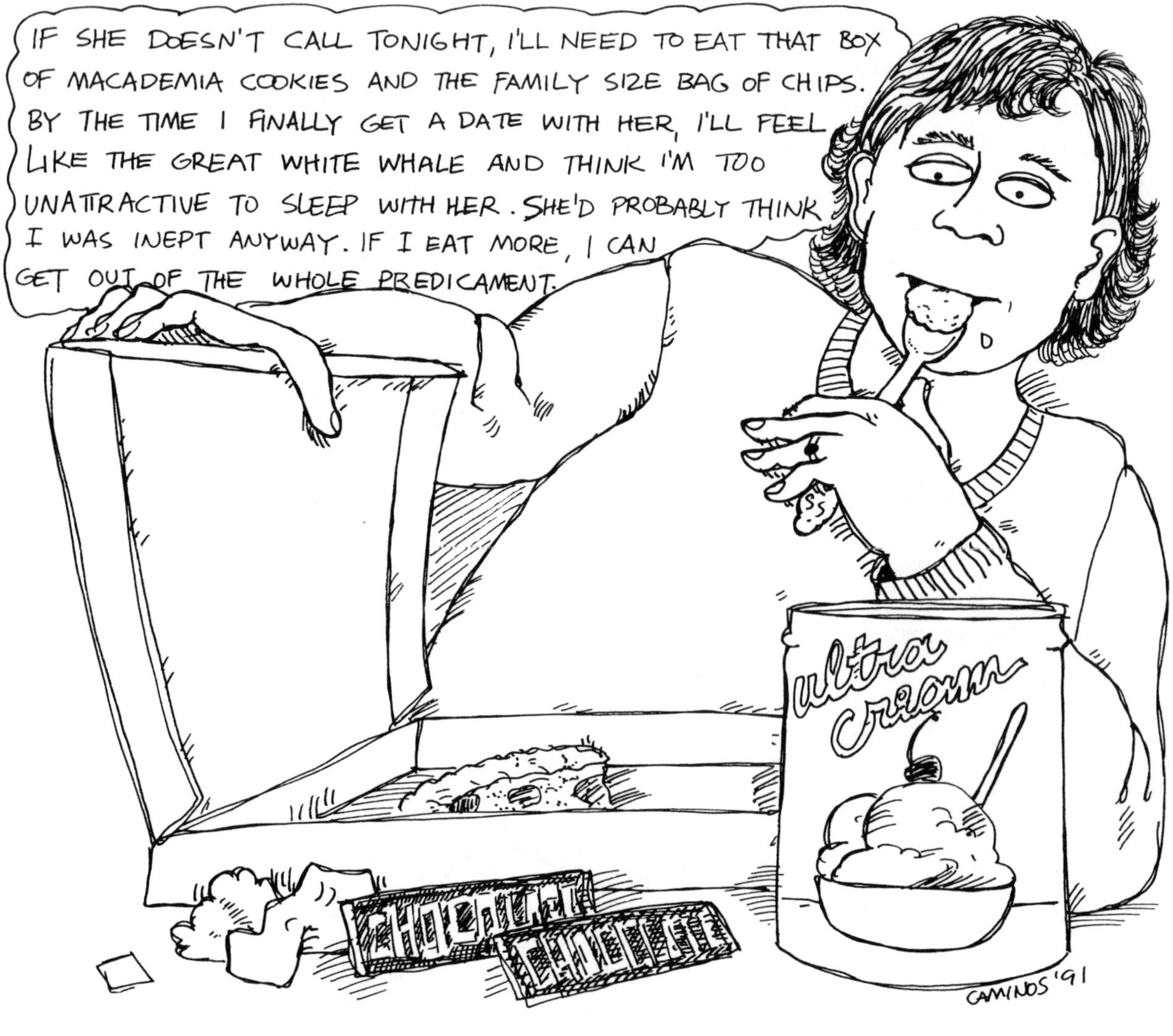
IF SHE DOESN'T CALL TONIGHT, I'LL NEED TO EAT THAT BOX OF MACADEMIA COOKIES AND THE FAMILY SIZE BAG OF CHIPS. BY THE TIME I FINALLY GET A DATE WITH HER, I'LL FEEL LIKE THE GREAT WHITE WHALE AND THINK I'M TOO UNATTRACTIVE TO SLEEP WITH HER. SHE'D PROBABLY THINK I WAS INEPT ANYWAY. IF I EAT MORE, I CAN GET OUT OF THE WHOLE PREDICAMENT.
ultra cream
CAMINOS '91

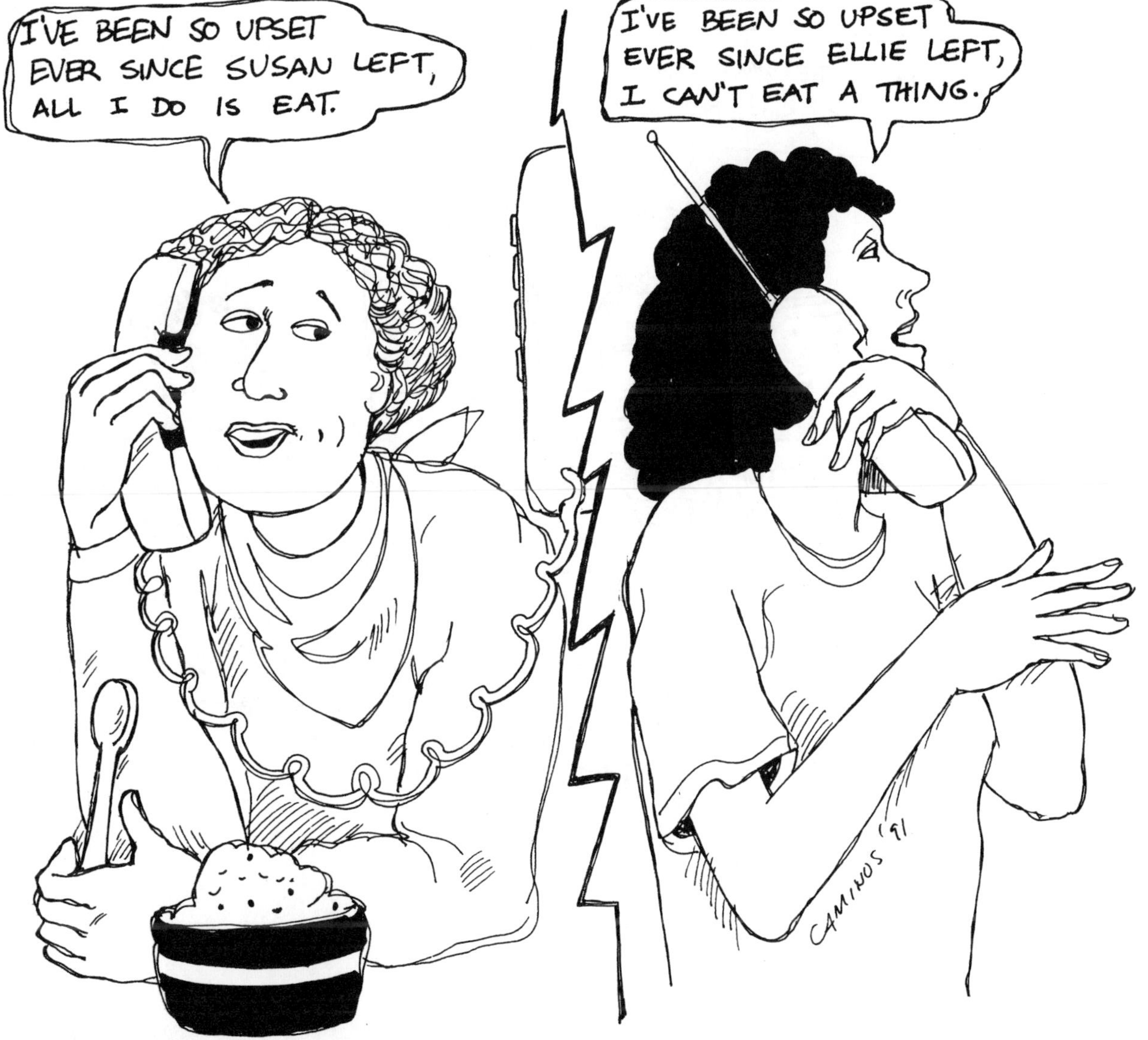
I'VE BEEN SO UPSET EVER SINCE SUSAN LEFT, ALL I DO IS EAT.
I'VE BEEN SO UPSET EVER SINCE ELLIE LEFT, I CAN'T EAT A THING.
CAMINOS '91

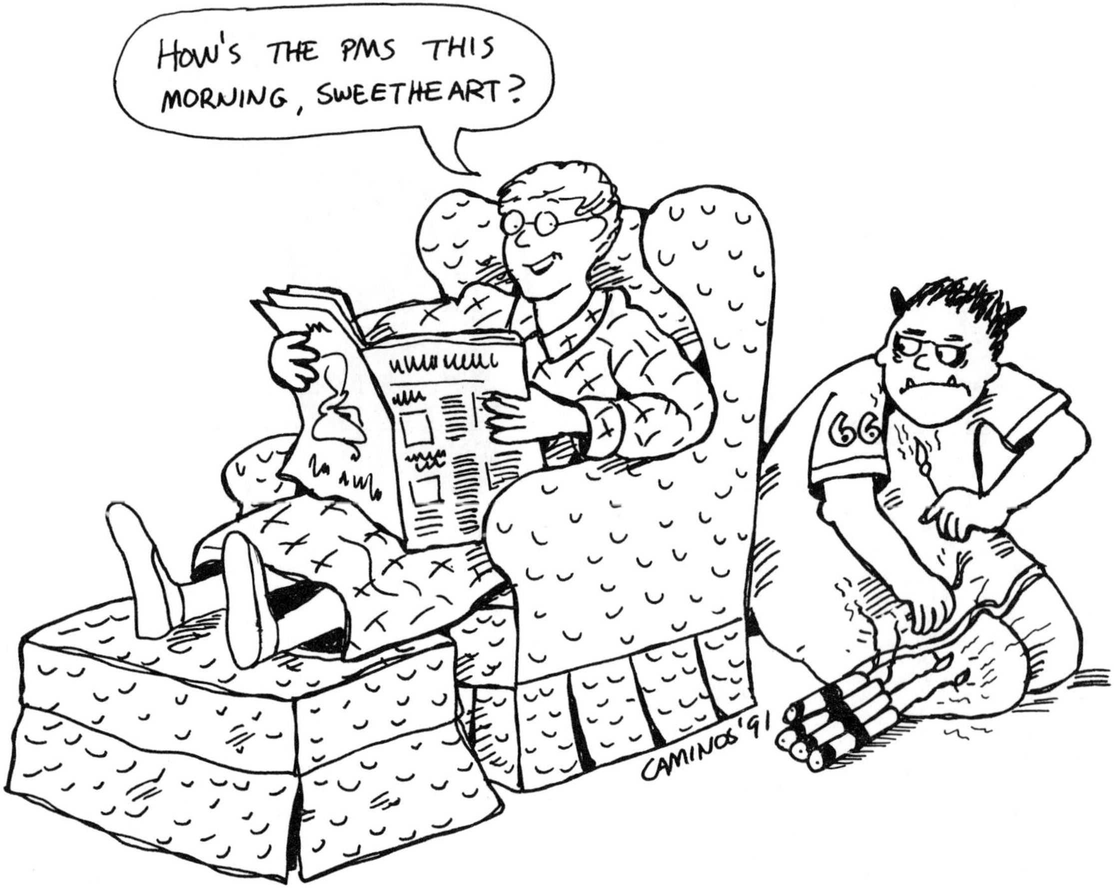
HOW'S THE PMS THIS MORNING, SWEETHEART?
66
CAMINOS '91

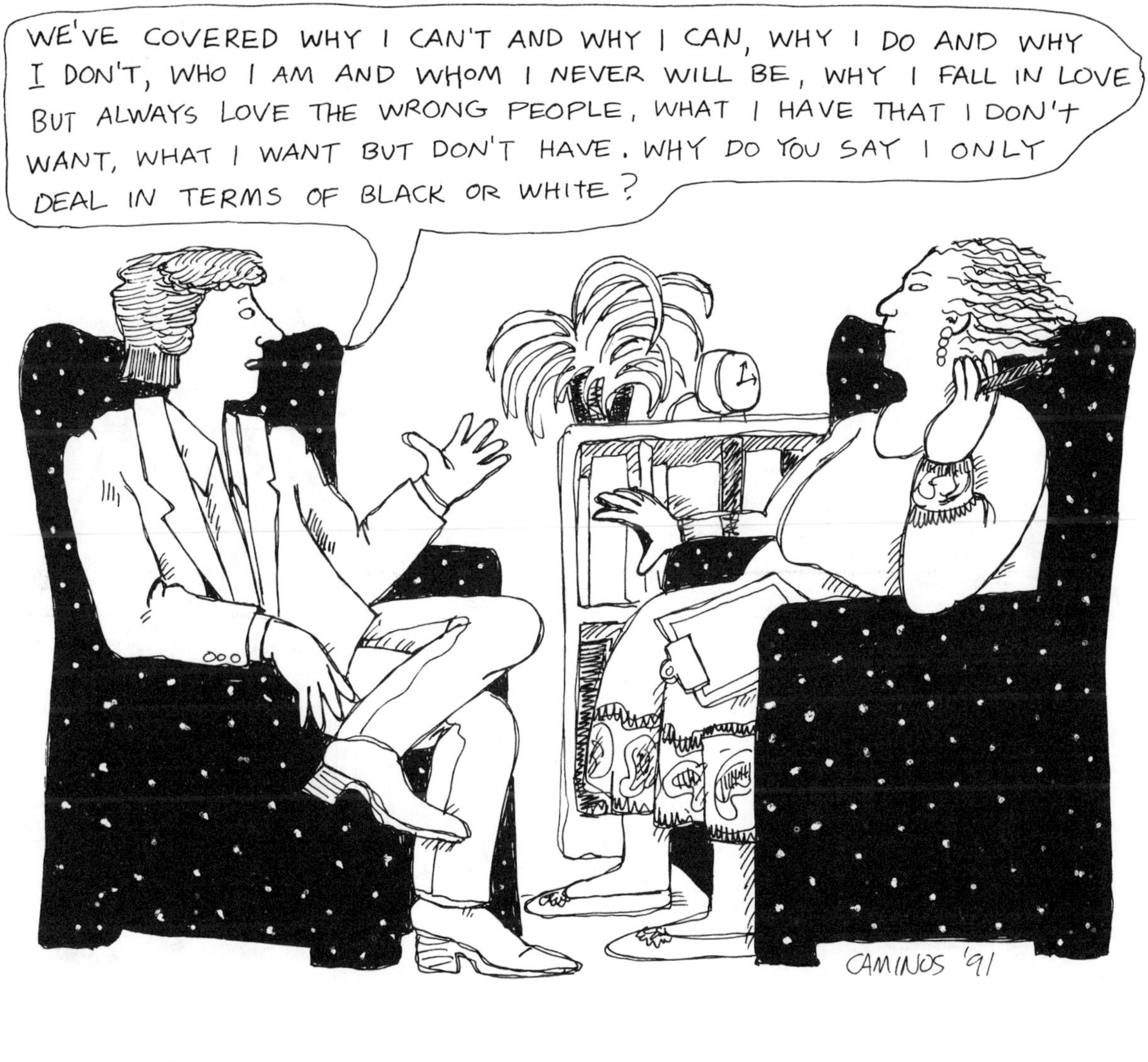
WE'VE COVERED WHY I CAN'T AND WHY I CAN, WHY I DO AND WHY I DON'T, WHO I AM AND WHOM I NEVER WILL BE, WHY I FALL IN LOVE BUT ALWAYS LOVE THE WRONG PEOPLE, WHAT I HAVE THAT I DON'T WANT, WHAT I WANT BUT DON'T HAVE. WHY DO YOU SAY I ONLY DEAL IN TERMS OF BLACK OR WHITE?
CAMINOS '91

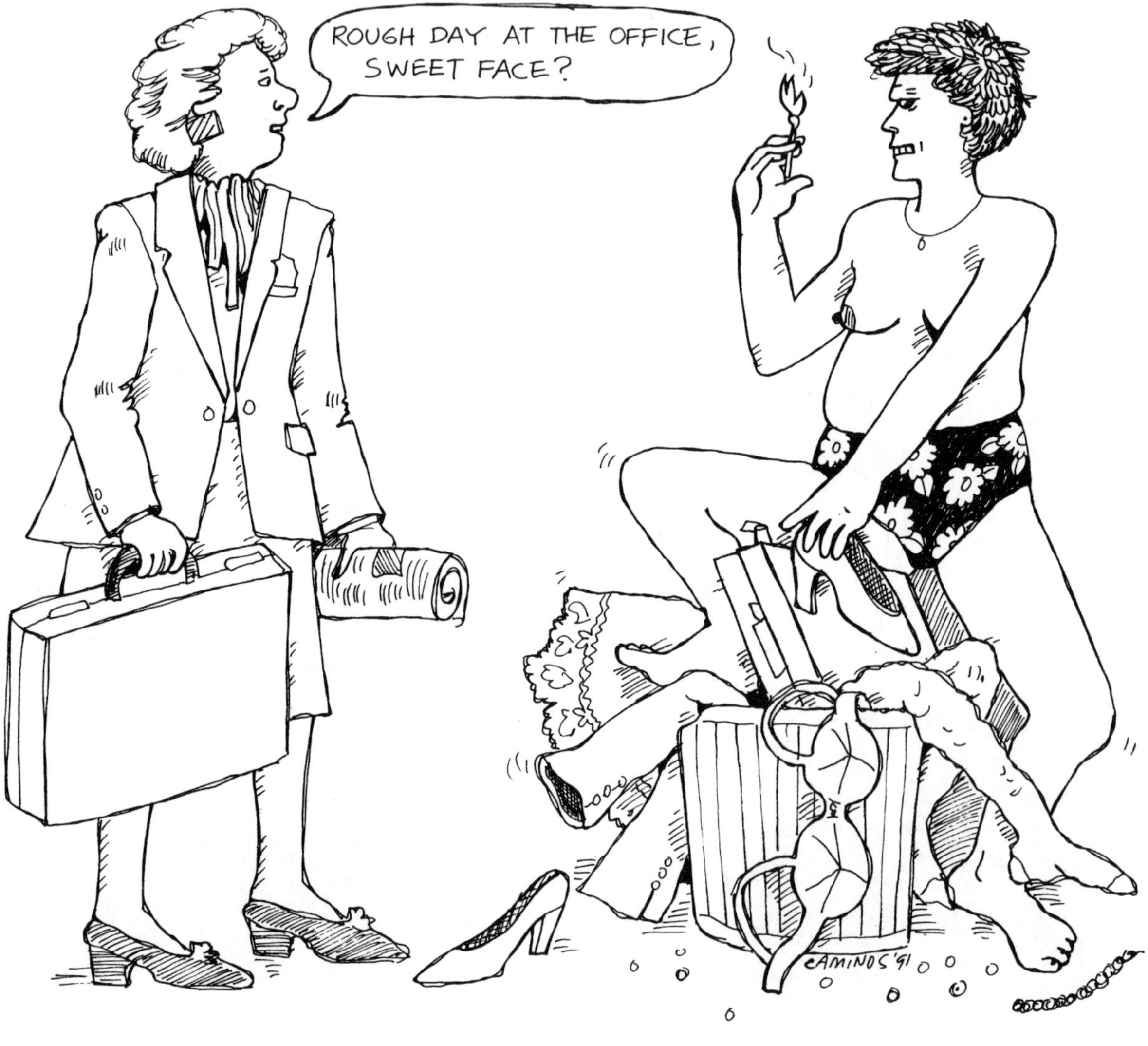
ROUGH DAY AT THE OFFICE, SWEET FACE?
CAMINOS '91

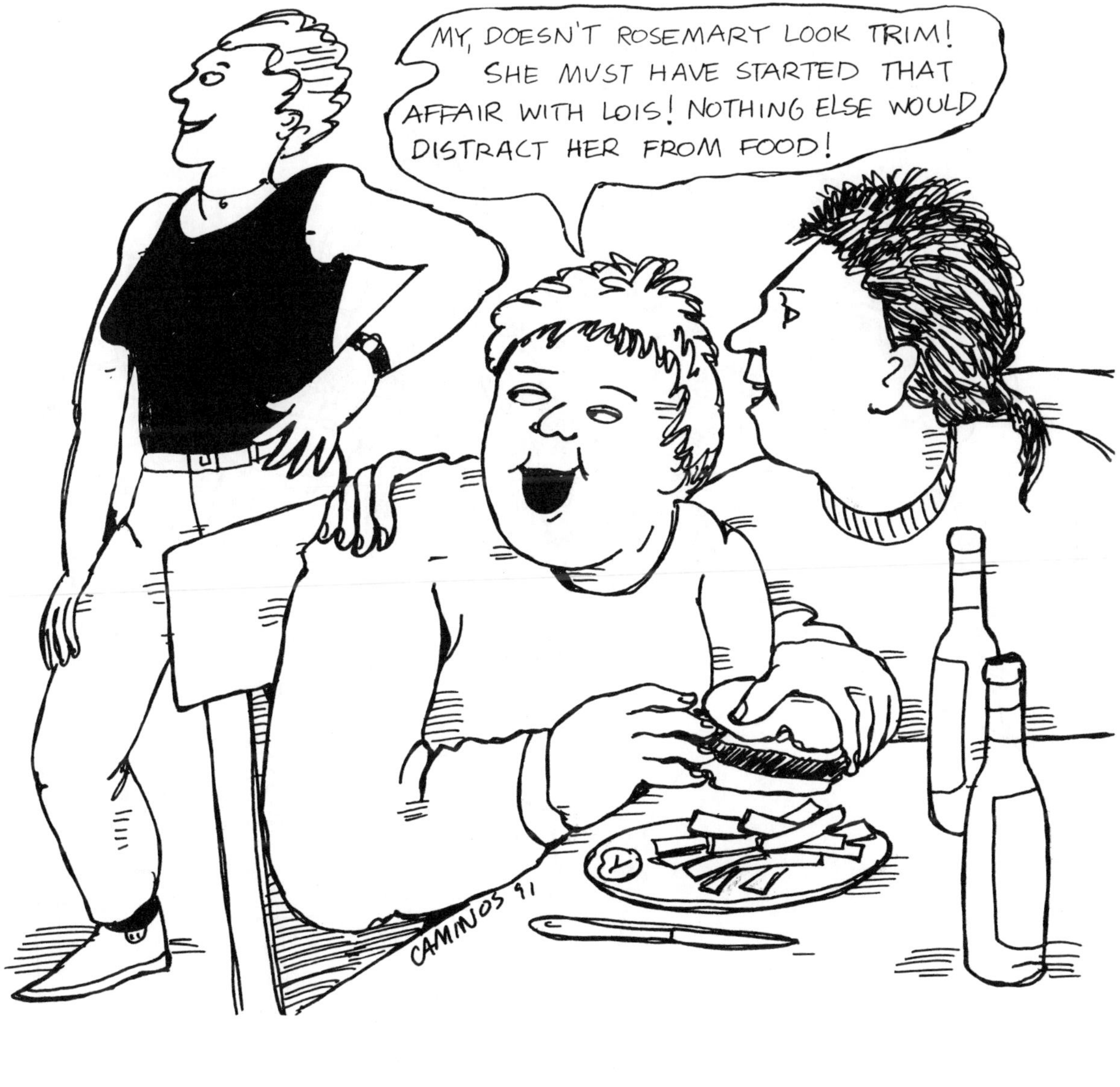
MY, DOESN'T ROSEMARY LOOK TRIM! SHE MUST HAVE STARTED THAT AFFAIR WITH LOIS! NOTHING ELSE WOULD DISTRACT HER FROM FOOD!
CAMINOS '91

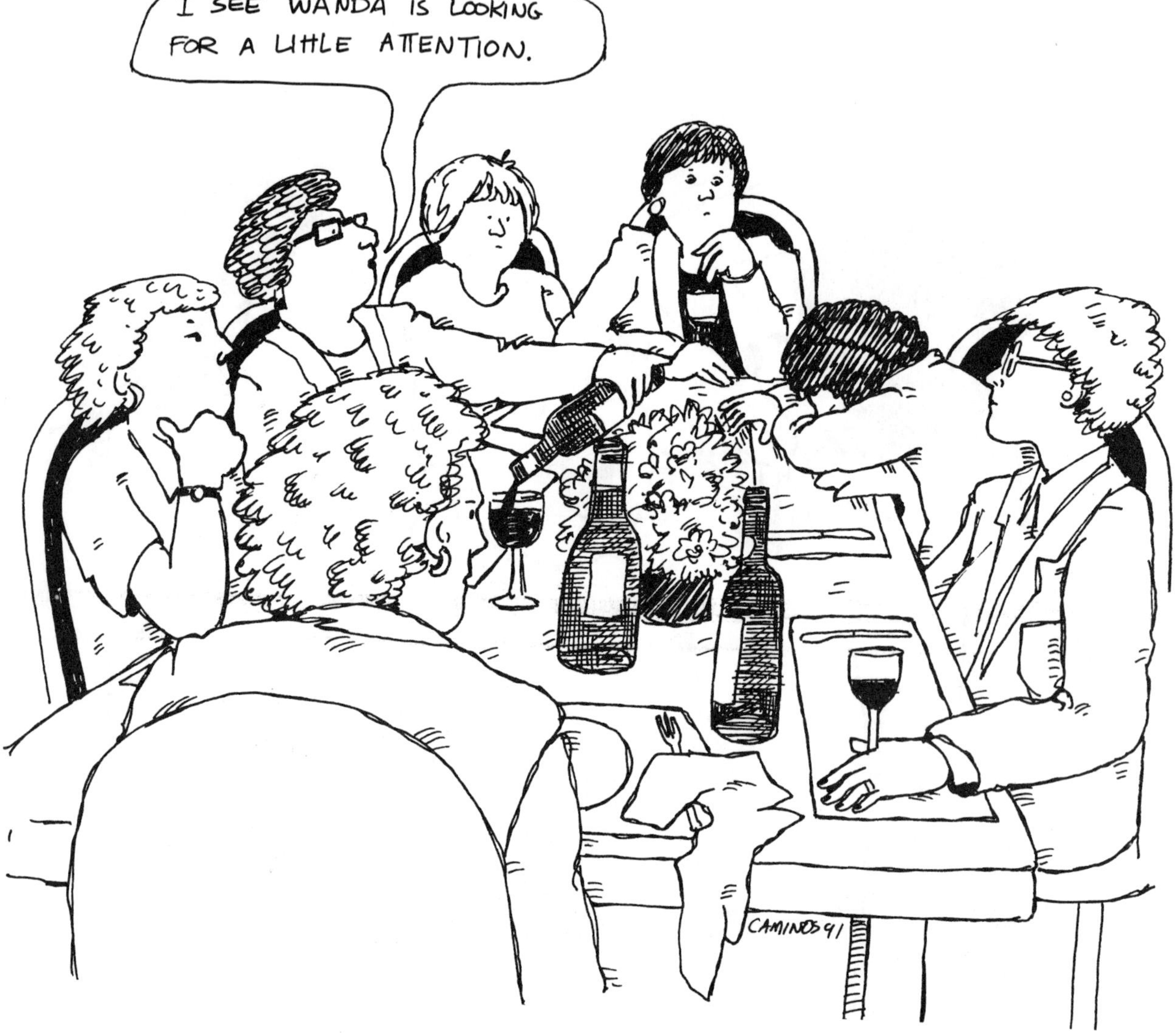
I SEE WANDA IS LOOKING FOR A LITTLE ATTENTION.
CAMINOS 91

NO WEDDING RING, READING THE NEW NOVEL BY MADWOMAN PRESS, AND FLYING INTO SAN FRANCISCO. AH HA!
CAMINOS '91

JANET, YOU KNOW OUR DEAL:
I DO BATS, MICE, AND NIGHT NOISES.
YOU TAKE CARE OF BEES, WASPS, AND SPIDERS.
CAMINOS '91

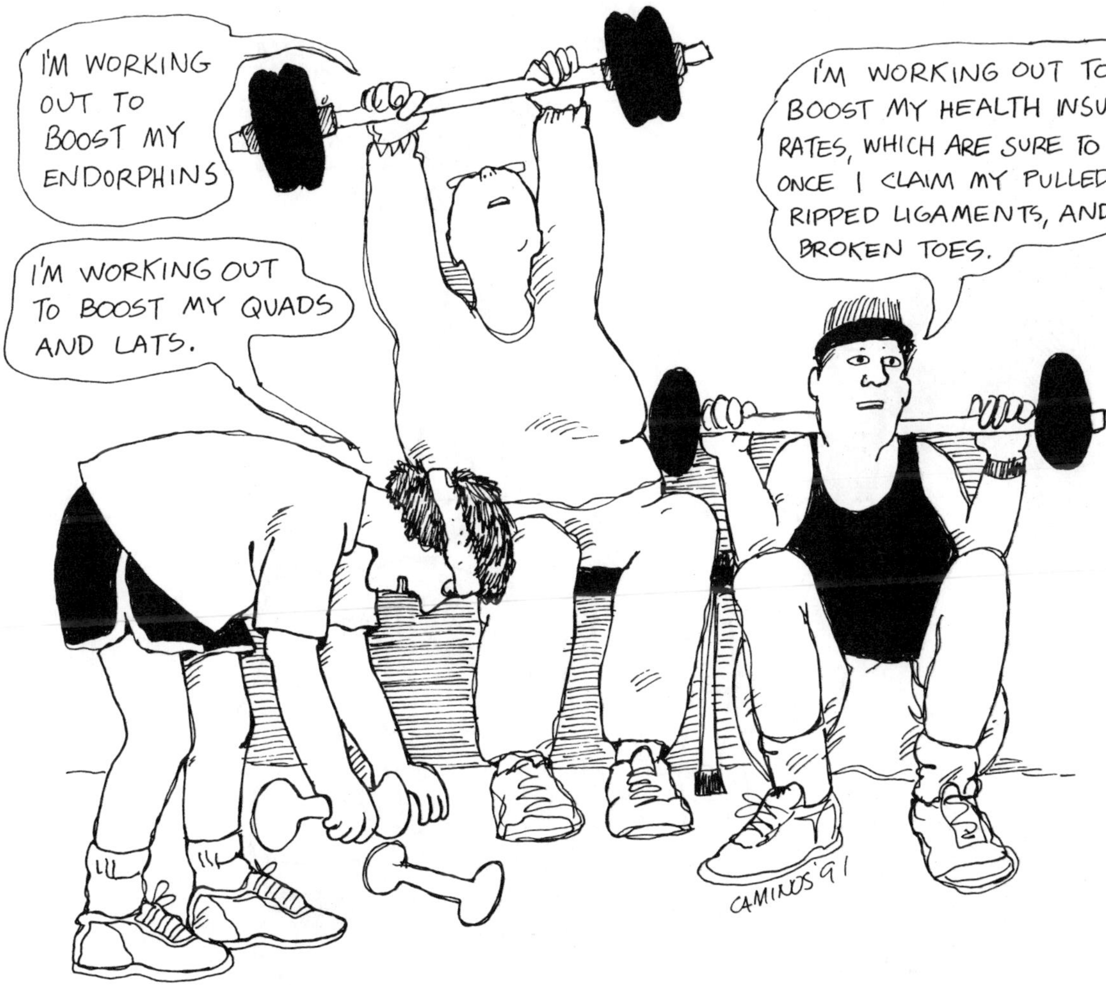
I'M WORKING OUT TO BOOST MY ENDORPHINS
I'M WORKING OUT TO BOOST MY HEALTH INSURANCE RATES, WHICH ARE SURE TO GO UP ONCE I CLAIM MY PULLED BACK RIPPED LIGAMENTS, AND BROKEN TOES.
I'M WORKING OUT TO BOOST MY QUADS AND LATS.
CAMINOS '91

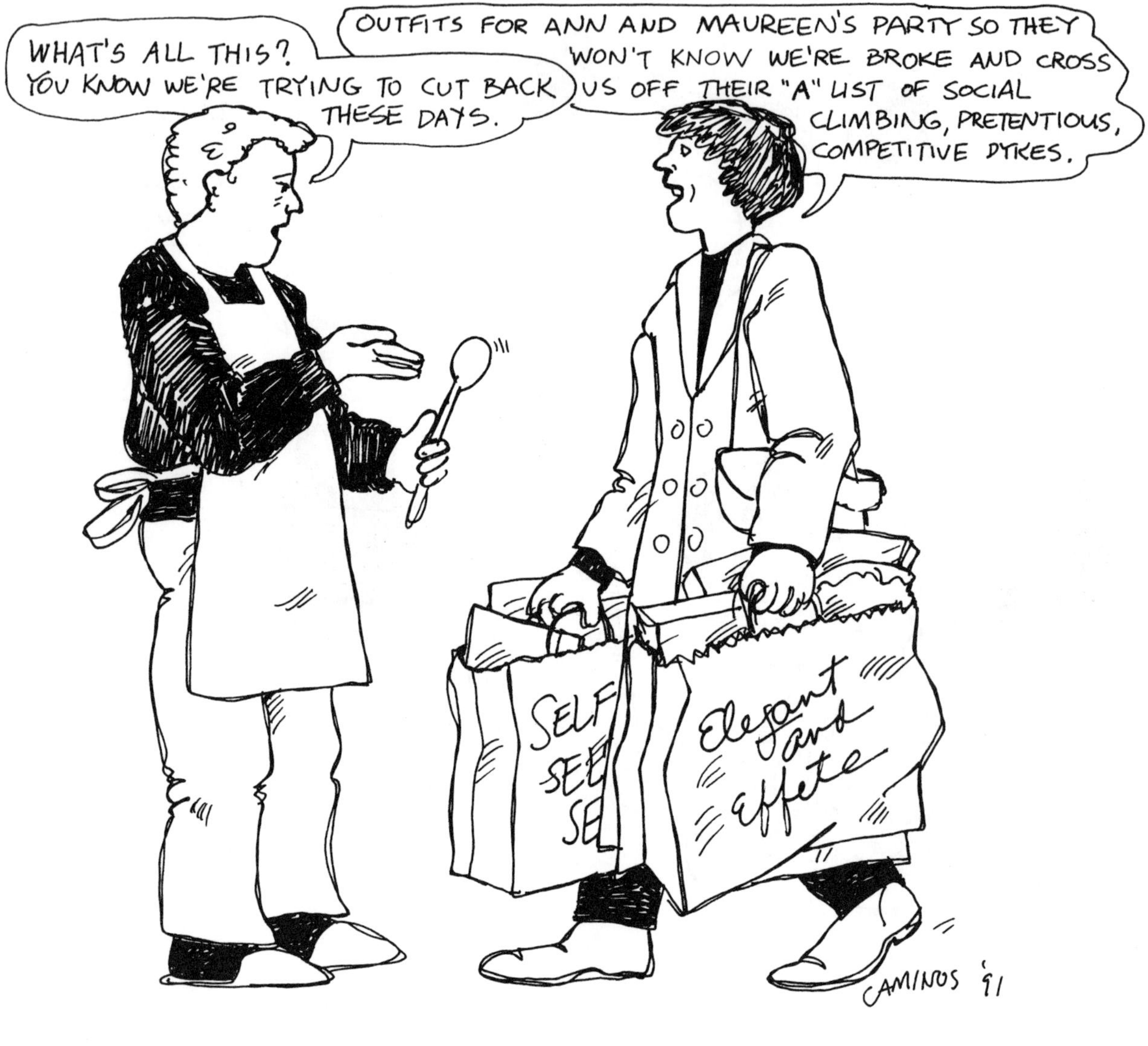
WHAT'S ALL THIS? YOU KNOW WE'RE TRYING TO CUT BACK THESE DAYS.
OUTFITS FOR ANN AND MAUREEN'S PARTY SO THEY WON'T KNOW WE'RE BROKE AND CROSS US OFF THEIR "A" LIST OF SOCIAL CLIMBING, PRETENTIOUS, COMPETITIVE DYKES.
SELF
Elegant and Effete
CAMINOS '91

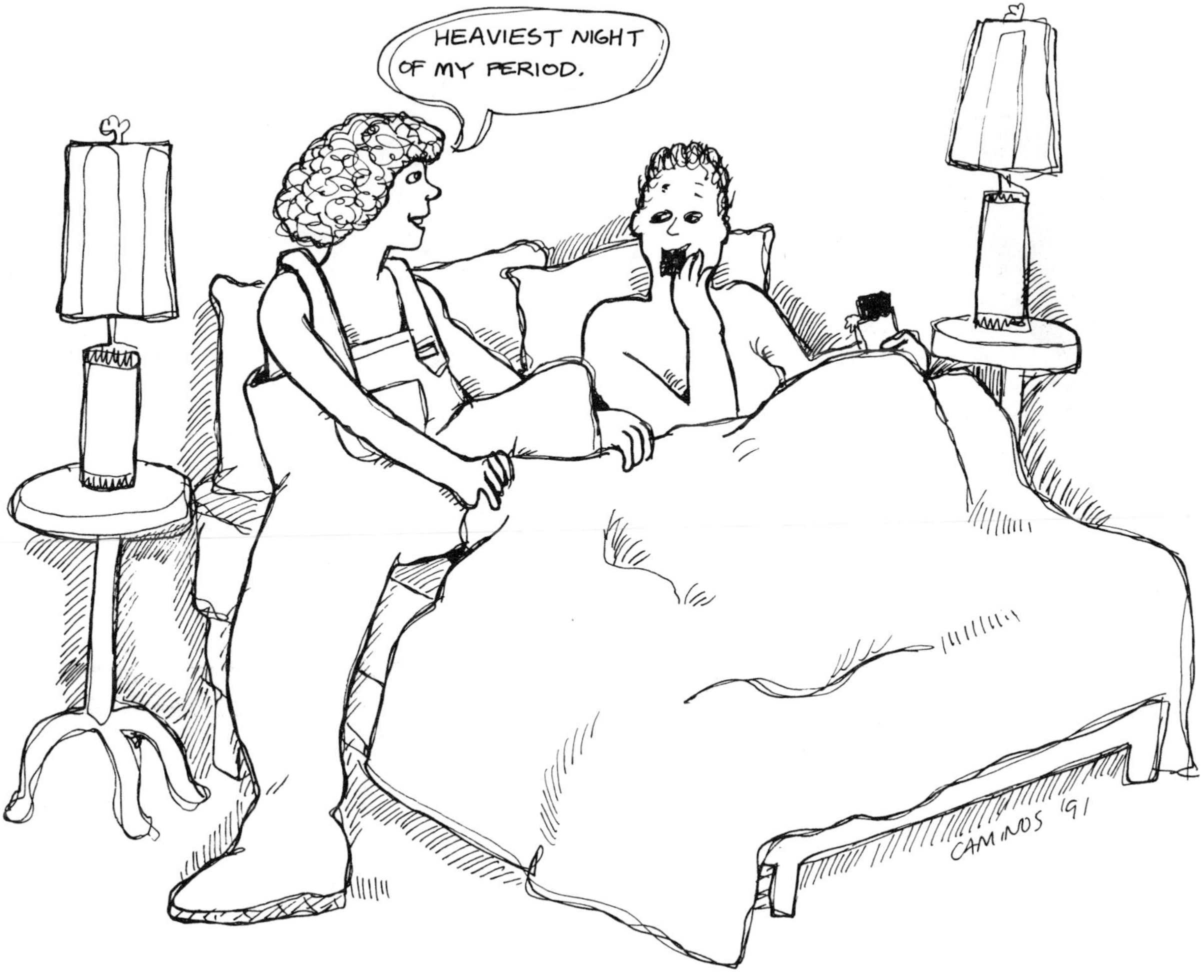
HEAVIEST NIGHT OF MY PERIOD.
CAMINOS '91

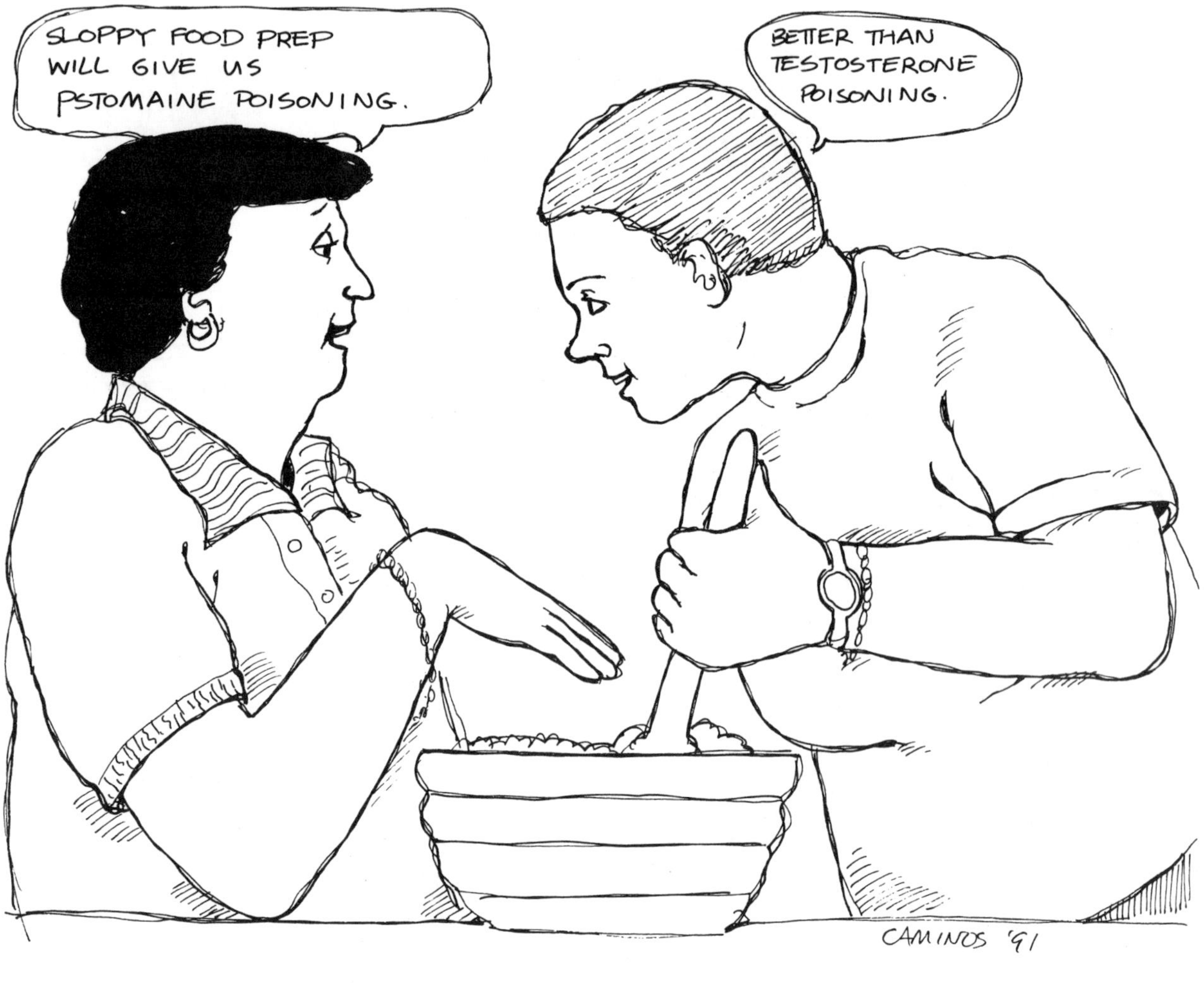
SLOPPY FOOD PREP WILL GIVE US PSTOMAINE POISONING.
BETTER THAN TESTOSTERONE POISONING.
CAMINOS '91

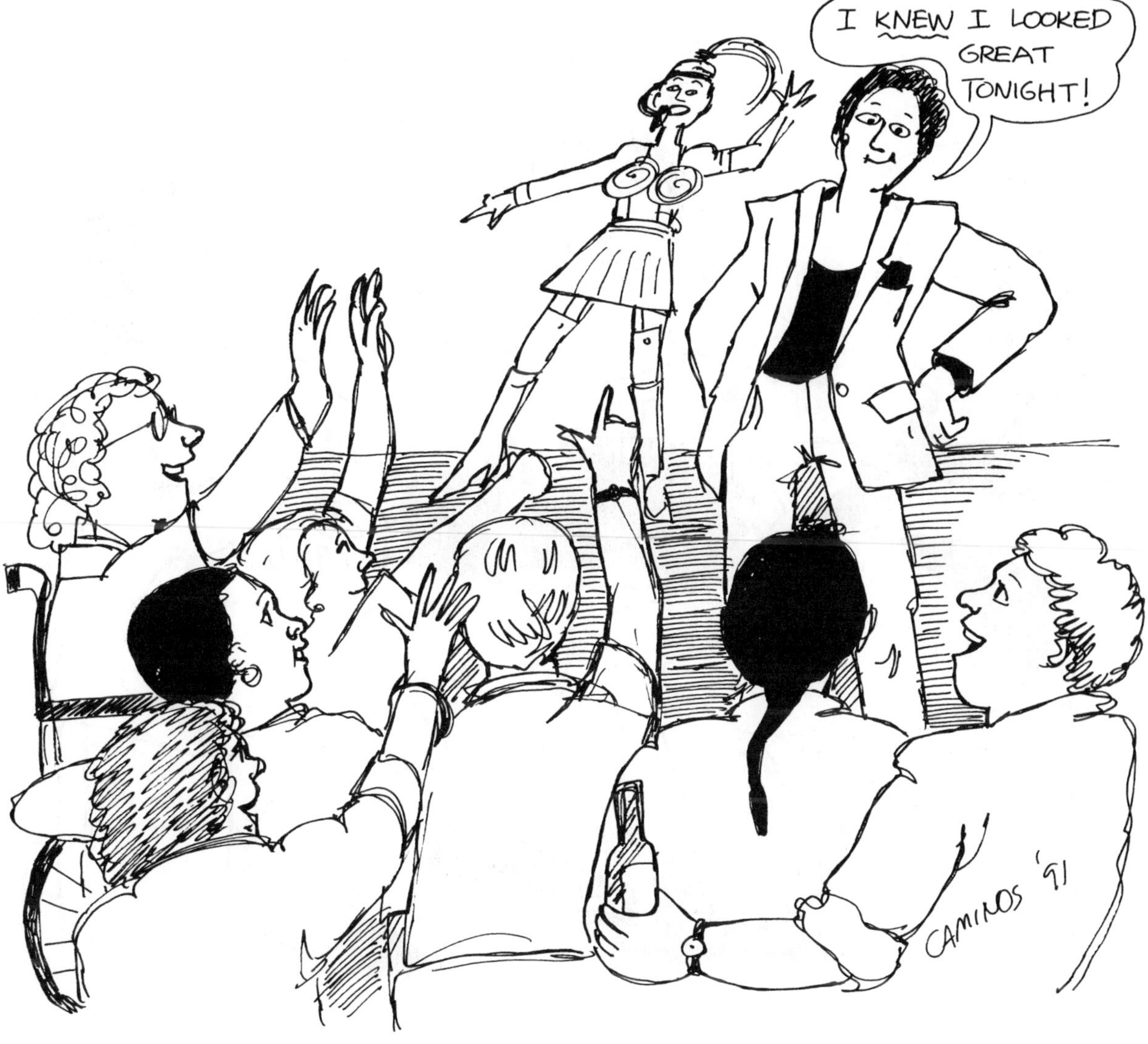
I KNEW I LOOKED GREAT TONIGHT!
CAMINOS '91

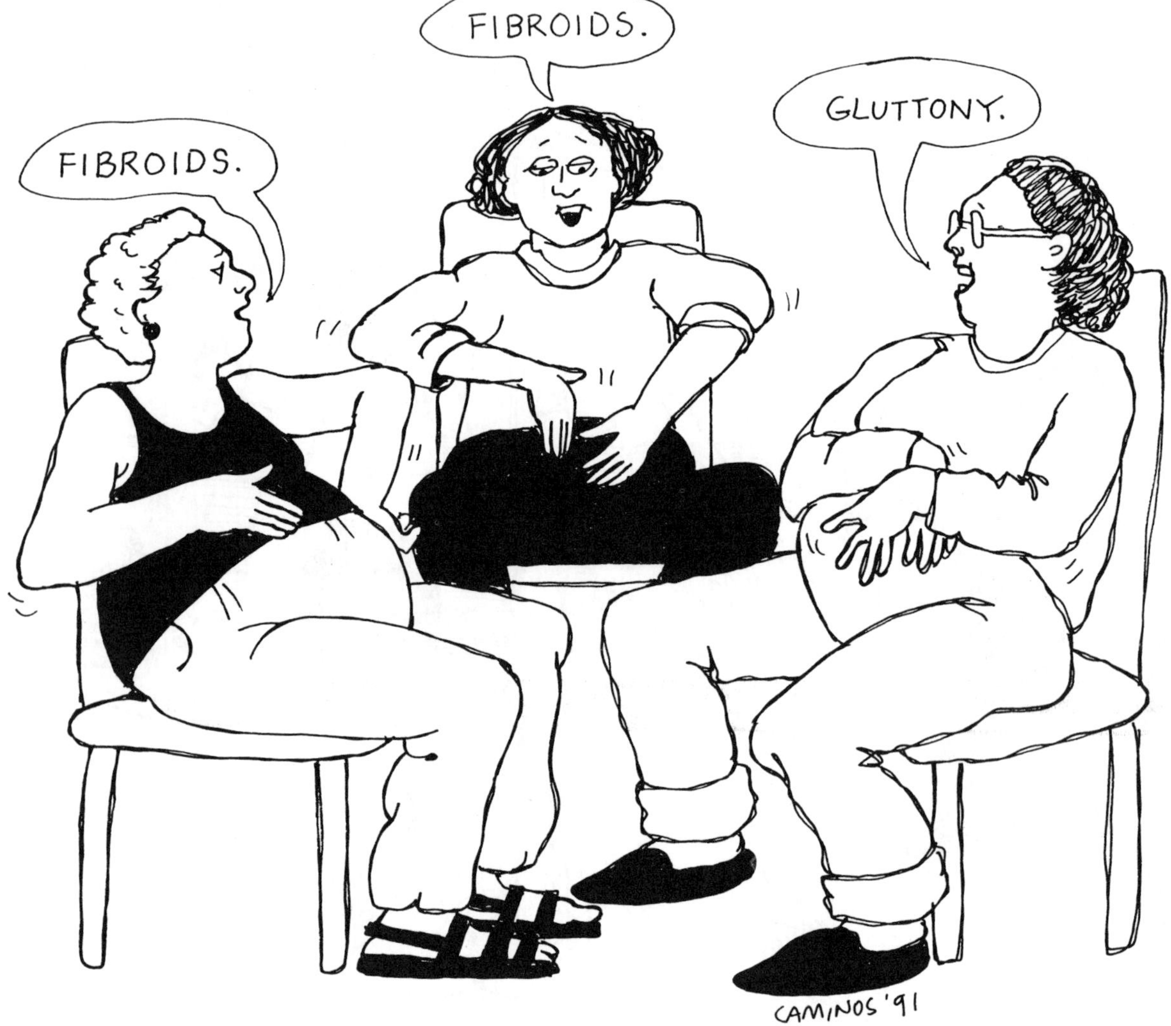
FIBROIDS.
FIBROIDS.
GLUTTONY.
CAMINOS '91

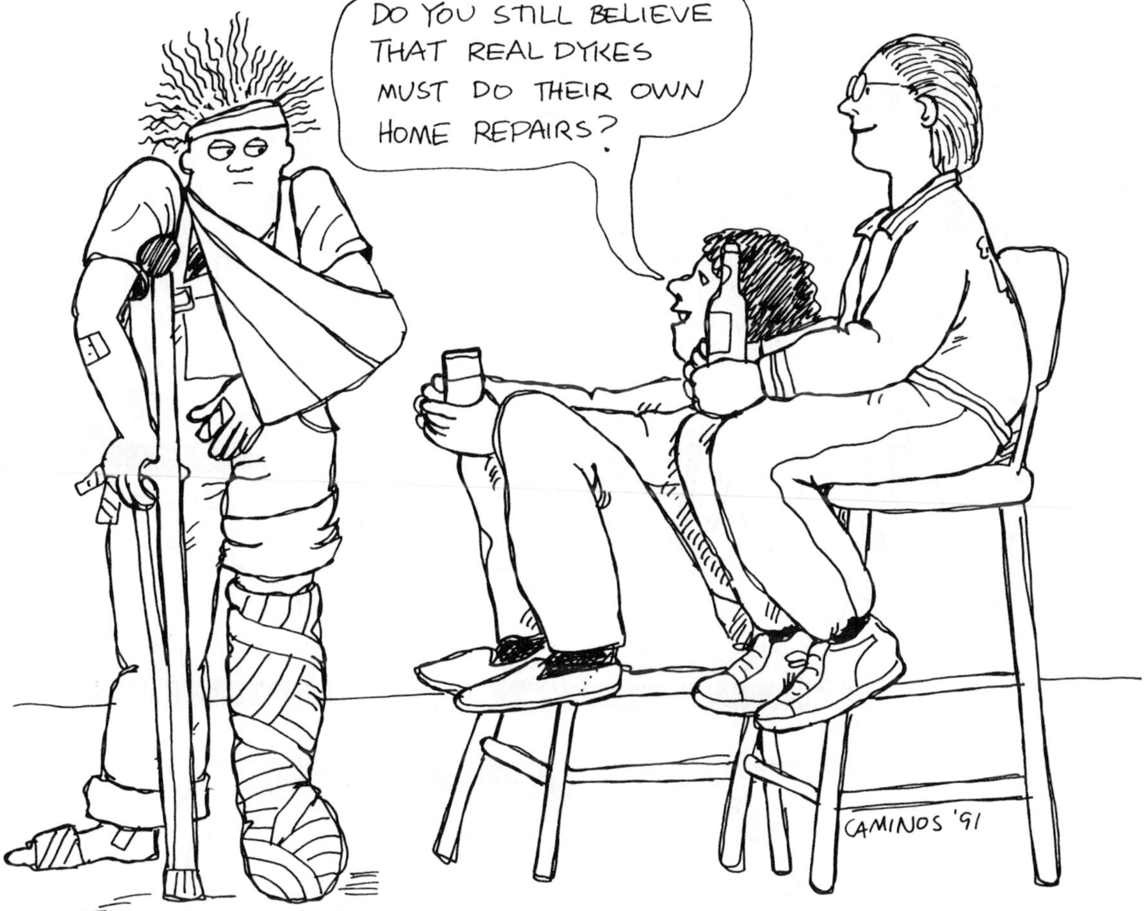
DO YOU STILL BELIEVE THAT REAL DYKES MUST DO THEIR OWN HOME REPAIRS?
CAMINOS '91

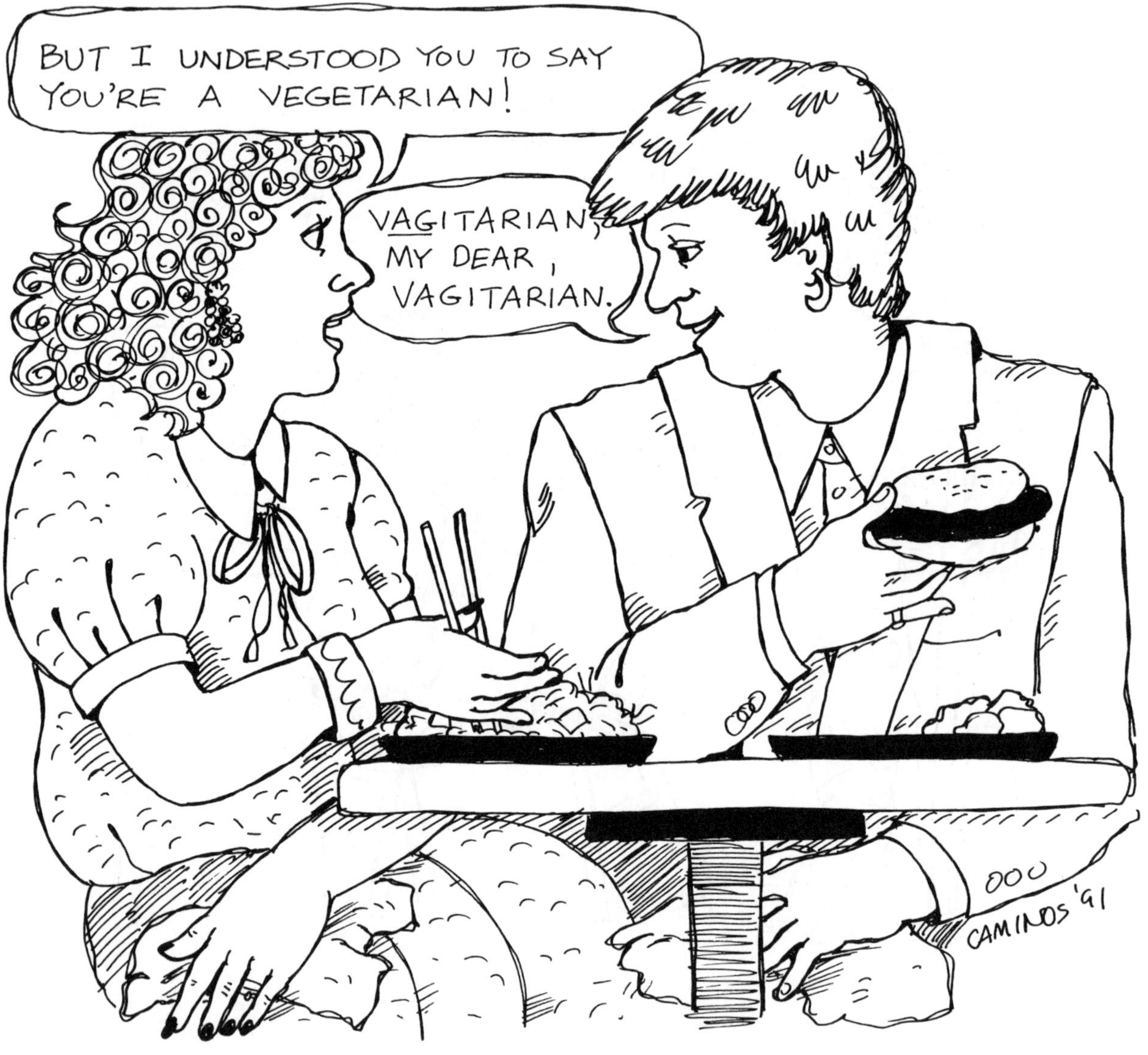
BUT I UNDERSTOOD YOU TO SAY YOU'RE A VEGETARIAN!
VAGITARIAN, MY DEAR, VAGITARIAN.
CAMINOS '91

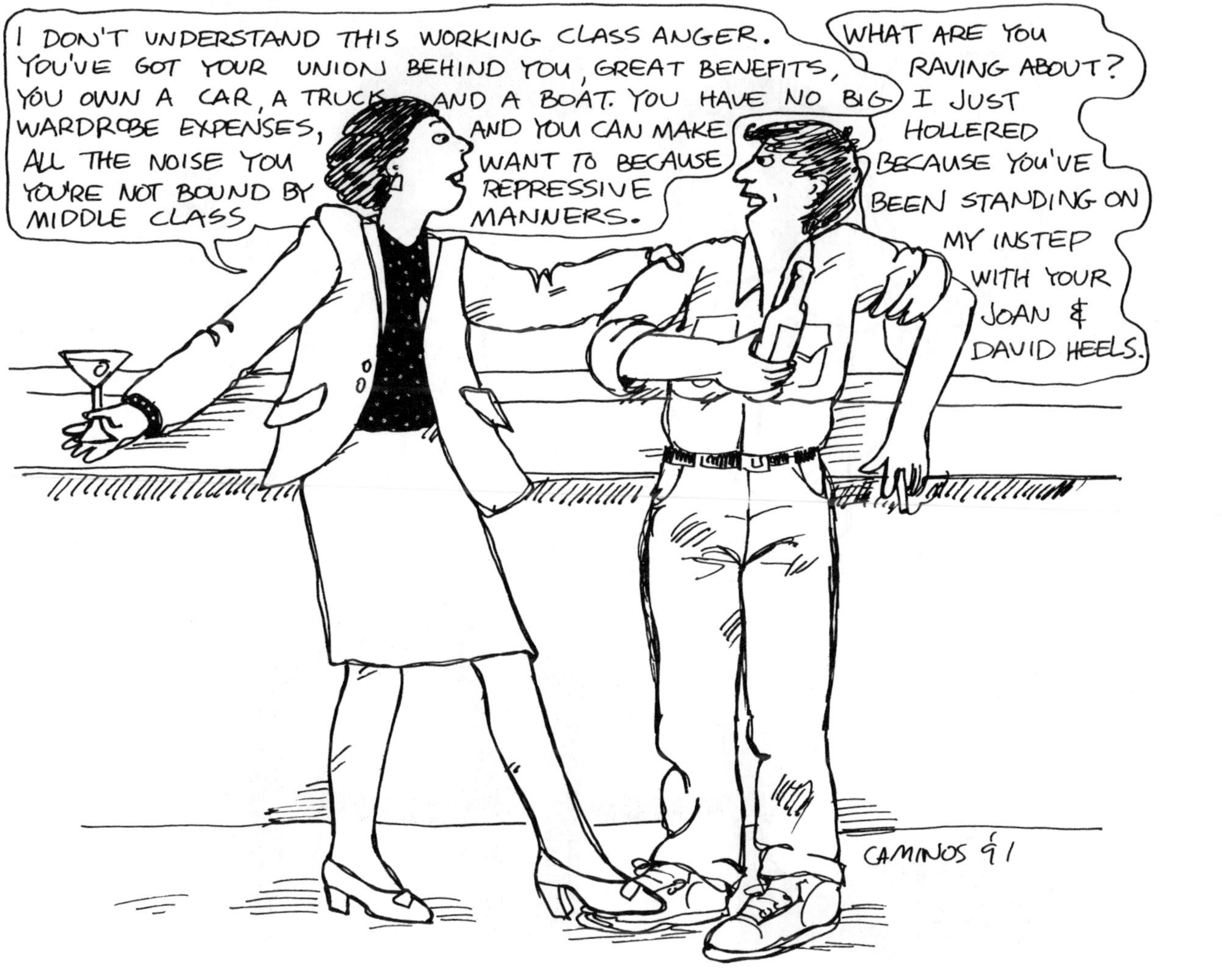

I DON'T UNDERSTAND THIS WORKING CLASS ANGER. YOU'VE GOT YOUR UNION BEHIND YOU, GREAT BENEFITS, YOU OWN A CAR, A TRUCK AND A BOAT. YOU HAVE NO BIG WARDROBE EXPENSES, AND YOU CAN MAKE ALL THE NOISE YOU WANT TO BECAUSE YOU'RE NOT BOUND BY MIDDLE CLASS REPRESSIVE MANNERS.
WHAT ARE YOU RAVING ABOUT? I JUST HOLLERED BECAUSE YOU'VE BEEN STANDING ON MY INSTEP WITH YOUR JOAN & DAVID HEELS.
CAMINOS '91

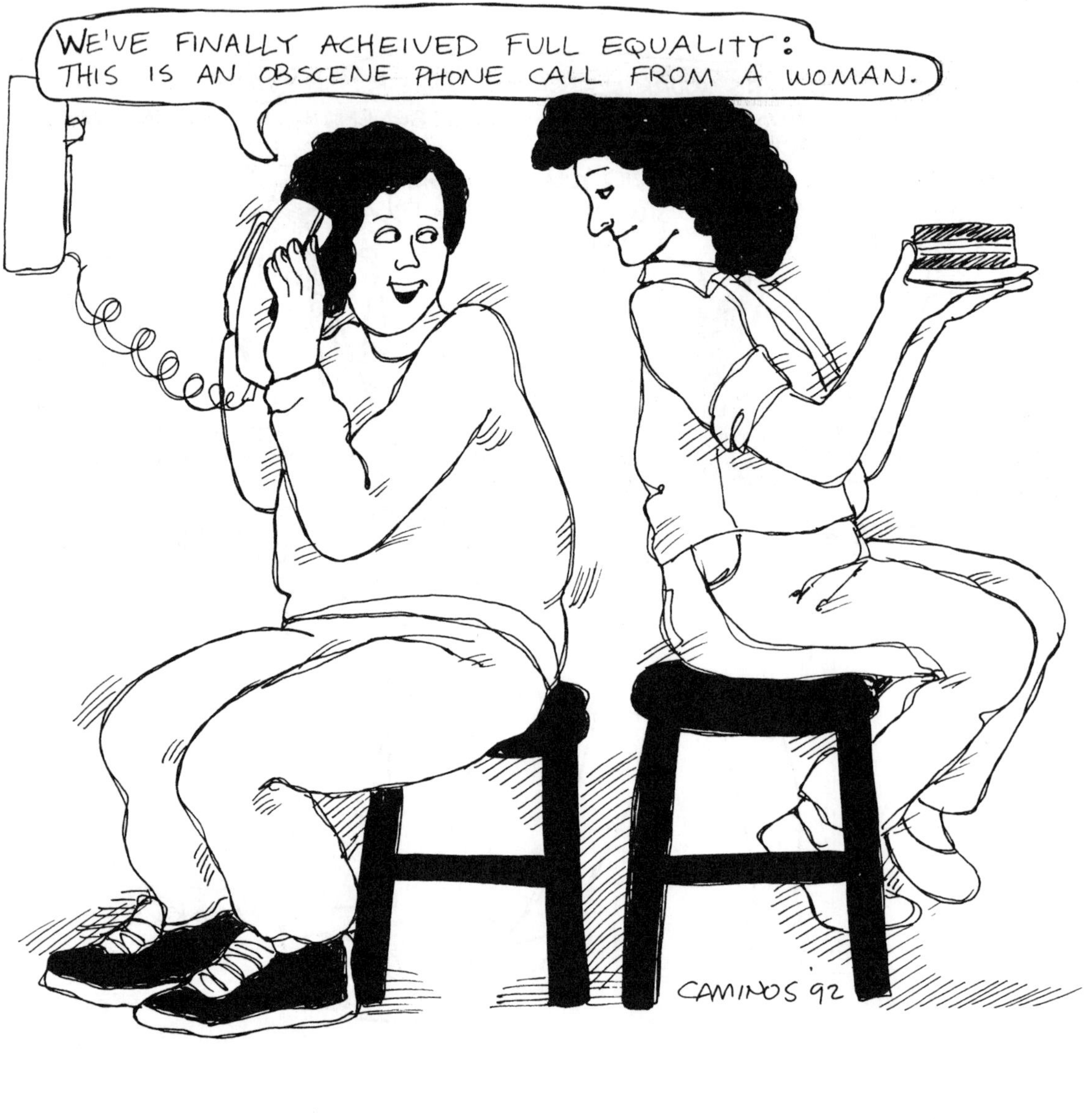
WE'VE FINALLY ACHEIVED FULL EQUALITY:
THIS IS AN OBSCENE PHONE CALL FROM A WOMAN.
CAMINOS '92

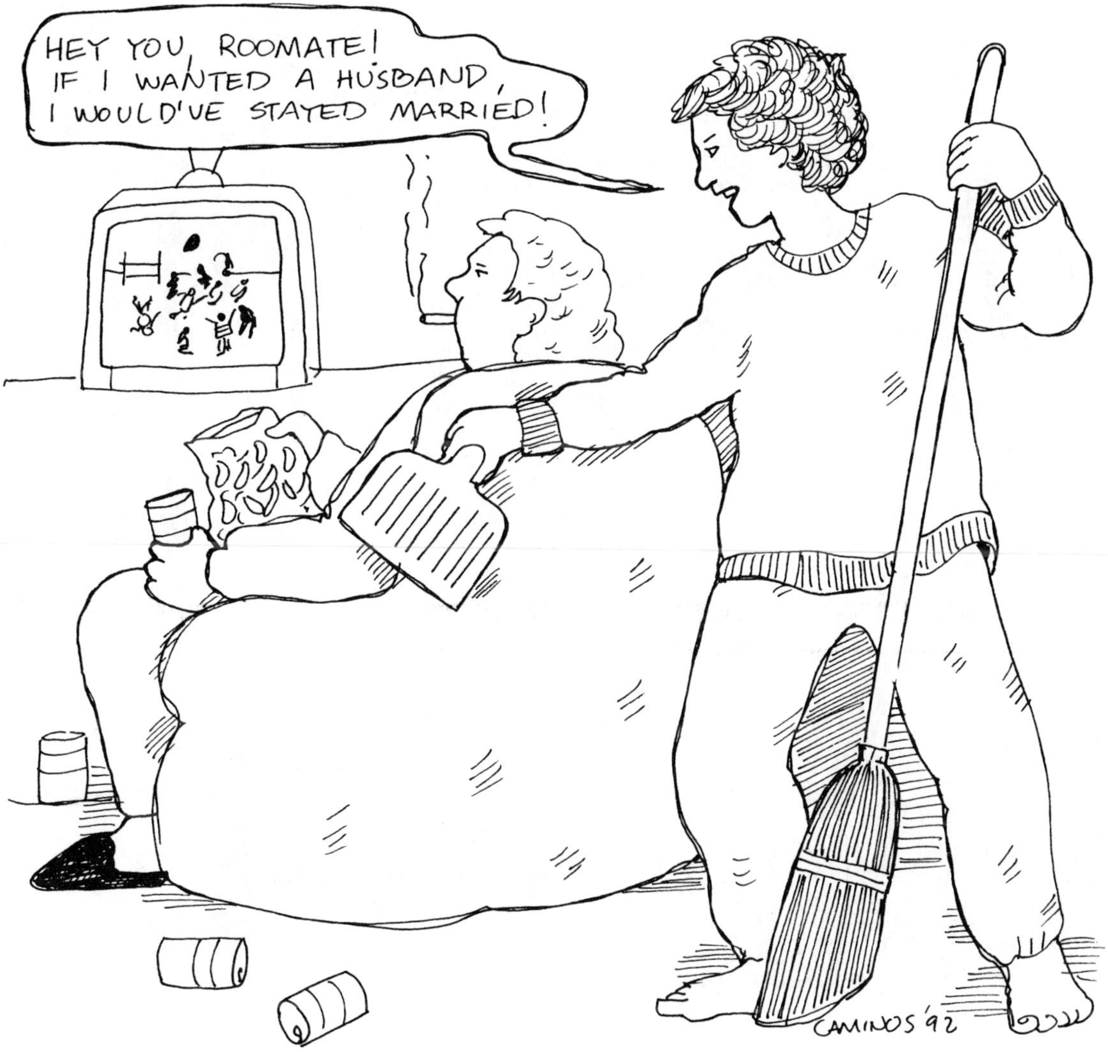
HEY YOU, ROOMATE!
IF I WANTED A HUSBAND,
I WOULD'VE STAYED MARRIED!
CAMINOS '92

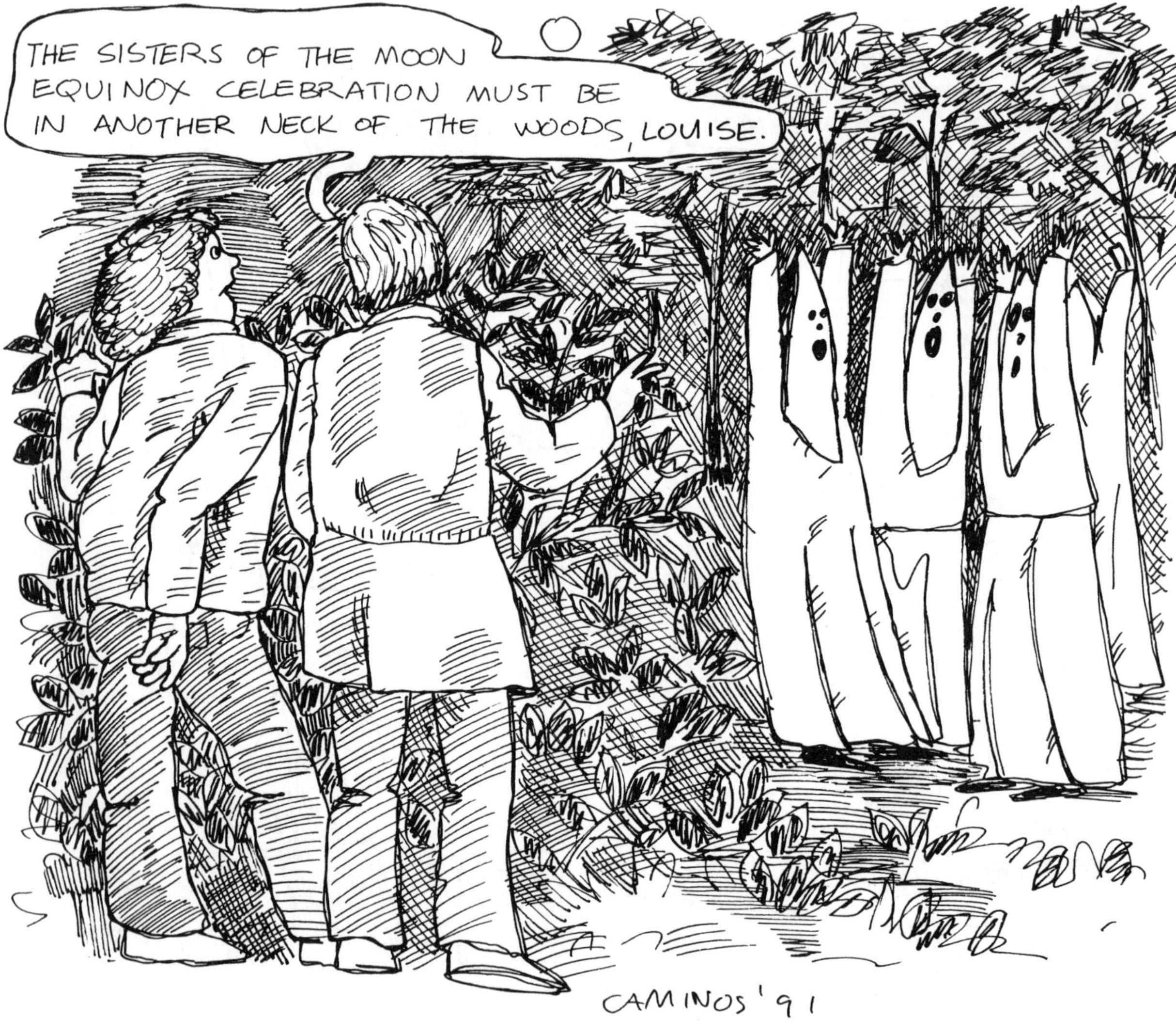
THE SISTERS OF THE MOON EQUINOX CELEBRATION MUST BE IN ANOTHER NECK OF THE WOODS, LOUISE.
CAMINOS '91

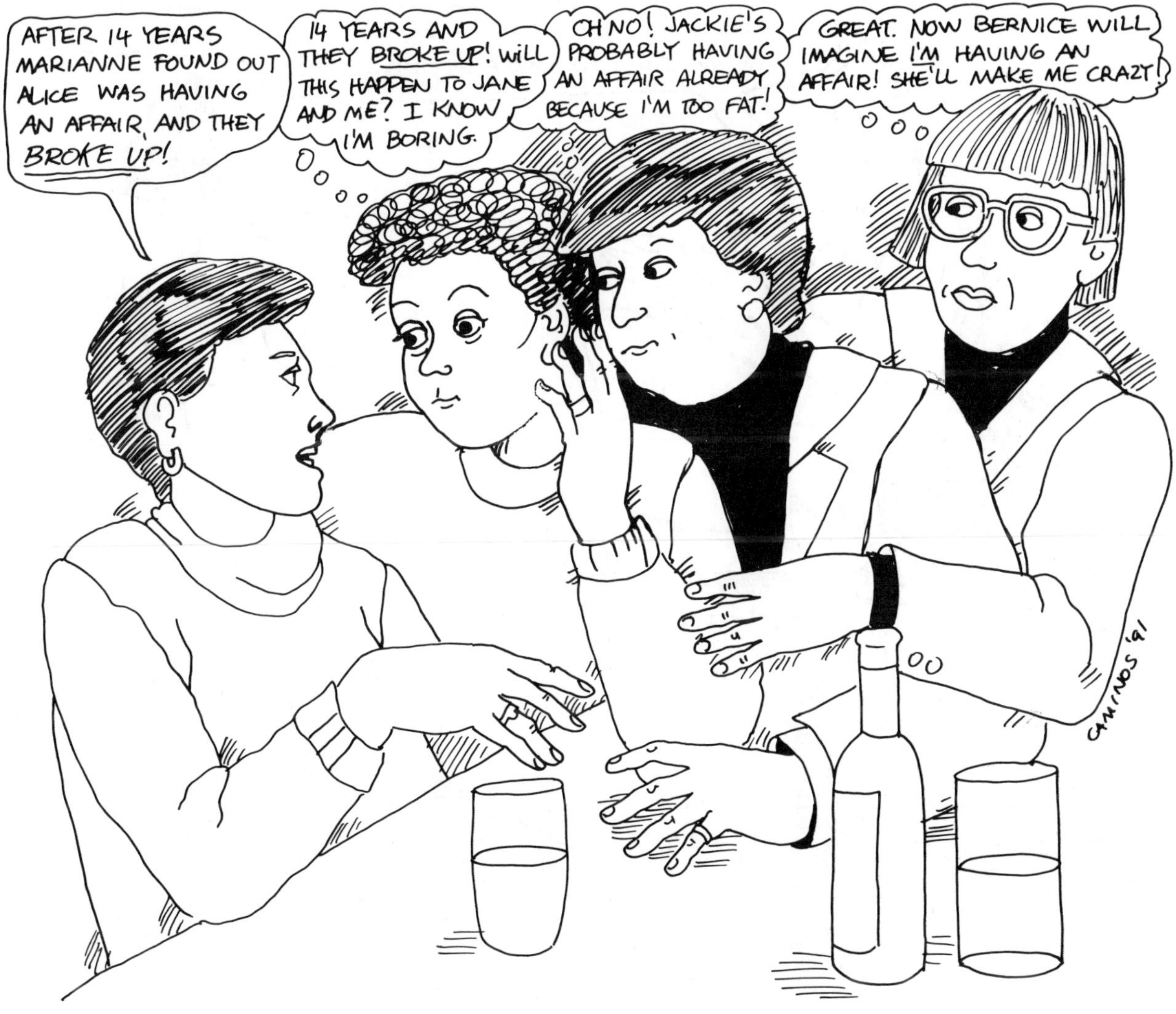
AFTER 14 YEARS MARIANNE FOUND OUT ALICE WAS HAVING AN AFFAIR, AND THEY BROKE UP!
14 YEARS AND THEY BROKE UP! WILL THIS HAPPEN TO JANE AND ME? I KNOW I'M BORING.
OH NO! JACKIE'S PROBABLY HAVING AN AFFAIR ALREADY BECAUSE I'M TOO FAT!
GREAT. NOW BERNICE WILL IMAGINE I'M HAVING AN AFFAIR! SHE'LL MAKE ME CRAZY!
CAMINOS '91

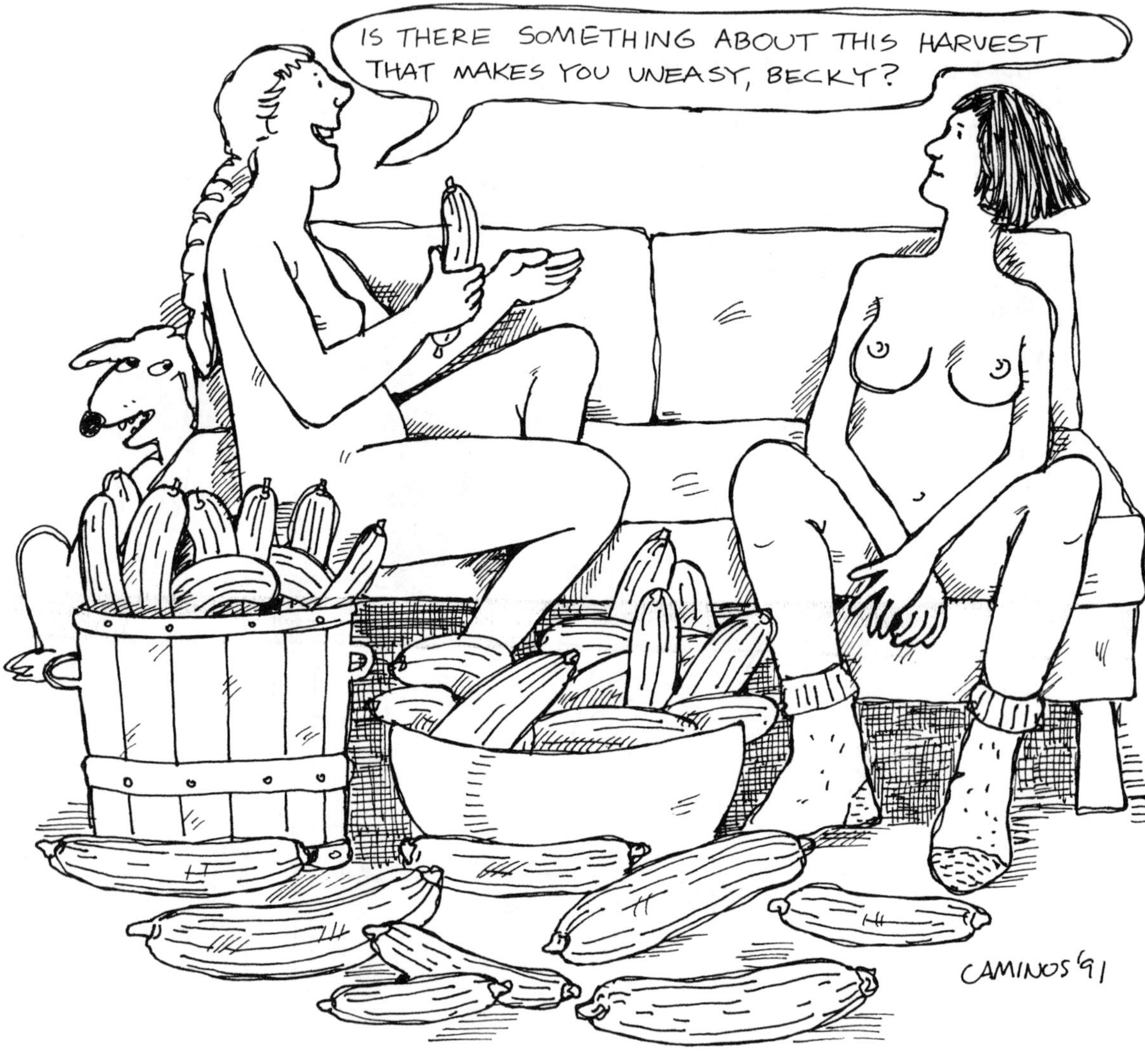
IS THERE SOMETHING ABOUT THIS HARVEST THAT MAKES YOU UNEASY, BECKY?
CAMINOS '91

YOU SAID YOU'D NEVER LEAVE ME! YOU SAID YOU'D ALWAYS LOVE ME! YOU SAID I WAS THE ONLY ONE! NOW YOU'RE GOING!
I'M GOING BECAUSE I WASN'T COMING.
CAMINOS 91

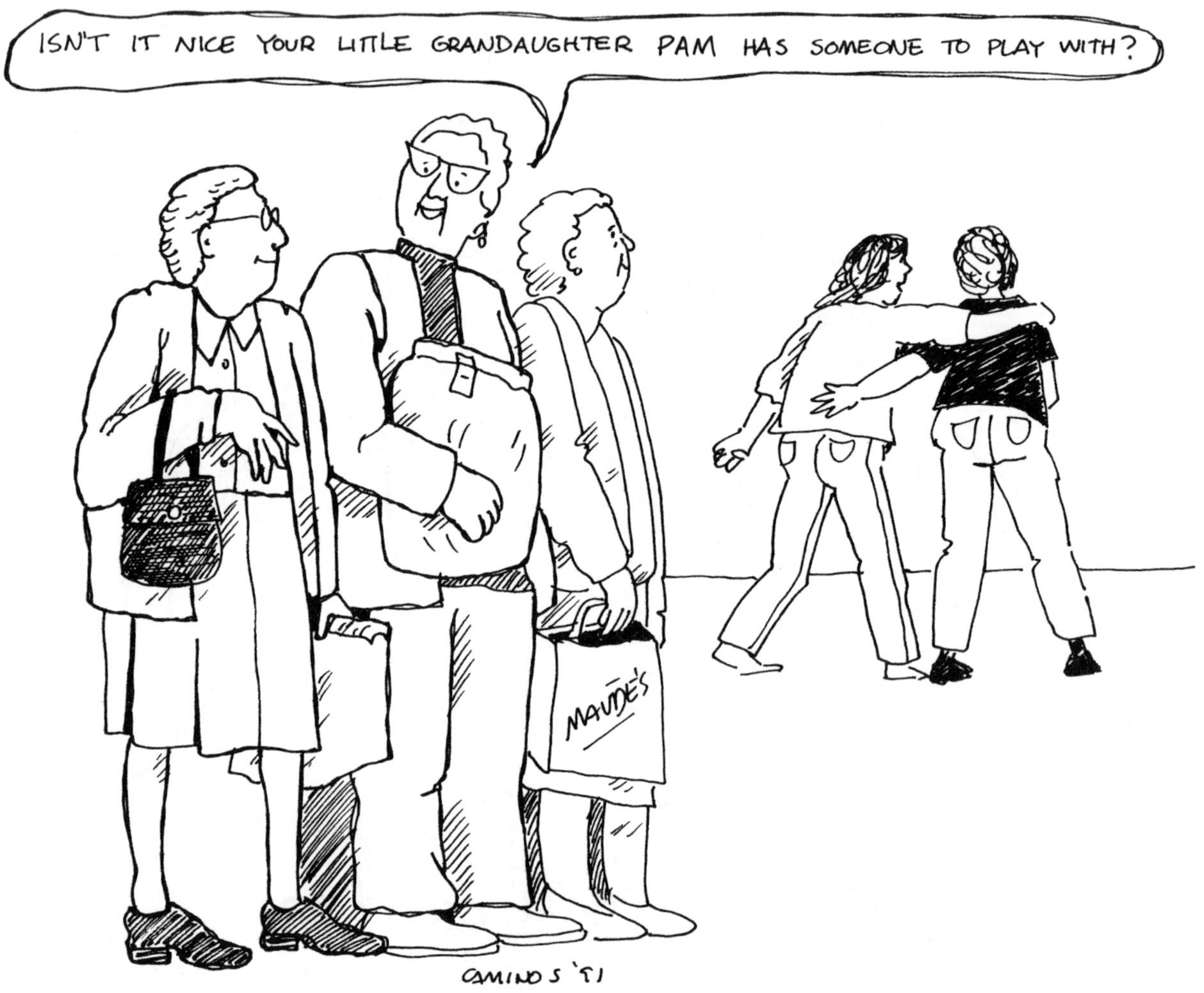
ISN'T IT NICE YOUR LITTLE GRANDAUGHTER PAM HAS SOMEONE TO PLAY WITH?
MAUDE'S
CAMINOS '91

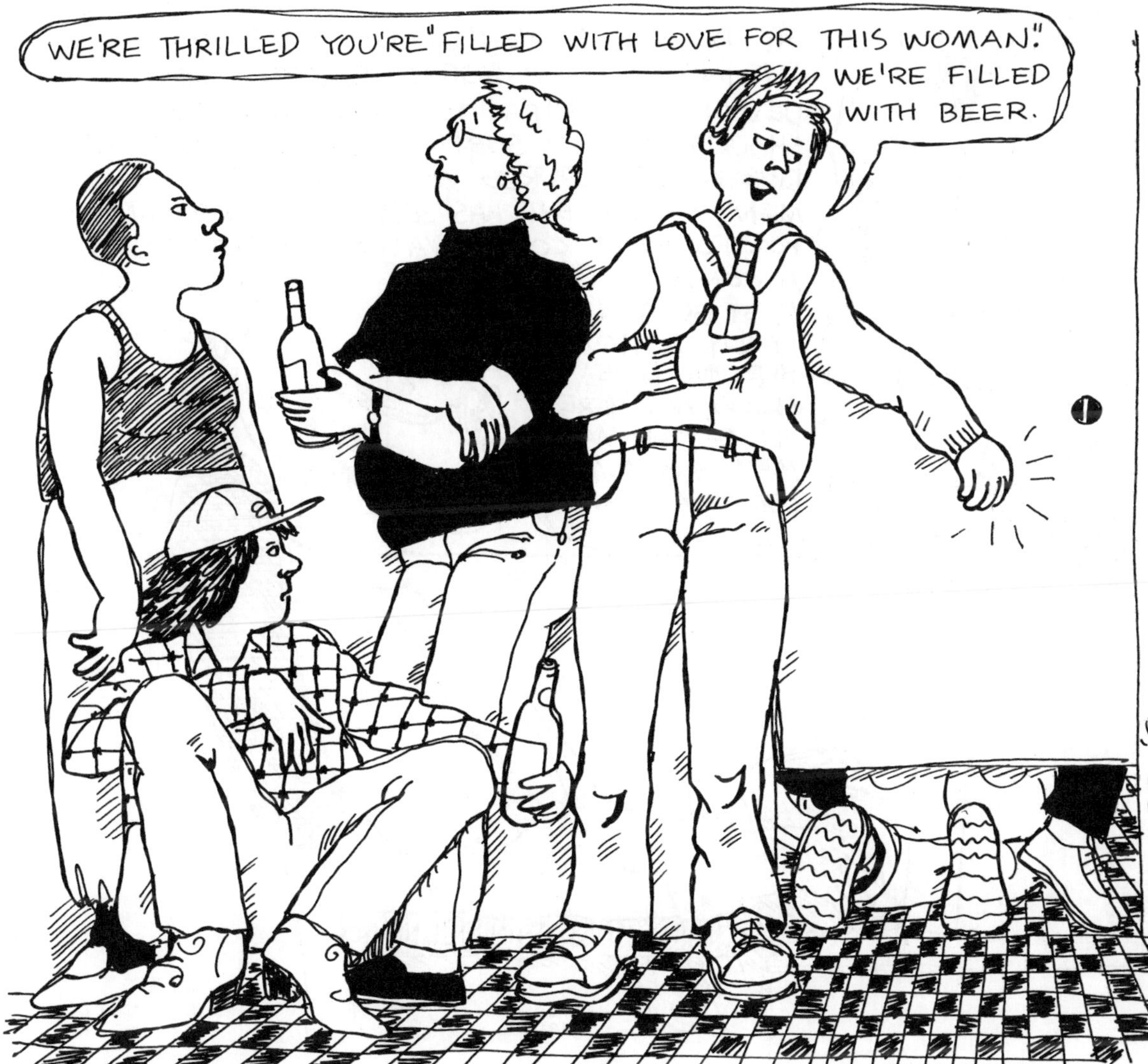
WE'RE THRILLED YOU'RE "FILLED WITH LOVE FOR THIS WOMAN." WE'RE FILLED WITH BEER.
CAMINOS '91

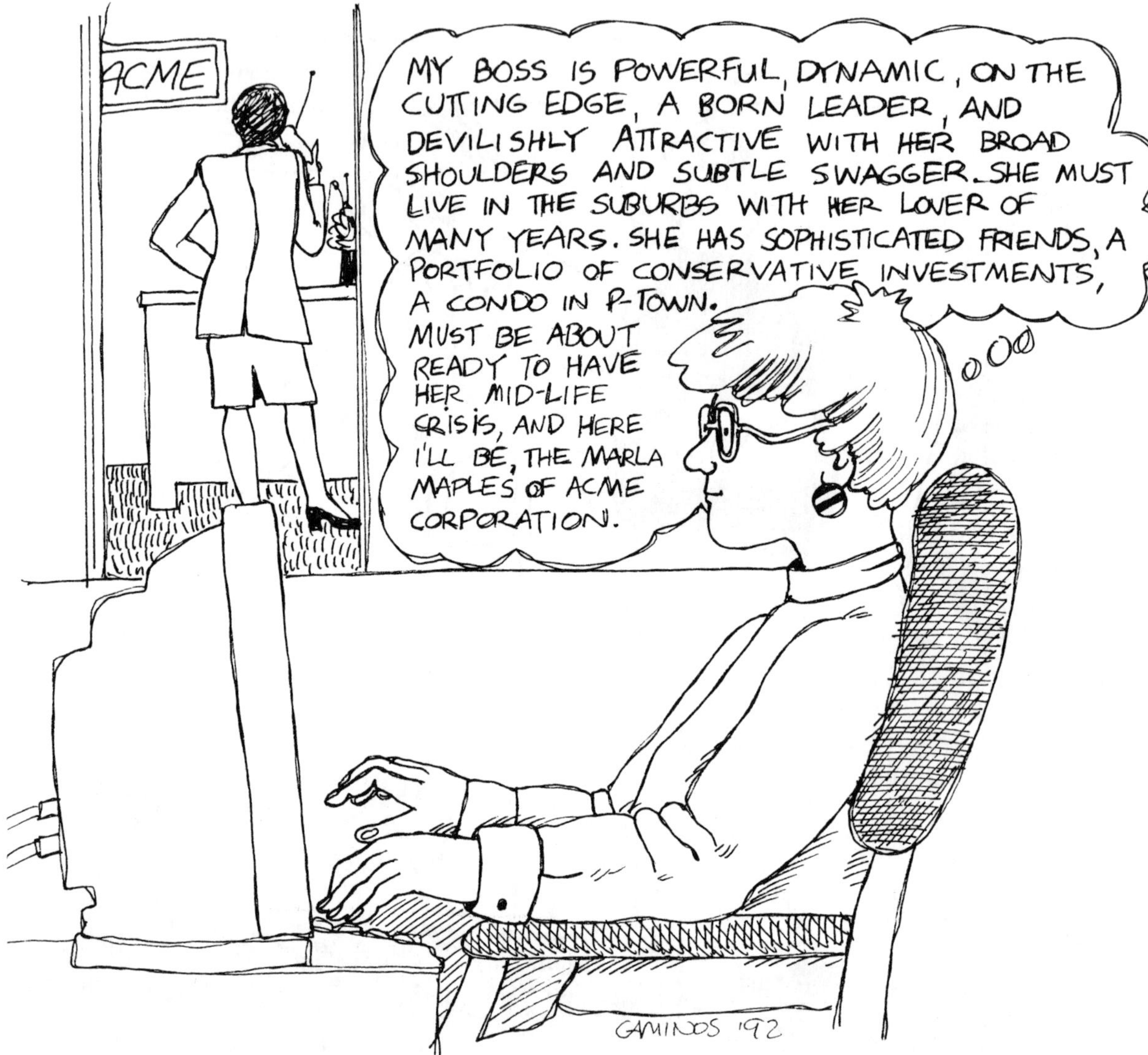
ACME
MY BOSS IS POWERFUL, DYNAMIC, ON THE CUTTING EDGE, A BORN LEADER, AND DEVILISHLY ATTRACTIVE WITH HER BROAD SHOULDERS AND SUBTLE SWAGGER. SHE MUST LIVE IN THE SUBURBS WITH HER LOVER OF MANY YEARS. SHE HAS SOPHISTICATED FRIENDS, A PORTFOLIO OF CONSERVATIVE INVESTMENTS, A CONDO IN P-TOWN. MUST BE ABOUT READY TO HAVE HER MID-LIFE CRISIS, AND HERE I'LL BE, THE MARLA MAPLES OF ACME CORPORATION.
GAMINOS '92

On the Road Again
The Further Adventures of Ramsey Sears

by Elizabeth Dean

Woman to Woman's irreverent columnist Ramsey Sears is on the road again. She's out of the office and out of sorts because she thinks her boss, Rita, is falling in love, but not with her. Her assignment is to report and write about lesbian life around the country. Ramsey smart-asses her way through sweaty foreplay on a hot basketball court in Texas before a wild woman teaches her how river rafting should really be done. Then her research trip to a holistic ranch forces her to share a room with Katy, the queen of whine, a politically correct health fanatic. A late night call from Rita ends Ramsey's travels through American Lesbiana and sends her on a driving marathon to meet Rita, and the mysterious Melissa in San Francisco.

On the Road Again, The Further Adventures of Ramsey Sears (223 pages at $9.95) is another book from Madwoman Press, and is available at your local women's bookstore or directly from the publisher. Send your order to **Madwoman Press**, P.O.Box 690, Northboro, MA 01532. Please be sure to enclose $9.95 plus $2.50 for shipping and handling. Add $.50 for each additional book.